GOD'S WORLD. NO STRING PUPPETS

GOD'S WORLD.
NO STRING PUPPETS

Providence in the Writings of Romano Guardini

Jane Lee-Barker

Foreword by Robert A. Krieg

☙PICKWICK *Publications* · Eugene, Oregon

GOD'S WORLD. NO STRING PUPPETS
Providence in the Writings of Romano Guardini

Copyright © 2022 Jane Lee-Barker. All rights reserved. Except for brief quotations in critical publications or reviews, no part of this book may be reproduced in any manner without prior written permission from the publisher. Write: Permissions, Wipf and Stock Publishers, 199 W. 8th Ave., Suite 3, Eugene, OR 97401.

Pickwick Publications
An Imprint of Wipf and Stock Publishers
199 W. 8th Ave., Suite 3
Eugene, OR 97401

www.wipfandstock.com

PAPERBACK ISBN: 978-1-5326-6321-5
HARDCOVER ISBN: 978-1-5326-6322-2
EBOOK ISBN: 978-1-5326-6323-9

Cataloguing-in-Publication data:

Names: Lee-Barker, Jane, author. | Robert Krieg, foreword.

Title: God's world. no string puppets : providence in the writings of Romano Guardini / Jane Lee-Barker ; foreword by Robert Krieg.

Description: Eugene, OR : Pickwick Publications, 2022 | Includes bibliographical references and index.

Identifiers: ISBN 978-1-5326-6321-5 (paperback) | ISBN 978-1-5326-6322-2 (hardcover) | ISBN 978-1-5326-6323-9 (ebook)

Subjects: LCSH: Guardini, Romano, 1885–1968. | Providence and government of God—Christianity.

Classification: B3254.G824 L43 2022 (print) | B3254.G824 L43 (ebook)

Dedicated to
my grandchildren
Ethan, Cailin, Isabella, and Connor

Jesus' message about providence also does not mean something like the Hellenistic world order, but rather the divine guidance of history which is directed toward the realization of the holy kingdom, but at the same time the guidance of the destiny of every individual so that the one takes place in and through the other. "Seek ye therefore first the kingdom of God and his justice, and all these things [necessary for life] shall be added unto you." (Matt. 6:33)

Romano Guardini, *The Virtues*, 155.

Table of Contents

Foreword by Robert A. Krieg ix
Preface xiii
Acknowledgments xvii

1 Introduction 3
    Romano Guardini 3
    Contemporary Theological Literature on Providence 15
    The Review of Critical Literature on Providence in Guardini's
        Work: The Contribution of Guardini Scholars 19
    The Central Research Question 24

2 Guardini's World: Relevant Biographical Details of Roman Guardini
    and Attention to the Socio-Historical Context 29
    Biography 29
    Prominent Areas of Interest in Guardini's Work 39
    People Who Influenced Guardini 44
    Collegial Influences 48
    Scholarly Influences 51
    People Guardini Influenced 54
    Relevant Socio-Historical Background:
        Changes in German Society During the Twentieth Century 56

3 Romano Guardini's Writing in His Early Life and Analysis 69
    Introduction 69
    The First Text on Providence 70
    Theme 1: Jesus Christ and Providence 77
    Theme 2: Providence Is Understood in Relationship with God 77
    Theme 3: The Individual Person Is Important to God 91

    Theme 4: New Creation and New Existence 97
    Conclusion 109

4 Guardini's Writing on Christian Providence in the Time of National Socialism 112
    Introduction: Guardini's Providence Texts in This Period 112
    Theme 1: Jesus Christ and Providence: How Jesus Understood Providence 116
    Theme 2: Providence Is Understood in Relationship with God 120
    The I-Thou Relationship and Development of Person 123
    Theme 3: The Individual Person Is Important to God 133
    Theme 4: New Creation and New Existence 146
    Conclusion 167

5 Guardini's Writing on Providence after 1945 and Analysis 169
    Introduction 169
    Theme 1: Jesus Christ and Providence 172
    Theme 2: Providence Occurs in Relationship with God—in the World 183
    Theme 3: The Individual Person Is Important to God 196
    Theme 4: New Existence and New Creation 205
    Later Texts of 1959–66 216
    Conclusion 222

Overall Conclusion: God's World. No String Puppets. Providence in the Writings of Romano Guardini 223

Providence—Guardini's Prayer 236

Bibliography 237
Index 249

Foreword

GOD'S WORLD. NO STRING *Puppets: Providence in the Writings of Romano Guardini* by the Reverend Dr. Jane Louise Lee-Barker is aptly titled. In five chapters, it presents Guardini's insightful and uplifting thought on divine providence (Latin, *pro-videre*, "to see ahead"): God's loving, wise and ultimately successful guidance of creation, history, and our lives.

This study is being published at a propitious moment. Romano Guardini (1885–1968) is a recent candidate for sainthood. In December 2017, the Archdiocese of Munich-Freising initiated the formal ecclesiastical process for Guardini's beatification and canonization. The Archdiocese took this initiative because this priest-theologian's life and writings are still instructing and inspiring thousands of people around the world, including Pope Benedict XVI (Joseph Ratzinger) and Pope Francis (Jorge Bergoglio, SJ).

God's World. No String Puppets is appearing in print at the right time, too, because today's crises—for example, regarding people's access to food, water and health care, the earth's climate change and environment, and human rights and justice—are quickening people's desire for the affirmation that God is walking with us and will eventually lead all of creation through every "darkest valley" (Ps 23:4) to the fullness of truth and life, to God's "kingdom." Today we yearn to hear anew St. Paul's words: "All things work unto good for those who love God"; indeed, nothing "will be able to separate us from the love of God in Christ Jesus our Lord" (Rom 8:28, 39).

To what may we liken Lee-Barker's book? Imagine that we are standing in front of a large, colorful tapestry of a garden and listening to a commentary on the tapestry's originator, its entire image and the crucial role of the forest-green threads that run through the tapestry, enriching and unifying the entire image.

Similarly, *God's World. No String Puppets* discusses the priest-theologian's life, his view of God, and his notion of God's providence. That is, it recalls that Romano Guardini was born in Verona, Italy, grew up in Germany, was ordained a priest in the Diocese of Mainz, and, after completing his doctoral studies, flourished as a pastoral leader, preacher, lecturer, and writer at the universities of Berlin (1923–1939), Tübingen (1945–1947), and Munich (1948–1964). It locates Guardini's numerous books and articles in relation to three periods: World War I and the Weimar Republic, the Third Reich and World War II, and the economic, political, and cultural success of West Germany.

Further, the book highlights the profound view of God that Guardini imparted in his writings over fifty years: that is, the God of Jesus Christ is "the living God" who is interpersonal in God's very being of Father, Son, and Spirit, and who is thus interpersonal with creation, especially with human beings. It is in relation to this Triune God that Lee-Barker's book presents Guardini's seemingly paradoxical understanding that divine providence guides us to our telos, God's new creation, while simultaneously respecting our human freedom. God does not treat us as puppets, but rather draws us into freely collaborating with God for the coming of the "kingdom."

In particular, thanks to Lee-Barker, this study shows that Guardini's notion of God's providence runs through the scholar's entire literary corpus. That is, *God's World. No String Puppets* examines the "threads" of Guardini's rich, multifaceted thought on divine providence beginning with his 1916 article on *göttliche Vorsehung* ("divine providence") and ending in 1963 with *The Wisdom of the Psalms*. During the intervening five decades, the theme of God's loving, wise, and effective guidance in nature, history, and our lives comes to prominence in a number of other books including: *Conscience* (1929), *The Living God* (1929), *The Lord's Prayer* (1932), *The World and the Person* (1939), *The Art of Praying* (1943), *Faith and Modern Man* (1944), *Freedom, Grace and Destiny* (1948), *Wunder und Zeichen* ("Miracles and Signs," 1959), and *The Virtues* (1963).

Finally, as Lee-Barker explains, Romano Guardini chose scripture as the primary source for his prayer, thought and theology. In this, he approached biblical texts in ways that promoted a renewed hearing of God's living Word. In particular, as shown in *God's World. No String Puppets*, Guardini anchored his reflections on God's providence in Jesus' teaching: "Therefore I tell you, do not worry about your life, what you will eat or what you will drink, or about your body, what you will wear. . . [I]ndeed your heavenly Father knows that you need all these things. But strive first for the kingdom of God and his righteousness, and all these things will be given to you as well." (Matt 6:25–34; see Matt 10:29–31; Wis 14:3–4; 17:2).

The Lord Jesus' teaching in the gospels on God's providence and also that of St. Paul in his Letter to the Romans impart assurance and hope to all people who long for the coming of God's new creation, God's "kingdom." These biblical words surely stayed with Romano Guardini as he faced personal challenges and global crises, and these words were the wellspring for this saintly man's wisdom on divine providence. Guardini's wisdom—especially, though not exclusively, in eleven of his writings—is now available to readers in Jane Louise Lee-Barker's *God's World. No String Puppets*.

Robert A. Krieg
Professor Emeritus, University of Notre Dame

Preface

THIS BOOK WAS INITIALLY my doctoral thesis in theology and has been slightly modified for other readers. Romano Guardini (1885–1968) was a twentieth-century Italian-German religious philosopher. His work was written for the educated layperson and therefore is accessible to many beyond the field of theology. I believe his work needs to be known by today's generation, especially in the English-speaking world where people didn't know his work as well as the Europeans did in Guardini's lifetime. The title, *God's World. No String Puppets: Providence in the Writings of Romano Guardini*, refers to Guardini's idea that the world is not just nature but God's creation, and in God's created and very sacred world, people are given the opportunity for discernment, decision, and action in relationship with God who guides but does not force, coerce, or thrust "fate" upon them. They are not string puppets. In that context, Guardini is able to show how a person can trust in God's Providence.

I first came to appreciate Guardini's writing when I was a Post-Graduate student at the Pontifical Gregorian University in Rome during the 1990s. I particularly liked the way Guardini was able to develop theology which was clearly spiritual yet not bound up in rigid language or formulas. I was also attracted to the way he could relate the experiences of the human person to an understanding of God and Jesus Christ. I believe his writing was the way Guardini exercised his pastoral care. I noticed that Guardini had often written about Providence in the course of his long career as a scholar. I wanted to explore that notion in his writing and see what it meant to him and why. I found that I needed to situate much of his writing within his social context, for he often addressed pertinent issues of the day. His notion of God's Providence didn't change enormously over that period of time, but there were *some* important changes and development within that entire writing period. These changes were particularly important in the time around the period of National Socialism, World War Two, and afterwards. The foundation for his understanding of Providence was laid down in his earliest Providence writing which had been written during the First World War.

This book, therefore, is a study of the development of the notion of Providence in the writings of Romano Guardini. I look at three major phases of his writing, roughly corresponding to the period before National Socialism arose in Germany, the National Socialist period, and the post-war period. Guardini's very early writing grounds Providence in the nature of God with the action of human persons also important. Each period examines his treatment of Providence under four major themes which have emerged from Guardini's Providence texts: 1) Providence in its relation to Jesus Christ; 2) Providence understood in relationship with God; 3) Providence and the individual human person as important to God; 4) Providence with new existence and new creation. This chronological treatment shows how Guardini's theology of Providence, understood in relation to these four themes, is significant at all stages of his work and also develops over time, partly at least in response to the shifting socio-cultural environments in which he is writing, but always grounded in a scriptural and theological account. The significance of this book is its challenge to those interpretations of Guardini which see Providence as a minor concept within his work or as one which remains fairly stable throughout his life. This book shows that Providence is a central notion for Guardini and indeed could be seen as a key to his theology. It shows that, while the basic pattern of his treatment of Providence was present already in his early works, his account develops over time in a dynamic way. By doing this, the book offers a fuller and more sophisticated interpretation of one of the most important figures in Catholic intellectual life in the twentieth century and of his notion of Providence.

In this book I have used a capital "P" for Guardini's use of providence to distinguish it from concepts of providence which someone else may have.

I agree with the use of inclusive language where possible. Guardini wrote in the first half of the twentieth century when gender issues were viewed differently although Guardini encouraged the participation of women in many of the activities he was responsible for. He wrote in German, where the gender is not always identified (*Mensch* can be used for both men and women). Annoyingly, Guardini's translators into English have used the male form. While I have not tampered with the citations this action may have affected the literary flow slightly. Nevertheless I have striven to make my own language inclusive.

I have studied Guardini's work in several languages. Where I have primarily used the English text (and checked the German one) I have listed it in the Bibliography under that title first. Likewise if I mainly used the Italian version I have listed it under that title. All other books are listed under their German title.

Acknowledgments

FATHER PROFESSOR DR. PETER Neuner offered invaluable research advice including the importance of showing the evidence for claims I was making and the need for a chronological study for understanding development in Guardini's notion of Providence. I learnt much from him.

The circle of Guardini scholars usually met once a year at Burg Rothenfels. In the early part of my research, I was privileged to be a part of this circle on several occasions and thus able to discuss my work with some of the world's leading Guardini scholars. Their advice was invaluable. In particular I am grateful to the late Professor Arno Schilson, who understood Guardini's work so well and offered advice and affirmation. Thank you also to Professor Dr. Alfons Knoll, Dr. Gunda Brüske, and Dr. Joachim Reber, each of whom offered information about Guardini that I had not previously known. In 2010, Professor Dr. Robert Krieg met me at a conference and offered affirmation and invaluable encouragement. I am thankful that he agreed to write the Foreword to this book. Fr. Dr. Alfons Klein, SJ, my spiritual director in Germany (now deceased), supported and encouraged me in this venture. Dr. Rosemary Leiderer (now deceased) gave constant encouragement to see this work through to its end.

My Australian thesis supervisor, Fr. Dr. Robin Koning, SJ, offered advice and correction of my writing style where necessary. He suggested comparing the actual themes Guardini used for Providence across the three periods which has made the changes in Guardini's work easier to see. Mons. Dr. Florian Schuller and others at the Catholic Academy of Bavaria gave me access to the Guardini archives, allowed me to work in the library and encouraged me in my research. Professor Lee Parker, Professor Katharyn Massam, and Dr. Janette Gray (now deceased) offered valuable research and writing advice.

My family, especially my adult children, Belinda and Jeremy, and my mother, Bess, were there for me and constantly encouraged me. I am thankful my mother was able to hear that the original thesis had been passed before she died several weeks later.

Finally, God has been with me. The "living" Providence that has been clear on many occasions has ensured that this book is by no means an academic venture alone.

∽

"Ooh! (eyes alight!) he taught us that we could have God in <u>this</u> world. Jesus Christ is important, and he was always completely positive."

Dr. Rosemary Leiderer (now deceased) talking to me about Guardini's sermons that she heard during her time as a student at the University of Munich.

One day while I was researching my thesis in Germany, I was looking at some literature on Guardini in the back of St. Ludwig's Church in Munich where Guardini had been the university preacher. A lively, elderly lady approached me and asked if I was interested in Guardini. I said that I was and was writing a thesis about his work. She became very excited and told me how important his books had been to the people there during the war and how much they had been helped by them. She then gave me enthusiastic encouragement to continue with this work.
J. LB.

1

Introduction

THIS BOOK IS ABOUT the development of the notion of Providence in the writings of the twentieth-century philosopher of religion Romano Guardini. I have studied his work chronologically in order to see this development. The chronological treatment of three sequential historical periods shows how Guardini's theology of Providence, understood primarily in relation to four themes, is significant at all stages of his work and, while retaining a stable form, also shows development or changes over time. These changes are partly in response to the shifting sociocultural environment in which he is writing, but nevertheless grounded in a scriptural and theological account. I will contribute to the current state of research on Guardini on Providence by: a) A comprehensive view of the relevant writings; b) Arguing that there is significant development in his work, especially during the National Socialist period; and c) Giving proper weight to the foundations of his views which he first lays down in the early period. We now turn to a brief outline of Romano Guardini and his work.

Romano Guardini

Romano Guardini was a Roman Catholic philosopher of religion, well known in Europe in his lifetime, who was born in Verona, Italy, in 1885 and died in Munich 1968.[1] His parents had migrated to Mainz when Guardini was a year old and he later considered himself to have had the

---

1. Guardini was the favorite theologian of Pope Benedict XVI and Pope Francis (see chapter 2).

best of both Italian and German education and culture. He was Professor of Philosophy of Religion and Catholic World View at the University of Berlin before World War Two. After the war he held the chair of Philosophy of Religion and Christian World View, first at the University of Tubingen and then at the University of Munich. It is clear from his own education ranging from choice of university to the choice of his own progressive teachers and then the type of his own research, that while committed to the Catholic Church, Guardini was following a path which was not constrained to the narrow parameters of Roman Catholic theology of the time.[2] In particular, his unconventional approach to theology was seen in his focus on human existence and experience enabled by his study of the phenomenology of the human person as found in literature and other texts.

Guardini used Scripture as his first point of reference which was also unusual for a Catholic theologian of that time. He wrote for the educated public and, in an endeavor to reach as many people as possible, he wrote in everyday language explaining each point in a way an intelligent layperson would understand. During his life, Guardini wrote over one hundred articles and over seventy books and was considered to be one of the leading thinkers in Germany. Now more than fifty years after his death, his work continues to be well known and to be researched in Germany and beyond.[3]

Guardini's Theology of Providence

Guardini's theology is focused on the human person living in the world. Both God and the world come together in his work and his notion of the world is life affirming not life-denying. Guardini's theology of Providence is consonant with the Biblical view of Divine Providence and shows how a person can live with God's Providence, as an individual, yet in harmony with the Providence of the whole. In Guardini's notion of Providence, rather than taking a cosmological approach, Providence is understood from the point of view of the human person. There is a vocational aspect to living with Providence. Guardini grounds his theology of Providence

---

2. Guardini wrote under a pseudonym (Dr. Anton Wacht) in the early part of his academic life because he was afraid of being censored by the Vatican. The word *Wacht* carries a sense of being on the watch or on guard.

3. Krieg, *Romano Guardini*, 2.

in the theology of God the Creator. The context of Providence is God's love which is both the path and the goal. One is held in relationship with God as one journeys to God's kingdom. Providence in Guardini's view is not a finished act or plan which God imposes on the world. Being open-ended it allows for the possibility of human involvement in its completion. Guardini specifically relates this aspect to human decisions in which the person has the opportunity to co-operate with the grace of God to form a new inner *Gestalt*; a new, internal dynamism and inner structure, to bring Providence to completion. One must be transformed by the grace of God in order to contribute to a transformed world. There is an illusive aspect to this action however as the human person is asked (in the manner of Matt 6:33) to focus on seeking the Kingdom of God and God's righteousness not their own Providential future. While Guardini's notion of Providence is consonant with mainstream Christian theology, Guardini's special contribution lies in his ability to articulate modern social and philosophical understandings of human existence and theological anthropology, bringing these things together with his theological understanding which, in addition to Scripture, is also informed by the early Church Fathers, Medieval Theologians, and others in the Christian Tradition.[4] The Catholic Church and its teaching was important to him.[5] He presents a contemporary synthesis of traditional and modern ideas which show feasibility for living with Providence in today's world. Guardini presents Providence as an alternative to destiny and this is well developed in his later work, *Freedom, Grace, and Destiny*. His worldview and theory of The Opposites demonstrate his belief in a fundamental unity of all creation in God. The focus in this thesis is about development of Guardini's notion of Providence; whether, how or why, his notion of Providence develops over time.

---

4. Although Guardini was not a dogmatic theologian as such, he nevertheless wrote as a theologian, and along with such scholars as Marie-Dominique Chenu and Yves Congar, could perhaps be said to be a Ressourcement theologian because his original writing bears many of the characteristics of resourcement theology methods but predates the time believed to be commencement of Ressourcement theology. The Ressourcement was a renewal movement in Catholic theology that sought to return to the original sources such as Scripture and the Church Fathers and involved the consideration of human experience. See Flynn and Murray, *Ressourcement*.

5. Ratzinger, *Fundamental Speeches from Five Decades*, 249.

Guardini's Methodology[6]

As a religious philosopher, studying anthropology, through the phenomenology of the human person, Guardini focused on human experience in the light of faith.[7] In order to see what was "distinctively Christian," in their work, Guardini studied the writings of St. Augustine, Pascal, Kierkegaard, Dostoevsky, Hölderlin, and Rilke.[8] His writing deals with the human person struggling with existence, and the meeting of Christian believers with the world.[9] "My approach is *Weltanschauung*, [Worldview] a vision of man and his world realized from the standpoint of faith," he said.[10] The world and every aspect of it was important to him and in developing a worldview which was never narrowly confined to dogmatic issues he says, "I didn't give the lectures from a textbook or traditional ideas, but sought to think about the particular problem itself and through it to attain the answer."[11] As a philosopher of existence[12] Guardini's study of Providence was made in the context of human living from the standpoint of the human person[13] ontologically open to the world and God. Therefore, everything in the world was important to him.

---

6. The theologian Paul Allen has noted that contemporary sources for theological method are commonly Scripture, Tradition, Reason, and Experience. Allen also notes that theologians usually bring their own priorities, hermeneutical principles, and styles to bear on a theological question and explore it using comparisons, contrasts, and correlations. Analogous language is often used. See Allen, *Theological Method*, 6.

7. The decision to study human experience was unusual for a Catholic theologian of that time. In the 1920s, the Catholic Church was in the throes of the Modernist crisis and sought to contain possible unorthodoxy or liberalism by using highly controlled theological methods and texts, not experience.

8. The decision to study human biography was the suggestion of the philosopher Max Scheler (see chapter 2).

9. Schilson, "The Major Theological Themes of Romano Guardini," 33. Schilson notes that Guardini didn't go directly to theology or philosophy but studied the meeting of Christian believers with the world so that he could take a view of the whole. See also Schilson, *Perspectiven Theologischer Erneurung*, 25.

10. Guardini's words to Gremillion, "Interview with Romano Guardini," 194.

11. Guardini, *Berichte über mein Leben*, 45 (my translation).

12. Giorgio Penzo argues that Guardini is a philosopher of existence rather than an existentialist as such. He notes that Guardini named himself in this manner as well. The philosopher of existence sees the level of authenticity only when there is an opening to the transcendent. For the existentialist, the dimension of existence is on the level of authenticity only in the act of existing. See Penzo, "L'Interpretation Di Hölderlin," 450.

13. Joachim Reber notes that Providence, in Guardini's understanding, is studied

Guardini's theology is inductive rather than deductive[14] which has enabled him to study the breadth and depth of human existence. His world is an ontologically contingent world with a concrete exterior. Guardini's books transcend the boundaries between theology, philosophy, literary criticism, and human biography and they touch on psychology, sociology, and numerous other areas. As such his writing is difficult to categorize and his eloquent prose was often refined in the crucible of the pulpit, before publication, bringing into his work a relevance to daily life and human experience (The spoken word has an immediacy which the well considered written word may not have).

Guardini dealt with themes rather than creating a systematic theology as such.[15] One could say that Providence is dealt with in the same way; Providence was a theme which Guardini repeatedly returned to throughout his long career. Much of the basic form was there from the beginning, yet the content changed slightly because the changing historical context meant that certain aspects of the subject assumed greater importance in a given text or time. My research shows that the concept of Providence, itself, is dynamic in Guardini's writing. In order to place Providence in its social context three historical periods will be studied and dealt with in turn.

Guardini's Use of Scripture

In 1934, Guardini said that the Christian Scriptures were his source of creativity[16] together with reflection on his own experience and an intensive encounter with things in the world. In 1928, he said, "Sacred Scripture belongs to the sphere of faith and experience at the same time."[17] In his study of human existence Guardini used Scripture as a source rather than working from a Dogmatic theme as such. Working in this way was unusual for a Roman Catholic scholar at that time and the move to do so enabled him to develop his more organic, relational ideas of God and

---

through the human person with the hope that it may be reached through living. See Reber, *Romano Guardini Begegnen*, 159. Gunda Brüske also notes that Guardini chose to write about Providence as anthropology and central to the person, rather than as part of world history. See Brüske, *Anruf der Freiheit*, 274.

14. Krieg, *Romano Guardini*, 18.
15. Krieg, *Romano Guardini*, 21.
16. Farrugia, "Romano Guardini," 403–6.
17. Guardini, *Würzeln*, 2:368.

the human person, without the restrictions of the predominant and rigid Neo-Scholastic system. In his early life, he wrote many books and articles about the Scriptures.[18] Christian discipleship and pastoral sensitivity was central to this pursuit. Most importantly, for this book, his notion of Providence is grounded in Scripture, and in a particular way in the classical New Testament text on Providence, Matthew 6:25–34.[19] Nevertheless, Guardini was a kerygmatic theologian and, along with other theologians who used this method, such as Karl Barth, Guardini's Biblical hermeneutics have been said to be "pre-critical" and pursued without regard for Scripture scholarship of the time.[20] Krieg argues that Guardini ignored the teaching of Pius XII's 1943 *Divante Afflante Spiritu* and, furthermore, that his Christology was out of date.[21] On the other hand, Krieg says that he made a significant contribution to Catholic spiritual life, especially Catholic life of the laity, which had not been well nourished with Scripture. In short, Guardini's Biblically inspired works made a valuable contribution to help change the future of Catholic Christianity.[22] Scripture and the study of human biography were not mutually exclusive and, in other works, Guardini was able to bring Scripture, literature, philosophy, and theology together. Phenomenology was integral to this task.

---

18. For instance, among many other works he wrote: "Der Weg zu Gott im Neuen Testament"; "Der Glaube im Neuen Testament"; "Die Liebe im Neuen Testament"; "Betrachtungen über Gestalten aus der Heiligen Schrift"; *Im Anfang war das Worte*; *Jesus Christus. Sein bild in den Schriften des Neuen Testament*; *Weisheit der Psalmen*.

19. In his first Providence text, Guardini cites the Liturgy of the Hours (Breviary) and uses relational language of God the Father in whom one could trust, while in subsequent texts, he uses the New Testament passage relating to Providence (Matt 6:25–34). In *The Art of Praying*, 130, he clarifies his concept with Romans 8:28, "All things work together for good for those who love him who are called according to his purpose."

20. Krieg, *Romano Guardini*, 142. Krieg notes that Guardini was a Kerygmatic Theologian. Such a theologian seeks to identify the individual whom Christians call "Christ" and to "know" him rather than "knowing about" him. In addition to Guardini, Karl Barth, Emil Brunner, Karl Adam, Engelbert Krebs, and Hugo Rahner, wanted to help Christians in this way. In this teaching, the Scriptures, Sacraments, religious devotions, and church teachings are used. Critics of this method argue that such an approach is pre-critical in its Biblical hermenutics or even fideistic. See Krieg, *Romano Guardini*, 144.

21. Krieg, *Romano Guardini*, 158.

22. Krieg, *Romano Guardini*, 159.

Phenomenology Based on Human History

Guardini searched for a way to understand human persons in the unity of the eternal world of God. He noted that in ancient times the dichotomy between rationality and intuition did not exist; the separation of the two aspects was a modern problem. In antiquity, there were strong links between the experience of lived mysticism and intuitive symbolic vision. The mystics were also Scholars.[23] Conversely in the modern world, ideas had been tied to only that which could be analyzed.[24] Guardini, chose a methodology which, in his view, would enable him in the presentation of his work, to move beyond Kantian dualism in a way that was real, and not just part of an abstract scheme; to resituate human persons in the totality of their existence, in God.

Firstly, then, Guardini worked phenomenologically with human history. That is to say he took human biography and described it phenomenologically. The phenomenological method is well known.[25] Edmond Husserl developed this method in his writings at the beginning of the twentieth century. The core of the phenomenological method is a description of consciousness without presuppositions and prejudices. Phenomenology is not concerned with facts, but essences, and phenomenology aims to "purify" phenomena from what lends them reality to consider them apart.[26] The "really essential" is sought.[27] All knowledge of the essence is arrived at by the suspension of judgement, an "epoche" whereby all that does not belong to the universal essence is bracketed.[28] That is, other things are suspended from judgement. After "bracketing" the pure phenomena can be described without distortion, as they are, in their essence.

Husserl sought to enlighten his study by considering the consciousness of objects. That is to say, what am I doing when I encounter a certain object? How do I think of it or relate to it? Intentionality is thus a part

23. Gerl-Falkowitz, *Romano Guardini*, 273.

24. Gerl-Falkowitz, *Romano Guardini*, 274.

25. The term comes from the Greek words meaning the setting forth or articulation of what shows itself. It was first used in the eighteenth century by Kant and Hegel and then popularized by Husserl. "Providence" in *The New Catholic Encyclopedia*, 11:780.

26. Husserl, *Ideas*, 43. Later, Guardini's work was influenced by Heidegger with his focus on meaning.

27. Guardini uses this terminology in his attempt to understand the human person and Providence.

28. Husserl, *Ideas*, 44–45.

of this method because Husserl believed that we have an intentionality towards objects. The relation to the object arises when we encounter it and the object is "given" in a "partial" sense. We do not encounter it in its wholeness but since only an aspect is given the remainder cannot be completely known with the same certainty. We may, nevertheless have an idea of the part we can't see. Other aspects of the object may be presented in turn or later and thus complete the knowledge of the object more. For instance a person might enter a room and see a book on a table. Only an aspect of the book is given and the remainder such as the other side of the book cannot be perceived with certainty. In order to see the book in its entirety a person would have to pick it up, turn it around or turn it over and perhaps open it to see all aspects of it. The person encountering the book would have intentionality towards the book. That is, the book would have some sort of significance for him or her. The person will not try to drink from it, for instance.

Consciousness, Husserl believed, lies between two poles; that of the ego and that of the object. The objects are independent of consciousness. Consciousness, on the other hand, may have a number of attitudes towards the object such as believing, doubting, considering, or willing. The object itself has a "sense" (*Sinn*) or ideal character. An intellectual intuition of the thing (*Wesenschauung*) may be taken in its entirety along with the presentation of it. Therefore we can say that the universals are wholly given. Phenomenology aims to realize reality in order to bring its self-givenness to immediate intuitive evidence. By givenness we refer here to those things which can't be reduced to other things or explained by them and are therefore "given" by reality. These are the phenomenological essences (*Wesenheiten*).[29] "Thus the perpetual object may be absolutely known because it is 'reduced' to what is immanent in the act of perception."[30]

Max Scheler, who encouraged the young Guardini to study human biography, defines phenomenological philosophy as that science:

> Which undertakes to look on the essential fundamentals of all existence with rinsed eyes, and redeems the bill of exchange which an over-complex civilisation has drawn on them in terms of symbol upon symbol.[31]

---

29. Brunner, "Foreword."
30. Perry, *Philosophy of the Recent Past*, 210.
31. Scheler, *The Eternal in Man*, 13.

Scheler believed that the essence of that which is religious cannot be reduced to anything else and belongs, in particular, to man. In this science in the place of empirical proof we have insight. Resonant with Guardini, Scheler believed that the divine and human spirit mingle in the spirit of man and the divine is a source for "new life" for human persons.[32] Guardini aims to show the existence of a "religious essence."

> When consciousness touches the essence, it wants to know the significance. In this structure and image, in which the "all" "becomes," every element conditions another. A magnetic attraction to the essence of something calls my attention. Signification in it touches signification in me.[33]

Phenomenology which is involved with human history is that which is discovered in the account of a person's experience and is therefore guided by that person's comprehension of their own situation. Guardini was not the first person to work with life itself. Around the end of the nineteenth century, there were a number of philosophers and theologians who were disenchanted with the intellectualist, more metaphysically based, way of thinking that many people used at that time. They developed their philosophy along the lines of personal being. Historically speaking, this way of thinking has been prominent in Hebrew and Jewish writing and later in, St. Augustine, Pascal, Dostoyevsky, and Kierkegaard.[34] Philosophers of Being, some of whom are more "existentialist" than others, seek to consider the whole being of a person in life itself.[35] Thus personal sentiments such as happiness, suffering, guilt, joy, are highlighted.

Guardini has similar ideas to some of these writers, yet distinguishes himself from others of that time. He objected to both Neo-Kantianism and the anti-metaphysical forms of the "philosophy of life" (*Lebensphilosophie*). Guardini believed that Neo-Kantianism reduced Christianity to subjective ethics whilst the anti-metaphysical forms of 'philosophy of life', such as that of Friedrich Nietzche and Henri Bergson, were too non-rational. Guardini thought the human capacity for reason and the rational dimensions of objective reality should not be overlooked. In

---

32. Scheler, *The Eternal in Man*, 10.

33. Quoted in Babolin, "L'Esperienza Religiosa in Romano Guardini," 314. In his book, *Das Wesen des Christentums*, Guardini argues that the essence of Christianity is Jesus Christ himself. See Guardini, *Das Wesen des Christentums*, 8.

34. Macquarrie, *20th Century Religious Thought*, 193.

35. Macquarrie, *20th Century Religious Thought*, 194.

his opinion, these people, and this includes the neoromantic Catholic theologian, Karl Adam, also lack a language to adequately describe the transcendence of God.[36]

In taking the approach he did Guardini was trying to enter a particular person's consciousness; to look at experience "from within." The experience may be unrepeatable or unverifiable, but Guardini hoped to draw some objective and more general principles out of it. The phenomenologist's method is comprehension rather than discursive scientific knowledge and since Guardini was working from concrete human history and biography the insights gleaned were able to illuminate a clear path because of the vicarious participation in the experience of another. Overall, the experiences studied are seen in the context of an entire life and therefore present with the unity and wholeness of that life in a self-contained framework. It was unusual for a theologian of that time to study human experience. Yet this approach would prove to be an important way of teaching his readers to trust their own experience.[37] The centrality of Christ, especially in the period of National Socialism, included the possibility of human experience as Guardini's incarnational theology trod a path pointing to discipleship. Indeed, the theosis which results from acceptance of Christ is lived with Christ as "innermost principle."[38] Each person, as a "door for God" in the world, is able to contribute to a spirit filled world. The experience of each person is invaluable. The understanding of human experience was also an integral part of Guardini's worldview. He held the chair of Catholic Worldview and, later, Christian Worldview and while not strictly methodology, as such, the area crucial to an understanding of his worldview and view of Providence is his notion of the Opposites, to which we now turn.

The Opposites

Guardini's work on the Opposites *(Der Gegensatz)* was published in 1925 and presents the idea of *Anschauung*: intuitive perception. *Anschauung*

---

36. Krieg, *Romano Guardini*, 13. Here Krieg also notes Guardini's indication of his own path from Plato through Dante and Pascal to Hölderlin, Mörike, and Rilke.

37. A former student of Guardini, the German Jewish philosopher, Hannah Arendt, notes that an inability to trust one's own experience contributed to the ideological thinking seen in the period of National Socialism. See Arendt, *The Origins of Totalitarianism*, 470.

38. See chapter 4.

is the act of knowledge which takes place in the extreme tension of the opposing poles of human life.[39] Guardini preferred to work with the "living-concrete"; phenomenologically working with biography or human history. His study of Augustine's confessions, Dostoevsky's characters or Pascal's biography, work towards this end. Out of the polarity of the opposites which together form the whole, living conceptions may be known.[40] Nevertheless, the living-concrete can only be known by the act of knowing which is conceptual and intuitive and therefore embraces the antithetical structure of human thought.[41]

Guardini believes, the act of knowing takes place in the extreme tension between opposing poles in human life. Furthermore, he searches for a way to understand reality while not rescinding from the concrete. That is to say, he moves from "conceptual conceptions" to "living conceptions" as understood by the ancients. He wants to include the richness of all reality while maintaining the awareness of unity and singularity which he believes the Divine has. Guardini sees opposition as polarity which is contained in all that lives, most importantly the concrete. The opposition is not just a characteristic but life itself and the opposition involves contraries but not contradictions. That is, both arise out of the unity of that which is but one does not negate the other. Rather, they co-exist and balance each other and in personal existence a person may bring the opposing elements into harmony with each other. Guardini indicates that the contradiction between good and bad cannot be mediated. For example good and evil are contradictions not contraries, because in principle they cannot co-exist at the same time, whilst silence and speech or solitude and community may be "two sides of the same coin" which complement and balance each other. Being an individual and member of a group can also exist simultaneously. Two things are implied at the same time; relative exclusiveness and relative collegiality of forces.[42]

Unlike Göethe, Herman Hesse, Carl Jung, and Thomas Mann, Guardini does not accept that evil is a necessary part of life. He considers that Romanticism wrongly placed good and evil in the category of opposition

---

39. Laubach, "Romano Guardini," 114. In another article outlining the work of German theologians, Gerald A. McCool describes "Intuitive Knowledge" as the presence to the intellect of an existing singular in the richness of its concrete unicity. McCool, "The Primacy of Intuition," 57–73.

40. Müller, "The Philosophy of Christian Existence," 50–54.

41. Laubach, "Romano Guardini," 114.

42. Gerl-Falkowitz, *Romano Guardini*, 269.

whereas, to him, they rightly belong in the category of contradiction.[43] Yet, contraries are necessary for a balance of the tension which arises in the totality and concreteness of life in time, because in time we are able to experience the clarity of singular aspects of life rather like a pattern that has been enlarged and brought in its singular elements to the fore. One–after–anotherness is possible. Making up the whole, the singular elements may be opposites in the sense of contraries but not in the sense of contradiction. Guardini's theory is that with contraries the multifaceted nature of things is held in tension without synthesis as such. Movement is needed in order to realize the contrary elements. Therefore life itself, having different modes of being, must necessarily have flexibility and movement arising out of the unity of the whole of life, in order to realize fulfillment. The "simple" arises here. There is unity but not synthesis which would reveal complexity. At another, deeper, level unity arises out of all that is; God himself.

Guardini's theory showed his intention to move from the abstract zone of logic to the concrete. The opposition occurs in a pre-cognitive way, in life itself, and thinking can be corrected because unlike the unilaterality of "scientific" approaches, concrete life is present in fullness. The pre-cognitive aspect, working symbolically, renders the system highly individual (particular for each person) since the multifaceted nature of symbol makes significance highly personal. Order within the living of our existence comes forth from the unity of God in which the person finds their true worth and meaning in the world. The order is a work of grace.[44] In the manner of Max Scheler, Guardini distinguishes different spheres of being but, unlike Scheler, Guardini places being before value; noting that the Logos holds supremacy over eros.[45] Against the dualistic thinking of Kant, he wants his notion of being to be neither linear nor hierarchical but holistic in the sense of the totality of existence lived physically, spiritually, in the world, since for him, it is the heart which is the organ of knowledge, and indeed, in its corporality, united with spirit which moves it to clarity of vision.[46]

It could be argued that the idea of unity in a work may lead to a determinist theory, yet in Guardini's work individual initiative and human

---

43. Guardini, *Diario-Appunti e Testi*, 245.
44. Guardini, *Christliche Besinnung*, 7.
45. Gerl-Falkowitz, *Romano Guardini*, 278.
46. Gerl-Falkowitz, *Romano Guardini*, 278.

choice are important. Since the Judeo-Christian tradition, especially from Augustine, has usually considered evil to be the absence of good, Guardini's contradictories stand more clearly in that trajectory. Guardini's work, especially on the life of Christ, makes no attempt to diminish the negativity or undesirability of evil. This aspect, in relation to Providence, will be considered later in the thesis and the centrality of Christ in Guardini's writing discussed in chapter 4. We now turn to a brief consideration of Providence in contemporary scholarship.

Contemporary Theological Literature on Providence

Divine Providence, in the Scriptures, refers to God's loving care of human persons. In the book of Job, the Hebrew word used for God's Providence means care or charge (Job 10:12) while the Greek term (πρόνοια) expressing the idea of Divine Providence means forethought (Wis 14:3; 17:2).[47] Theologically the term refers to the act by which God "causes cares for, and directs all creatures to their proper ends, in attaining which each one contributes to the final purpose of the universe – the manifestation of His external glory."[48]

Providence is a classical theological theme and still relevant to contemporary theology.[49] A number of well-known authors come to mind.[50] Other scholarship on providence includes books looking at the Scriptural view of providence such as such as the aforementioned Wright's, *Divine Providence in the Bible*. Since Guardini worked primarily from Scripture it is worth noting, in some detail, Wright's research on the notion of providence in Scripture. Wright's work reveals God as 1) Sustainer of the universe who guides the world, out of love, sustains it in being and brings it to its final goal which is God; 2) The universe achieves this goal as it reflects the glory of God and intelligent creatures render service and praise; 3) Salvation of intelligent creatures occurs as they share in divine life through resurrection of the dead, vision of God and love; 4) God guides the world by an overall plan of providence that directs all that

---

47. "Providence," 11:780.
48. "Providence," 11:780.
49. For recent examples, see Wright, *Divine Providence in the Bible*; see also Tiessen, *Providence and Prayer*.
50. Including John Hick, Maurice Wiles, Christoph Schwöbel, Colin Gunton, Denis Edwards, and Ian Ramsey.

happens to God's purposes rather than determining each event ahead of time.[51] Importantly, in the Bible, God does not achieve God's purposes by divine action alone as human persons are also asked to act to promote the divine purpose.[52] This view concurs with Guardini's position.

Some of the literature which has developed in response to the debate on "Open Theism" is also Scripture based. Open Theism, as a movement, developed in the last twenty years, as a reaction to the ideas arising out of Calvinist, Greek and Latin ideas of God. These theologians argue that the God of the Bible is a living God and therefore did not have the attributes that classical theism focused on such as immutability, impassibility and timelessness. In that sense they can argue that God is living, personal, relational, Good, and loving. Open Theism argues for a personal God who is open to the future.[53] Guardini's theology bears some similarities to the work of these openness theologians, although that statement has to be qualified. Guardini presents a living, personal, relational God and he believes God is omniscient. God knows the future but he leaves human persons free to make their own decisions. Human person are thereby afforded integrity and dignity. Providence is experienced in that context. How that occurs will be developed in other chapters. Since it may be said that God is the ground of a person's being and ever-present in a person's existence, a critic may question whether in Guardini's mind enough freedom is given to the human person or if the human person is autonomous enough. In asserting that Providence is not a finished, fixed plan for the future, but is open for completion by human persons, Guardini shows that while people are free to make their own decisions God is aware of what the future will bring and there is a path which will bring providential fulfillment and is open for each human person to discover.

Providence in Guardini's Writings, and Where It May Be Found

1. "Siebter Sonntag nach Pfingsten" ["Seventh Sunday after Pentecost"]
2. *Conscience*

---

51. Wright, *Providence in the Bible*, 2:258.

52. Wright, *Providence in the Bible*, 2:261. This human action is seen in Guardini's work and will be discussed below.

53. For instance, see Rice, *The Openness of God*; Pinnock, *The Openness of God*; Sanders, *The God who Risks*; Hasker, *God, Time, and Knowledge*; Hasker, *Providence, Evil and the Openness of God*.

3. *The Living God*

4. *The Lord's Prayer*

5. "Was JESUS unter Vorsehung Versteht" [What JESUS Understood about Providence]

6. *The World and the Person*

7. *The Art of Praying*

8. *Freedom, Grace, and Destiny*

9. *Wunder und Zeichen* [Miracle and Sign]

10. *Gebet und Wahrheit* [Prayer and Truth]

Guardini's Notion of Providence in Relation to the Providence Theology of His Time and Before

In the nineteenth century, a dichotomy was often seen between the things of the world or human persons, and God or spiritual things. To some theologians the world or God was "other." Guardini argues that neither the world nor God is "other" to human persons because all are inextricably linked (see later in the book). The world is to be welcomed rather than disparaged in our relationship with God. The world is God's world, created and intrinsic to the relationship between God and human persons. Guardini's human world is an ontologically-contingent world and it is with this argument, intrinsic to Guardini's notion of Providence, that Guardini is able to address Kant's dualism and neo-Scholasticism's over-rationalized schema. In this sense he is able to present a view of Providence which does justice to God and the world.

Guardini grounds Providence in the theology of God the Creator. Accordingly, Michael A. Hoonhout argues that this action, on the part of any theologian of modern times, is significant.[54] Writing on the exemplarity of St. Thomas Aquinas, Hoonhaut notes that while Christianity, in the tradition of the Bible has, from the beginning, grounded Providence in the theology of the Creator, the emergence of Nominalism in the fourteenth century spelt an end to this connection. Some scholars linked Providence (incompatibly) to the human will and freedom as absolutes. In short, these arguments considerably truncated the argument

---

54. Hoonhout, "Grounding Providence," 1–19.

about Divine Providence while intensifying the arguments about freewill and freedom. Although Guardini discusses freewill and freedom in the post war period, he still grounds Providence in the theology of God the Creator where the place of grace is important. Guardini is still therefore able to maintain the integrity of his notion of Providence. In Guardini's thought both human will and freedom are compatible with Providence especially as both are grounded in the grace of God. Guardini's assertion is that the human person's response to God who is the ground of their being, testifies to a unity which would not be possible in a conception of the human will and freedom as absolute. Furthermore, by grounding Providence in the theology of the Creator God, Guardini is able to address the difficult area of nature and grace which nineteenth century theology was unable to adequately deal with without giving way to a dualism.

God is not only the ground of all being but a God of communion and while not termed by Guardini as such, the meaning embodied in the theological concept of *Theosis* is integral to Guardini's theology of Providence and illuminates his argument. In some of his later work the term Christification could be used because of his focus on the link with the indwelling Christ.[55] Krieg notes that Guardini chose to use the language of Existentialism[56] and not the theological language of Neo-Scholasticism. This assertion would concur with Macquarrie's statement that, "Belief in providence like belief in creation is founded existentially." In this sense Guardini chose language appropriate to writing on Providence.[57]

Guardini presents Providence as an alternative to "destiny."[58] Destiny in his work is transformed into Providence and this aspect is well developed as an argument in his later work *Freedom, Grace, and Destiny*. His theology of Providence is consonant with mainstream Christian theology on the subject and defends the belief in secondary causes. That is to say, Guardini's notion of Providence has a double agency although ultimately the grace of God has primacy.[59] Thus it is possible to say that

---

55. A Christological approach to *Theosis*, as understood in biblical and Patristic sources, is discussed in Cooper, *Christification*, 15.

56. Krieg, *Romano Guardini*, 11.

57. John Macquarrie argues that it is through happenings which strengthen our being, regardless of our own actions, that a person comes to believe in providence. See Macquarrie, *Principles of Christian Theology*, 241.

58. Which may be understood as akin to "fate."

59. The notion of secondary causation was brought to prominence by St. Thomas Aquinas who argued for God as the primary cause of reality, while nature and human

Providence according to Guardini is grounded in the theology of God the Creator acting with the co-operation of human beings.[60] He shows how Providence for the individual person can be understood to proceed with that of Providence in human history. Guardini presents a contemporary synthesis of traditional spirituality (present in the work of early Christian theologians) and modern philosophical ideas which are able to show feasibility for living with Providence in today's world. The world itself with its nature, socio-historical-cultural context and people themselves, is important. Guardini held that human persons are held in the being of God who gives them freedom, who lets them be, yet paradoxically, God continues to show interest in each person and be involved in every aspect of their lives. Human persons, regardless of ethnic or social background, are called to exercise personal decisions, to respond to the call to relationship with the personal, transcendent yet immanent God while that same God is able to guide and show involvement in their lives and the world.

The Review of Critical Literature on Providence in Guardini's Work: The Contribution of Guardini Scholars

While Guardini scholars have considered Guardini's notion of Providence to be an important component of his overall work, in most cases they have written on his idea of Providence as part of a larger work. Each has made a very valuable contribution and we will consider each scholar's work in turn.

---

persons have causal powers of their own. See Robson, *Ontology and Providence in Creation*, 119.

60. Guardini's theology of Providence resonates with the words of Macquarrie, who notes that the doctrine of creation need not refer to creation only in a single moment of time but can mean the dependence of the being at all times on the Being who lets them be. Where creation is seen as an event in the past, the doctrine of Providence is able to establish a link and show God's continuing interest in God's world. Macquarrie notes that "Faith in God's providence asserts that [divine] creativity has a positive character ... is ... not just a random creativity.... [R]ather it is an ordered movement into ever fuller and richer kinds of being." Macquarrie, *Principles of Christian Theology*, 239. This statement by Macquarrie is commensurate with Guardini's notion of Providence.

Gunda Brüske

Gunda Brüske, a German scholar, includes a section on Providence in her book, *Anruf der Freiheit*. Her book focuses on the theological anthropology of Guardini and considers the significance of human persons in his theology. In the book which comprehensibly covers his thought in a number of areas, she puts the discussion about Providence under the overall heading of "Christian Existence in Time." Providence immediately precedes her section on the Saints and the fulfillment of humanity, which reflects Guardini's priorities and way of thinking. She rightly notes that Providence has played a very large role in Guardini's overall thought. Her analysis treats the concept as a whole in the sense that although she notes the special importance of the National Socialist Period for his writings on Providence, she does not treat the other periods of time as being different in any way. Brüske relates Providence to being and says that in Providence-living a person lives from the being of the Father. She notes that Guardini is able to show how the being of the Saints changed. The Christian person can change in the same way as the Saints did. Purity of faith and love of the Kingdom of God are important in Providence-living and the link between nature and grace in his writing is from Godly grace and human freedom. For Brüske, Guardini's world is a world of being and is "my own concrete world."[61] The world of being has a concrete form (*Gestalt*) but Guardini puts this with a person's interior, and says that when a person focuses on the Kingdom of God the person will have a changed being. The environmental social sequel is a changed environment; a changed "whole." Guardini has chosen to speak about Providence and make his contribution to the field, unconfined by Dogma, in reflecting on the human person. Here, she notes, Providence occurs through the I-Thou relationship rather than a cosmological world picture and in this way it has been developed with an environmental-psychological focus in order to clarify the effectiveness of God through this participation.

Alfons Knoll

In the comprehensive work, *Glaube und Kulture bei Romano Guardini*, the German scholar Alfons Knoll put his section on Providence in the category of "Concretization in Christian Existence." Knoll focuses on

---

61. Brüske, *Anruf der Freiheit*, 275.

Providence as found in *The World and the Person* and *Freedom, Grace, and Destiny*. He writes that Guardini sets out a spatial model of Providence rather than a temporal one. In that sense it is possible to speak about Providence from an ahistorical position.[62] When the "whole" is seen in the concrete, notes Knoll, it remains an idea.[63] Nevertheless, that which is seen in history must ultimately be thought of in the temporal sense. This is dealt with in the existential approach that Kierkegaard, Jaspers and Heidegger used. Only in the exercise of choice can the world of human persons be constructed in certain situations as historical.[64] Knoll writes that Guardini addresses the importance of personal choice, grounded on the Creator and Redeemer, over the other possibilities of Autonomy (radically self-reliant independence) and Heteronomy (a person's center lies outside of him or herself and is manipulable).[65] For the fullness of Providence, the Creator can guide the human person, as the Sermon on the Mount, the center of the Christian message, says.[66] Christ wanted unity between the human person and the world, thus in Christian being, the history of the individual and history in its entirety go together at the same time yet only in relationship with God. Knoll considers Guardini's view of Providence to be forward looking, rather than a reflection of the Middle Ages or early Christian period, because of the concentration on the New Heaven and New Earth.[67]

Joachim Reber

Joachim Reber, another German Scholar, wrote his doctoral work on the philosophical notion of world in Guardini's work.[68] In his book, *Romano Guardini Begegnen*, he devotes a chapter to Guardini's notion of Providence, taking most of his argument from Guardini's ideas, in *The World*

---

62. Here Knoll cites the Guardini scholar Eugene Biser who argued that Guardini wrote from the entirety of the world rather than from history, as such, because there would be a cognitive reorienting when the reality of history appeared in it. See Biser, *Interpretation and Veranderung*, 92.

63. Knoll, *Glaube und Kultur*, 371.

64. Knoll, *Glaube und Kultur*, 371.

65. Knoll, *Glaube und Kultur*, 372. Guardini explains these terms in his work see below.

66. Knoll, *Glaube und Kultur*, 373.

67. Knoll, *Glaube und Kultur*, 375.

68. Reber, *Die Welt des Christen*.

and the Person. He notes Guardini's insightful awareness of the difference in the environment that each person has. The environment around a loving person, for example, will be different to that around a person who is hard of heart. Providence is a result of choice while destiny is just what happens. Whatever is carried out in the world is not only from the outer world but also the inner world and not only from things but also from people. The important thing for each person is their attitude of mind which determines their destiny. The "Kingdom of God" attitude is inner-worldly and particular for each person. Such an attitude is an opening for God's work. Every human heart is a door for God in the world. When one sets their mind on the Kingdom of God and God's righteousness, in belief and trust, the door is open and God begins the new creation.

The new creation of the world is from the new creation of each person and from each person God makes the new world. The creation of the world is not a closed or finished act and is much more than the idea of *creatio continua*. Guardini is convinced that from the beginning God makes an opening from possibilities. The new creation and fulfillment of the world doesn't come from God's act over the world but from every individual human person bound to this attitude and freedom. Such people receive God's strength and power to make the world new. God wants the person's being to be holy but that can only be so through freedom. Guardini develops his miracle-thinking from an ontological point of view. This approach enables a "going beyond" with new possibilities. In the case of miracles God creates from natural things and the potential which is already in the world. The Saints demonstrate the way the world can change as the attitude and environment around a person is influenced to an extraordinary degree.

Hans Urs von Balthasar

Other Guardini scholars have made references, albeit brief, about Guardini's notion of Providence. For example, the Swiss scholar, Hans Urs von Balthasar, wrote a study on Guardini in 1970, *Romano Guardini: Reform from the Source*, and says that the first in a series of three favorite themes that permeate Guardini's, work is Providence. He writes that Guardini wanted to clarify the place of chance and destiny which do not lose their ambiguity in this world until there is providential guidance of the "eternal Father's providence, which guides from above with the co-operation of the Holy Spirit in the Divine Word and Son, [which] allows all things to work out for the best for all who truly believe and love."[69] Balthasar notes that the meaning of our incomplete world points to the ultimate cosmic meaning which is the "eschatological recreation of the world in the risen Christ."[70] Through Christ human persons are able to bring their life into accord with God's eschatological design as they seek the Kingdom of God and show a desire to share God's care and responsibility for the world. In this way things around the person will be ordered from God's providential hand to the "ultimate centre of meaning which lies in God."[71]

These Guardini scholars have given a comprehensive and insightful glimpse into Guardini's writing on Providence. A brief consideration of the work of other Guardini scholars will be found in chapter 2. We turn now to an overall critical review of literature on Guardini's work and my contribution.

Gaps in the Literature on Guardini's notion of Providence and the importance of this book

The review of critical literature on Providence in Guardini's writing has demonstrated that there is still some room for scholarly research especially in the area of conceptual development and a comprehensive view of Guardini's notion of Providence. Most of the books written about Guardini treat Providence as a small section in a much larger work on another topic and are therefore relatively brief in their comments. Some studies of Guardini's writing treat Providence as a concept which is consistent through all of his work. They tend to concentrate on one or two texts for this assessment or a single period in time. Although Brüske names the 1916 text as one of the texts on Providence, none of the writers refer to this text beyond that reference as part of their writing on Providence in Guardini's work.[72] I, conversely, consider the text to be axiomatic for the argument that Guardini's concept of Providence is based primarily on Scripture and the doctrine of God, in the first instance, and which shows the importance of the nature of God. This book addresses these problems.

69. Balthasar, *Romano Guardini*, 48.
70. Balthasar, *Romano Guardini*, 48.
71. Balthasar, *Romano Guardini*, 48.
72. Nevertheless, it was Dr. Brüske who first told me of the existence of this text.

The significance of this book is its challenge to those interpretations of Guardini which see Providence as a minor concept within his work or as one which remains fairly stable and a moderately significant concept throughout his life. This book, on the development of Guardini's notion of Providence, shows that Providence is in fact a central notion for Guardini, and indeed could be seen as a key to his theology. It also shows that, while the basic pattern of his treatment of Providence was already present in his early works, his account develops over time in a dynamic way. By doing this, the thesis offers a fuller and more sophisticated interpretation of one of the most important figures in Catholic intellectual life in the twentieth century.

The Central Research Question

Studying Guardini's writing on Providence spanning more than forty years, it became clear that the passage of time demonstrated changes in Guardini's notion of Providence and the texts in which those writings were found, yet that was not reflected in the publications of the Guardini scholars who wrote on Providence in Guardini's writing. Therefore my central research question is: *Did Guardini's writing on Providence change or develop in each period of Guardini's writing, and if so, how and why? How did his notion of Providence change?* In order to answer this question I asked the following questions: Are those changes actually development? If there were differences revealed in different periods, what were they related to? Did those differences reflect the socio-historical context or something else such as theology and if so, how? If the socio-historical context is important what is the place of the "world" in Guardini's notion of Providence? Does one need to turn from the world to experience God's Providence? Was his writing a reaction to the context or did he follow it or learn from it? Was his writing counter-cultural and if so why? If the socio-cultural context was important what was the place of tradition in Guardini's writing? What is the tradition, and source of the tradition, which informs Guardini's Providence writing? What is the relevance of the development of Providence to human lives? What is the relationship of the Providence texts in each period to other texts Guardini wrote in the same period? What is the importance of the context or other themes in the texts where chapters on Providence are situated?

Methodology

The book is a study of the development of Romano Guardini's notion of Providence. In order to study this development I have worked chronologically, looking at three major time periods of his writing, roughly corresponding to the period before National Socialism arose in Germany, the National Socialist period, and the post-war period. Taking the texts chronologically has enabled a comparison to be made from one text to another and differences to be seen. The textual comparison has proved to be significant. The consideration of each of Guardini's texts, including the earliest text written before World War II, shows that Guardini's notion of Providence is firmly grounded in the Scriptures and Doctrine of God. Therefore when Guardini addressed issues during the period of National Socialism and presented an alternative view of Providence to Hitler, his view of Providence had been developed from his earlier work rather than simply being a reaction to Hitler, although Guardini's writing on Providence was certainly an important means of opposing Hitler and challenging Hitler's use of the term.

I have sought to work systematically through each of the major texts on Providence, studying not only the explicit text but also the overall text in which it was presented. I have chosen to work inductively, allowing the texts to reveal the themes and focus of Guardini's writing on and around Providence (rather than taking a deductive approach which might have considered classical Providence themes and then searched for those categories in Guardini's texts) although I have considered some classical Providence themes such as Predestination. Guardini's very early writing grounds Providence in the characteristics or nature of God, and in each period, I have examined his treatment of Providence under four major themes that appear in his Providence writings. They are: 1) Providence in its relation to Jesus Christ; 2) Providence is understood in relationship with God; 3) Providence and the individual human person are important to God; 4) Providence is new existence and new creation. The chronological treatment shows how Guardini's theology of Providence, understood in relation to these four themes, is significant at all stages of his work and also develops over time, partly at least in response to the shifting socio-cultural environments in which he is writing, but always grounded in a scriptural and theological account. I have critically evaluated Guardini's concept of Providence in the overall context of his theology and the socio-historical background linking Guardini's theological response to challenges of the society of the time. A comparison of *various editions of the same texts* show differences that reflect the context of Guardini's writing[73] as he sought to address the issues in society. Working on the phenomenology of human biography meant a focus on human existence or human experience. Guardini drew his theology of Providence primarily from Scripture. Furthermore, in the sense that he paid attention to the social context in which he worked, Guardini worked contextually, although, often, counter-culturally, leading me to seek to understand the *mileu* in which Guardini's desk and pulpit were situated. Guardini's work involves theological anthropology, which has assumed importance in this book.

My own archival work extends to Guardini's books, articles, audio recordings and sermons although the concentration has been on the texts listed earlier in this chapter. Guardini held positions in philosophy of religion and dialogued quite extensively with philosophers. Therefore it has been necessary to pay attention to the writings of some of these philosophers such as Kant, Nietzsche, Buber, and Heidegger. Guardini was a colleague of both Buber and Heidegger and regularly exchanged texts with them. Their influence is seen in his work and my comments about that can be found in the next chapter.

Theological Anthropology and Phenomenology

We have mentioned, above, the contemporary sources of theological investigation, namely, Sacred Scripture, tradition, human experience and reason. Guardini is a philosopher of human existence. In the existential method meaning is discovered during the act of existence while for the philosopher of existence, meaning occurs when human understanding is thrown open to the whole of being in encounter with the absolute. Guardini argues that human persons, made in the image or likeness of God, can become "children of God" after repentance and conversion to God. Recent theological research on theological anthropology notes the importance of the concepts of "difference" and "the other."[74] While Guardini will not say God is "other" because God is the ground of our being,

---

73. Guardini's work is often countercultural and as Bevans notes, the true communication of the gospel may involve a conversion, "a radical metanoia, a U-turn of the mind." Bevans, *Models of Contextual Theology*, 117. In this assertion, Bevans is taking up the ideas of Newbigin, *The Gospel and Western Culture*, 5–6.

74. Tolliday and Thomson, *Speaking Differently*, 1.

"the other," in another sense, assumes importance in our own openness to human persons and to God.

Phenomenology, as understood by Edmund Husserl, is the philosophical study of the structures of experience and consciousness. Martin Heidegger, although initially a student of Husserl, modified this study to a study of ontology in the belief that the existence of the human person (*Dasein*) was more central than thoughts about his or her consciousness. In his mind a person's state of mind is not determined by existence but is an effect of it. Guardini's writing shows both the method of Husserl and, later, that of Heidegger who was an academic colleague whose influence is discussed below. The historical, social, theological and academic context are all important to this study and form a valuable background which has been attended to and referred to where relevant.

Biography and History

The book is a work of Theological Anthropology within the discipline of Systematic Theology, but entry to the thought of Romano Guardini on Providence is inextricably related to his life story—his biography. Focus on the individual or turn to the subject in contemporary writing has seen a trend towards "life writing."[75] Furthermore, contemporary trends in historical research show a turn to a biographical approach. An historian has argued that, "For too long, too many historians have been too concerned with impersonal forces, underlying structures and long-term developments. Now, 'people' are back."[76] Biography enables the person to be seen in a context while the historical and theological details are able to move beyond mere structuralism.

Structure of the Book

The book has been divided into five chronological chapters. This chapter, chapter 1, is the Introduction to the thesis. In it I have identified Guardini the man and his work. In chapter 2, I have considered Guardini's biographical details and influences on Guardini while noting those whom Guardini has influenced. Significant aspects of the socio-historical background are presented. In chapter 3, I have considered the early period

75. Caine, *Biography and History*, 6.
76. Blanning and Cannadine, *History and Biography*, preface.

of Guardini's work from 1916 to 1929. Providence is studied under four themes. Within chapter 3, *Theme One* focuses on God and God's nature instead of the experience of Jesus which is found in the other chapters. chapter 4 deals with the Nationalist Socialist time from 1930 to the end of the war in 1945. Clear changes are seen in this period, and although Hitler came to power in 1933, changes appropriate to Guardini's response to the regime started in 1930. In chapter 5, I have analyzed Guardini's writings in the post war period, 1945 to 1963.

In his last Providence text, Guardini noted that Providence means much more than the text, which has been lifted out from the whole but means: the epitome of guidance, the life of human persons, the individual and the group, the development of all God had wanted in creation and in redemption. The text, with a special connection to the proclamation especially emphasized by Jesus, is taken from the whole.[77] It is all of these things, brought together, that will speak of Providence in this book.

---

77. Guardini, *Gebet und Wahrheit*, 121.

2

Guardini's World

Relevant Biographical Details of Romano Guardini and Attention to the Socio-Historical Context

Biography

GUARDINI WAS BORN IN Italy but moved to Germany with his parents when he was one. His cultural and formal education was both Italian and German and there were a number of factors in his life, and education, which helped to shape the content and method of his work, which we will now consider.

Member of a Literary Circle

As a bright young man at high school (*Gymnasium*),[1] Guardini had been invited to participate in a cultural group which met together regularly to discuss history, the arts and religious belief.[2] This proved to be formative for his future writing because it opened up areas of thought which he would draw on later, such as the writings of Rilke, John Henry

---

1. A "Gymnasium" education in Germany does not refer to a sports school but a specifically academic one which is offered to good students who can expect to go on to university.

2. They studied writers such as John Henry Newman, Léon Bloy, and the medieval mystics. Krieg, *Romano Guardini*, 4.

Newman and the medieval mystics.[3] This link between cultural interests and theology is important for understanding Guardini's approach to theology because in refusing to develop an abstract theory which was not grounded in the lived experience of the human person, he was able to develop his notion of the "living concrete," looking phenomenologically at human lives, especially those in literature. These studies provided him with ample material with which to develop his theology and also involved the existential phenomenology of the human person.

Higher Education

As a high school student Guardini had been enriched by the literary circle but, at university, he initially chose to study chemistry and economics which did not really match his personality and he eventually moved to the study of theology following a religious experience and renewal of faith. Initially, he sought to study with the progressive theologian Herman Schell but the University of Würzburg, where Schell taught, did not accept him and he found a place at the University of Freiburg. It was there that Guardini discovered his love for theology and decided to transfer to the University of Tübingen with its unique, creative theological faculty which was seen by some as radical. The university had its own contribution to make to Guardini's formation.

Tübingen University, spread over the picturesque university town of Tübingen, was founded in 1477 by a regional prince and authorized by Pope Sixtus IV. Three chairs were established in theology. The Protestant theologian and reformer, Philip Melanchthon also studied there. Significantly, "The whole university was stamped with a Lutheran orthodoxy" and the eminence of some of the teachers ensured its place and importance as a theological faculty.[4] Nevertheless, there was a Roman Catholic Faculty. In 1817, a Catholic faculty of theology was established and became one of the most important Catholic Centres of theology in

---

3. In 1908, while he was a theology student at the University of Tübingen, he and a friend formed their own circle for the study of world literature. Krieg, *Romano Guardini*, 5. See also Schilson, *Perspectiven Theologisher Erneurung*, 25. Schilson notes that Guardini didn't just simply go into theology and philosophy but studied the meeting of Christian believers with the world order so that he could take a view of the whole.

4. Numerous well-known philosophers and theologians such as G. W. F. Hegel and F. W. J. Shelling were also educated there. *New Catholic Encyclopedia*, 233.

Germany.⁵ The faculty has a combination of historical and speculative methods, with an emphasis on relating modern thought to doctrine of the faith.⁶ Characteristically, Guardini had chosen a university which specialized in the type of theology he would develop well.⁷ Yet, there was a price for his choice because, after he was ordained, he found he was denied the possibility of teaching in the Diocese of Mainz because even the *Catholic* Faculty at Tübingen did not ensure the Roman Catholic orthodoxy the diocese was looking for. Nevertheless, Tübingen had other benefits for Guardini's work. While there, Guardini had become acquainted with a Benedictine monastery nearby which was to have a formative effect on his life and work.

Benedictine Oblate

Guardini was a lifelong Oblate of St. Benedict. His Oblate vows of reading Sacred Scripture on a daily basis, the Rule of St. Benedict and praying the Liturgy of the Hours, contributed to a large number of publications, particularly in his early writings, which reflected this commitment.⁸ For instance, as early as 1916, reflecting both his interest in Scripture and his life as a priest and Benedictine Oblate, he wrote, "The Psalms from the Breviary on Thursday and the Spiritual Life."⁹

The Rule for which St. Benedict is famous presents an organic pattern for the balance of work and prayer, action and reflection.¹⁰ The goal of the Rule is God, a goal to be achieved by keeping a clear focus on the centrality of Christ and, in the light of Christ, recognizing the sacredness of people and things as integral to God's creation—a world made sacred.

---

5. In addition to Guardini, many other prominent theologians including J. A. Möhler, K. Adam, and H. Küng were former students.

6. "Tübingen School," in *The Oxford Dictionary of the Christian Church*, 350.

7. His teachers there will be discussed below.

8. Some of these publications are: "Der religiöse Gehorsam" (1916); "Die Bedeutung der Psalmen vom feriae quintae für das geistliche Leben" (1913); "Zum begriffe des Befels und des Gehorsams" (1916); "Die Liturgie und die psychologischen Gesetz des gemeinsams Beten" (1917); "Lex orandi" (1919); "Von Sinn des Gehorchens" (1920); "Das Objective in Gebetsleben" (1921).

9. Guardini, "Die Psalmen," 54.

10. The Rule taps into the aesthetic beauty of the world and the significance of its depth. It is intended to be a primer of the practical application of living the Christian life in community.

The importance of conversion (*metanoia*) runs right through the rule from beginning to end. Guardini's theology of Providence reflects the importance of each of these points testifying to his belief that his vocation was to bring the spirituality and insights gained in the monastery to the parishes and would ultimately be spread to the wider world.[11]

Liturgical Leader

Guardini's involvement with Benedictinism also led him to his appreciation of liturgy. In his autobiographical "report" on his life, *Bericht über mein Leben*, Guardini recorded his first impressions during his visit to the Benedictine Abbey of Beuron in 1906. Since the guest house was still being constructed, Guardini stayed within the cloister itself. He writes:

> My first visit there remains vivid in my memory.... The church was already dark with only a few candles in the choir. The monks stood in their places and prayed by heart the beautiful psalms of Compline which was then monotonal. Mystery moved through the whole church, sacred and simultaneously soothing. I eventually saw that the liturgy has a great deal of power and glory. At the beginning it was the simple door of Compline rather than the portals of majestic liturgical action (at Mass) that led me more intimately into the heart of the liturgy's holy world.[12]

Thus it was at a Benedictine Abbey that Guardini discovered in the liturgy's simplicity and mystery, a sense both of God's presence and of the incomprehensibility of God. These themes of God's simultaneous immanence and transcendence are reflected in his later work. More significantly, for this book, Guardini's sense of the important role liturgy and communal prayer had in discerning God's guidance was reflected in his writing on Providence. His experience of God in the liturgy of the monastery not only found expression in his writing, but in his work with the Liturgical Movement in which he was a leader.

Guardini's ideas on liturgy are reflected in his publication in 1918 of *The Spirit of the Liturgy*. The work was an immediate success and contributed to liturgical renewal in a major way. Max Scheler praised the book[13]

---

11. Krieg, *Romano Guardini*, 80.

12. Kreig's translation of Guardini's words in *Berichte über mein Leben*, cited in Kreig, *Romano Guardini*, 74.

13. Gerl, *Romano Guardini*, 109.

and so many Catholics bought it that it had to be reprinted twelve times in the first five years.[14] The sources in the book are clearly footnoted from Scripture and it speaks, with seriousness, to a person's spiritual needs. Furthermore, the book shows the differences and relationships between communal liturgical action and individual worship

> The Church is self-contained, a structure-system of intricate and invisible vital principles, of means and ends, of activity and production, of people organization, laws. The faithful are actively united by a vital and fundamental principle common to them all. The principle is Christ. (The Holy Spirit) governs this living unity grafting the individual onto it, granting him a share in its fellowship and preserving this right for him.[15]

This passage demonstrates the interaction of Guardini's theology with individual and community experience. The role of the Church and tradition from which it springs, was to make the Triune God present to human persons. Krieg notes that, in his pastoral leadership, Guardini was able to show what the liturgy could be, as he involved the students in the responses at Mass and faced the congregation, long before Vatican II instituted the practice.[16] Guardini had spoken of the painful experience of saying the Mass while the entire congregation remained absorbed in their own devotions.[17] Most importantly he was able to show the integration of personal piety and communal action in the liturgy so that neither aspect was excluded or isolated from the other.

In this book, Guardini demonstrated that Christ was the center of the liturgy. Christ leads the community's worship as head of the mystical body and enables the community to give thanks and praise in the Holy Spirit to God the Father.[18] The importance of Christ, to Providence, was to be developed considerably in Guardini's writing in the following period of National Socialism. *The Spirit of the Liturgy* thus reflected Guardini's attempt to recover the true nature of worship and involve the people in it. The influence of this work and Guardini's other writings was considerable and the effect of Guardini's work on renewal in the Catholic

---

14. Krieg, *Romano Guardini*, 79.

15. Guardini, *The Spirit of the Liturgy*, 142.

16. Krieg, *Romano Guardini*, 71. In this way Guardini had understood the relational aspect of the liturgy and was able to present it as much more than a rigid ritual or form.

17. Guardini, *Berichte über mein Leben*, 96.

18. Krieg, *Romano Guardini*, 78.

Church cannot be underestimated. Particularly through the Benedictine led liturgical movement, of the 1920s and 30s, Guardini, as a diocesan scholar-priest, was seen as a prominent leader of liturgical reforms.[19] O'Collins and Farrugia note that the 1947 encyclical, of Pius XII on the liturgy, *Mediator Dei*, endorses the work of Guardini and the other pioneers of this movement.[20] In the time leading up to the Vatican Council, he was invited to be a member of the Preparatory Conciliar Commission on the Liturgy but was unable to take up the opportunity because of bad health. Nevertheless, along with a number of other liturgical leaders, his work paved the way for Vatican II's Constitution on the Sacred Liturgy, *Sacrosanctum Concilium*. When the Vatican's liturgical commission meeting in Rome in 1968, heard that Guardini had died they, fittingly, prayed with thanks for his life of service in liturgical renewal.[21] Even in his early work, whether writing on the liturgy or citing the breviary, one thing distinguished Guardini from many of his Roman Catholic colleagues. It was his use of Scripture as an initial source for his theology. This source was to establish a certain, God centered, orientation to his work.

Youth Group Leader—Catholic Youth Groups

Just as Scripture and liturgy influenced Guardini's work and also prompted him to engage in liturgical reform, so too were the Catholic youth groups he led. Guardini was the national leader of the German Catholic youth groups. There was a dual effect. These groups had an influence on his work while he offered guidance and influence to the development of the groups themselves. In Germany, in Guardini's lifetime, many young people belonged to youth movements. Not all of these were religiously orientated[22] but all were orientated towards the renewal of society seeking to return to a simpler, more authentic way of life.[23] They called

---

19. O'Collins and Farrugia, *Catholicism*, 323.

20. O'Collins and Farrugia, *Catholicism*, 323.

21. Krieg, *Romano Guardini*, 90.

22. The youth movement was an important formative experience. Many of the groups have continued in modern Germany, but since Hitler wanted the young people to join his own youth movement, many were disbanded during the period he was in power. See Ruppert, *Quickborn*. In contemporary Germany, I observed that the Catholic Youth groups, in uniforms and carrying large flags, often take part in liturgical ceremonies in the Church.

23. Mosse, *Crisis of German Ideology*, 172.

themselves *Wandervogels* ("migratory birds") and in the idealism of their youth wanted to live in a different way to the previous generation, with self-determination and an appropriate capacity for decision-making and responsibility.[24] In some ways the groups were radical and sought to take a renewed path but in other ways they were considered to be conservative[25] because they placed tradition in a central role.[26]

By 1933, 1.5 million young Catholics were involved in thirty-three such organizations called *Katholische Jugend Deutschelands* (Catholic Youth of Germany).[27] While sharing some basic features with the other youth groups, the Catholic groups were different in certain ways and notably in their stress on commitment to Jesus Christ in the Catholic Church. Like the other groups they searched for a more authentic way of life but unlike the others they had an ecclesial dimension and looked to the religious tradition of the Church. Along with the other groups, they sought simplicity in food, dress and lifestyle but supplemented these things with abstinence from alcohol and tobacco. Frequent Mass attendance was encouraged and adhered to.[28] The important link between these groups and the Church was their sense of the authority of the Church and a desire for recovery of its essence. The groups were heterogenous with both priests and laity represented, but those such as *Quickborn* (Fountain of Youth) were essentially lay movements to prepare young people to move into the world. Students from the intellectual world participated together with workers from the technical sphere. It was this group, *Quickborn*, that Guardini was asked to lead in 1920 and he soon took over as national leader of the German Catholic youth groups. The meetings took place at an old castle, Burg Rothenfels, where the priests had a more fraternal role with the laity than elsewhere. In this way, Guardini's work with the youth

---

24. Mosse, *Crisis of German Ideology*, 172.

25. Some would argue that a turn to the "right" was clearly discernible. Mosse, *Crisis of German Ideology*, 17.

26. The political orientation of these young people demonstrated that in the notion of the Fatherland they had found an outlet for a natural patriotism encapsulated in the German "Heimat" (home town) and love of German culture. The ideal was to be "rooted" in one's home of origin and the Jews were seen to be inadequate because they did not seem to have their own country and were therefore "rootless." See Hudel, *Die Grundlagen des National Socialismus*, 94. Hudel, a Roman Catholic bishop and staunch Nazi supporter, used the argument of Jewish "rootlessness" to support his anti-Semitism.

27. Krieg, *Romano Guardini*, 50.

28. Gerl, *Romano Guardini*, 178.

movement formed his self-identity as a "fraternal" or brotherly type of priest. Guardini wrote of his own interpretation of the priesthood in this way:

> I found myself the type of brotherly priest who does not act out of his official position but carries the priesthood in himself as a pastoral force; who does not confront the faithful as the owner of authority but stands next to them. He is reluctant to offer them firm results and directions but joins them in their searching and asking in order to arrive with them at common results.[29]

Thus a key to Guardini's success may well have been his more relational and egalitarian approach rather than being authoritarian. Krieg notes that Guardini resisted ecclesial control of these groups, thus freeing them to develop and contribute to the Church at large without undue inhibition.[30] Like Guardini, their mentor and teacher, these young people were spiritually and religiously concerned with the pursuit of truth. Comparing the members of these groups with other young Catholics Guardini notes:

> The students who were members of the Catholic youth movement were recognizable by their very spiritual presence. The students who were members of the official Catholic student associations usually took little or no interest in my lectures unless they were also active in the Catholic youth movement. This lack of interest was a sign that many of the Catholic students were not engaged in a pursuit of the truth. Their religious ideals fitted with their concern for wearing the right clothes and pursuing their careers. The official members of the Catholic academic community ignored my lectures. From the outset, I was denied every form of official support. For this reason I was free from oversight by church authorities.[31]

Guardini led those who, like himself, were concerned with what lay behind appearances. His practiced ability to pursue a path which was God-focused rather than ecclesial focused, *per se*, stood him in good stead for the Nazi period which lay ahead where he would protect the movement from pressure to join the Hitler youth, long after other groups had given way. The words of one of his students, Heinz Kühn, illustrate his experience of being part of such a group:

29. Guardini, *Berichte über mein Leben*, 99. Kühn's translation in Kühn, *The Essential Guardini*, 3.

30. Krieg, *Spiritual Writings*, 26.

31. Guardini, *Berichte über mein Leben*, 93.

> If I wanted to explain in a few words what drew me and the small congregation that came from all parts of Berlin to Guardini's Mass, it was simply this: He was a person who by his words and actions drew us into a world where the sacred became literally and convincingly tangible. His mere appearance radiated something for which I have no other word than *luminous*; in his presence one fell silent and became all attention. With him on the altar, the sacred table became the centre of the universe.[32]

Kühn, a Christian with a Jewish mother, goes on to speak of the strength and courage the students were given as they faced a world in which the "forces of evil, Satan and his demons, were running rampant"[33] He notes that the sacredness had a more profound impact because Guardini celebrated the Mass "facing the people at which people responded aloud to the presider's prayers, something still new in those days."[34] Guardini's support and nurture of the Catholic youth groups meant that the Catholic youth organizations were strong and that is why they were eventually able to resist the pressure to join the Hitler youth much longer than other groups.[35]

Guardini—Educator

Guardini's pastoral support was closely intertwined with his pedagogy. He saw himself primarily as a priest-educator and spiritual leader. Thus his work reflects the altruism of one who knows he will inspire and influence young minds. Availability to his students was an important value for Guardini:

> I would say that this duty for an academic teacher is more urgent than writing thick books and shining at congresses. I would give him an appointment at home and see that I set him on the right path.[36]

One former student, Regina Kühn, notes the impact of such an appointment at Guardini's house:

---

32. Kühn, *The Essential Guardini*, 7.
33. Kühn, *The Essential Guardini*, 8.
34. Kühn, *The Essential Guardini*, 8; Krieg, *Proclaiming the Sacred*, 7.
35. For information about the resistance of the Catholic groups against pressure from the Nazis, see Evans, *The Third Reich in Power*, 271.
36. Guardini, *Berichte über mein Leben*, 66.

> Everything in the house was functional, of great simplicity, of the essence of beauty, and an intuitive absence of everything that would detract from the innate nobility of a piece of furniture or art. Everything was in order. He spoke to me about the soul of a house, about words spoken within the walls which would remain and cling to the walls and never again disappear. He spoke about the care one should take to make these lasting words into a shelter where the sacred would want to dwell, where word patterns of kindness, humility, respect and truth could become a grid to holiness, and where culture and sanctity could be synonymous. I found it difficult to be in his presence. There was no way out; one had no choice but to burn in the fire of his intensity and be totally absorbed.[37]

This passage illustrates Guardini's aim to work towards a Christian and sanctified world a real "city of God," because he believed that nature, human persons and society, in short the whole world, were important and permeated with the grace of God.

Young students were not the only group learning from Guardini. The population at large had contact with him and his lectures were full of non-official students, many of whom were not Roman Catholic. Hundreds of people, including students and staff from other faculties, housewives and people from every walk of life, helped to fill the largest lecture hall in the university (The Great Hall) to capacity. Writing about his lectures at the University of Berlin from 1923 to 1939, Guardini writes:

> My lectures were attended [not only by students but] also people from completely different faculties and walks of life. With them were other professionals who also came to my lectures. Now and then there appeared a colleague who simply wanted to listen to me, to this unusual "lecturer."[38]

After the war, at St. Ludwig's Church in Munich, where he was the "university preacher," the church was filled to overflowing, every Sunday, as people squeezed in to hear him preach. Guardini's preaching was an important part of his work and significant for his writing, since much of his published writing was preached or taught in lectures before it appeared in print. After the war, in an interview for the journal, *America*, commenting on his recovery from illness Guardini said:

---

37. Kühn, "Encounters with Romano Guardini," in Krieg, *Proclaiming the Sacred*, 90.

38. Guardini, *Berichte über mein Leben*, 44.

> I will preach again each Sunday in St. Ludwig's, the university church.... I am a professor but to me the pulpit is most dear. Mine is the basic principle of the two voices, the two chairs: lecture and sermon, podium and pulpit, natural truth and revelation, human science and God's must be equally studied, related, proclaimed.[39]

There is a wholeness in his approach and characteristically, Guardini's way of educating was not narrowly confined to spiritual matters. He believed the whole of life matters and he gave advice for many "everyday" tasks. For instance in 1921, Guardini, who like his mother suffered from depression, gave advice for overcoming melancholy tendencies that remains relevant today:

> At night before going to sleep, in a quiet and confident way, we should say: Tomorrow I will be happy . . . uplifted and going through the day, working, playing interacting with people: "That's how I'm going to be tomorrow for the whole day" [and] in the morning everything is much sheerer than it would otherwise be.[40]

Yet Guardini also wrote that to dwell with God in one's innermost being is to experience the source of true happiness.[41] These references show how totally Guardini regarded his work. He was not there for shallow "God talk" but for the holistic task of helping the human person to be more fully human and therefore more fully available for God. God's world is a sacred-world or world-made-sacred. Guardini's research and pedagogical tasks enabled him to educate for sanctity.

Prominent Areas of Interest in Guardini's Work

We have already adverted to the importance of Scripture for Guardini's writing. His work may also be more fully understood with an awareness of his position in the following two areas. They are the centrality of Jesus Christ and his employment of the life of the Saints. Each of these areas is important to living with Providence.

---

39. Gremilion, "Interview with Romano Guardini," 194–95.
40. Guardini, *"Von der Freudigkeit des Herzens,"* 6 (my translation).
41. Guardini, *"Von der Freudigkeit des Herzens,"* 3.

Jesus Christ in Guardini's writing

As early as 1919 Guardini had published his fourth book, *The Way of the Cross of our Lord and Saviour*. The book is a series of Lenten Reflections on the Stations of the Cross. Guardini's reflections on the Lord continued in 1929 with his book, *The Essence of Christianity (Das Wesen des Christentums)*,[42] where he presented the living-concrete Christ with the intention of recreating, anew, the response of the "living Christ." In searching for the "essence" of Christianity Guardini found that the "essence" is Jesus Christ himself, a historical person and not just a principle or value.[43] He wrote:

> There is no abstract definition of this essence. There is no doctrine, no basic structure of ethical values, no religious attitude and order of life which separates the person of life and the Christian reality. The Christian reality is Christ himself.... The Christian reality is therefore not a teaching of truth or the meaning of life. To be sure, it includes this but therein is not its essential kernel. Its essence is Jesus Christ himself, his concrete existence, his work and his destiny – this means therefore a historical person.[44]

Guardini's major book about the life of the Lord was published in 1937. Called *The Lord*, it was, alongside *The Spirit of the Liturgy*, to become his most famous, and globally recognized, book. The German title of *The Lord* reads *(Der Herr: Betrachtung über die Person und das Leben Jesu Christi)*. The word Betrachtung, carries a sense of meditation, examination or consideration about the concrete, living Christ who is present to believers in faith.

Consistent with his belief that knowledge begins with "living-concrete" persons, Guardini presents Christ as he lived his life. That is to say, he narrated the events and circumstances of Christ's life, phenomenologically, without recourse to lengthy formulas, theological language or abstract notions. Rather, he wanted Christ, in his person, as he was in his life, to shine out and allow the human person to encounter Him so that he or she would believe. For him, Jesus is the only mediator to God and

---

42. Guardini, *Das Wesen des Christentums*, 129–52.
43. Guardini, *Das Wesen des Christentums*, 5.
44. Guardini, *Das Wesen des Christentums*, 5, 68. Schilson's translation given in "The Major Theological Themes of Romano Guardini"; Krieg, *Proclaiming the Sacred*, 39.

everything should be seen in relational terms; the relationship of Jesus with the Father, the relationship of Jesus with people, the relationship of people with God. Krieg notes a number of themes in *The Lord*, all of which relate to personal existence. These include, "the "fallen" world, Jesus Christ as revealer, the uniqueness of Jesus Christ, the humanity of Christ and Christian conversion.[45] The response Guardini wanted in his presentation was the response of the heart.

As such Guardini aligned himself with several other theologians who have reflected on the proclaimed word of God with the intention of enabling the person today to know the living Christ. Among them were Karl Barth, Emil Brunner, Karl Adam, and Hugo Rahner. These were the "kerygmatic" theologians who sought through Scripture, the Sacraments and Church teaching to allow the real Christ to be present to the seeker after faith.[46]

Presenting Christ in a way that people could relate to did have some disadvantages for Guardini. Guardini has been said to have been inconsistent with his use of literature and Scripture because when he studied literature he considered the whole context in which it was written, such as the life situation of Höderlin, but didn't do the same for Scripture.[47] Furthermore, in the opinion of the same theologian, "Guardini treated the infancy narratives as though they were newspaper reports."[48] Possibly Guardini wanted to distance himself from the concepts associated with the abstract, distant Pre-Vatican II Christ of Neo-Scholastic theology.

---

45. Krieg, *Romano Guardini*, 148.

46. Krieg, *Romano Guardini*, 144. While Guardini's Christology has been said to be kerygmatic, his method should not be confused with the approach of a theologian such as Bultmann who extracted the kerygma from the person of Jesus Christ in order to attend to his message more. The result of Bultmann's method was rather like a wall chart labeled "kerygma." While such an approach would seem, at first glance, to be more sophisticated, his method of demythologizing could be near to an abstraction and relativization of Jesus Christ that Guardini rejected. On the other hand, the approach of Gerhard Ebeling, with his presentation of Christ as "word-event," would seem to be much more similar to that of Guardini. For him, the kerygma should not be understood as a formula which would be fixed and unchangeable but should be true to the Biblical notion of proclamation in which kerygma is a part. Faith, conversely, should be faith in Jesus Christ which is directed to the kerygma as its confession. Guardini's writing on Jesus Christ had brought out that very truth a number of years earlier. See Ebeling, *Theology and Proclamation*, 31.

47. Krieg, *Romano Guardini*, 142. Perhaps this difference also reflects an ecclesial wariness.

48. Krieg, *Romano Guardini*, 153.

Furthermore, he believed that the historical Jesus was a mental construct of modern theology. Guardini had already suffered because his ecclesial superiors had been worried about possible progressive tendencies in his work. If he had adopted the historical-critical method, of the time, he may have been under suspicion by anti-modernists again and his readers may not have been able to relate to Christ in the same way. Therefore, in my opinion, Guardini chose to adopt a pre-critical approach to Scripture, choosing to develop his Christology without reference to the Biblical criticism, of the time, especially historical criticism even after the encyclical of Pius XII, *Divino Afflante Spirito*, in 1943. What Guardini had hoped to gain was for God's word to be the focus of the orientation.

Guardini is adamant that faith must be in the living Christ and he therefore seeks to reveal Christ in as real a way as possible. In Christianity he saw that there is no abstract determination of essence, doctrines or structures of moral behavior for an order of life that can be separated from the person of Christ. Although written in a theological world dominated by Neo-Scholastic theology, Guardini manages to avoid the inherent rigidity of that system and also that which a more critical approach would have engendered, namely a concentration on the arguments about the theology or legitimacy of a system rather than the person. His movement to biography enables him to study the concrete Christ in his life, in order to phenomenologically elicit the whole seen first in the particular. As such he achieves his aim of presenting the Lord as he is in himself rather than an idea.

The Life of the Saints and the Laity

Guardini made frequent references to the Saints and the lives of the Saints because they were concrete examples of Christian believers in the world. In 1924, Guardini wrote, "Heilige Gestalt: Von Büchern und mehr als Büchern." In 1927, he wrote, "Die Heilige Franziskus zum Gedachtnis." Other articles on the Saints followed, and Guardini used the example of the Saints in various books. The choice of Saints favoured by Guardini appear to reflect his own theological position. For instance, he made frequent reference to St. Francis especially Francis' relationship with creation which spoke of the sacredness of the world. St. Francis was able to relate to the whole. It was St. Francis who exemplified the person living in the world and in contact with the whole of creation, both the world of animals and birds and the natural world in which they dwelt. It was St. Francis who was able to live in the way a person with Providence lives and his life showed he was a door for God in the world. Guardini was not concerned with miraculous stories in the life of Francis or any other Saint and there is little ecclesial emphasis. In the chapter on Providence written in one of his last works, Guardini urges his readers to follow the example of the Saints in their lives.[49]

Associated with the subject of the Saints is the vocation of every person and the place of the laity in the world. Regina Kuhn writes:

> I never heard him remark on the different tasks of ordained and lay people. We were all *Gottesvolk*, people of God, with our individual baptismal mission to participate in the "bringing home of the world into Christ's kingdom"[50]

Nevertheless, the question of the laity was addressed in Guardini's 1956 publication, *The Saints in Daily Life*,[51] where he writes:

> What kind of Saints will lay people be? Certainly not the saints of the exceptional, for whose existence there must in general be an atmosphere favouring the extraordinary . . . . Their surroundings are standardized: they work in laboratories, factories, in administrative agencies and organizations which function in a predetermined way; they live in homes which are often the same to the slightest detail . . . subject to uniform "packages" of education, entertainment, legislation . . . . How could they lead a Christian way of life . . . ? There is a way of sanctity which is open to all . . . . It is founded on the premise that the laity is answerable for the world . . . . religion is not simply the private relationship of a man or a woman with God but also involves the right ordering and developing of the world.[52]

Guardini's refusal to deny the world in the spiritual quest is an integral part of his theology. His argument for ethical, lay responsibility in the development of this world, is complemented by his argument for lay involvement in prayer, teaching and the church's sacraments. A personal relationship with Jesus Christ, is an integral part of that involvement.

---

49. Guardini, *Gebet und Wahrheit*, 129.
50. Kuhn, "Romano Guardini in Berlin," 89.
51. Guardini, *Saints in Daily Life*, 62.
52. Guardini, *Saints in Daily Life*, 79. This passage also addresses the concerns of anyone who might argue that Guardini does not have a lay theology.

People Who Influenced Guardini

The lives of Guardini's theological teachers say something about their pupil. They were progressive theologians who engaged with the society around them and the political forces which shaped it. Thus theology was not done in a vacuum or exclusivity. Their involvement in society and politics was not without a price as they sought to live with responsibility and integrity in a Church and society that had their own problems. This action shaped Guardini yet also reflects his own orientation in his choice of teachers and path. We turn now to the first of the people who influenced Guardini.

His Theological Teachers

Engelbert Krebs

Engelbert Krebs (1881–1955) supervised Guardini's dissertation on the Franciscan theologian and philosopher, St. Bonaventure, and thereby had a definite influence on Guardini's life and work. Krieg notes that both Krebs and Guardini were two theologians who had resisted Hitler.[53] A brief look at Krebs' life, can tell us something about the person Guardini learnt from and who almost certainly inspired him. Krebs, a priest and Professor of Dogmatics at Freiburg University, was by no means a scholar who kept his interests exclusively in the academy. He was politically involved in society from early in his life. Krebs studied at the University of Freiburg and entered the seminary during his first year there. Later he studied in Rome. While at university he became involved with the Görres *Gesellschaft* (Görres Society). Joseph von Görres (b. 1776) had gained international recognition for his defence of civil liberties and writing in history, literature and politics.[54] He combined his political interests with arguments for a greater role for the Catholic Church in society. Krebs was inspired by this religious-political combination in Görres and chose to write his academic work in a similar way by developing work on the theology of the Middle Ages; mystical theology with religious and local history. In addition he was an activist who clearly considered it important to address difficulties in society with practical assistance of one kind or another. During World War I, he wrote articles on Catholicism

---

53. Krieg, *Catholic Theologians in Nazi Germany*, 132.
54. Krieg, *Catholic Theologians in Nazi Germany*, 132.

and German patriotism and after visiting the front he personally drove wounded soldiers to hospital.[55]

After World War I, Krebs worked as a chaplain and wrote articles advocating more respect for women. In addition, he visited countries all over the world and wrote about the Church as a global community. His most comprehensive theological work was *Dogma und Leben* (Dogma and Life). This work dealt with the faith of the Church and how the salvation of our lives are (positively) grounded in the context of Dogmas. At the end of the book, Krebs argues that love of neighbor means that God loves all people including Jews to whom God's grace also extends.[56] In 1926, Krebs wrote a paper in which he argued that Catholic students shouldn't be involved in Anti-Semitic activities. The correct attitude to Jews was Christian love and respect. The "fleshly" Christ was Jewish.[57] Then, in 1927, Krebs wrote that Christians must regard Judaism as the home from which they were born and respect for their origins must continue. According to him, St. Paul and his co-workers had not renounced their Jewish roots and neither should contemporary Christians. When the Nazis took over in 1933, Krebs showed that he was unwilling to remain silent with a series of public issues related to the Nazi state including the delivery of a lecture in which he argued that the State should respect the authority of God and the Church. In 1934 he said to someone that Germany was being governed by "murderers, robbers and criminals."[58] The remark was overheard by another person who reported him to the Reich. In 1936 he was prevented from teaching and in 1937 he was put into retirement. 1943 saw him prevented from public speaking and saying Mass. Sadly, after the war he was too sick to give formal lectures again and was made emeritus. He died in 1950. Engelbert Krebs had studied the works of Wilhelm Koch who was also one of Guardini's teachers.

---

55. Krieg, *Catholic Theologians in Nazi Germany*, 134. In this book, Krieg argues that Engelbert Krebs and Romano Guardini were the two Catholic theologians who publicly opposed Hitler while the other four, dealt with in the book, did not.

56. Krieg, *Catholic Theologians in Nazi Germany*, 136.

57. Krieg, *Catholic Theologians in Nazi Germany*, 138.

58. Krieg, *Catholic Theologians in Nazi Germany*, 146. At this time Guardini had already been called to the Reich's Office to explain himself after the publication of his book making a veiled attack on Hitler (see below).

Wilhelm Koch

Wilhelm Koch also taught Guardini at Tübingen University. In Guardini's autobiography he writes that he felt a lifelong debt to the theologically progressive Koch who had taught him about the development of the Church's teaching. Guardini believed Koch "witnessed to the truth."[59] Furthermore, it was Koch who helped Guardini to overcome his scrupulousness which had greatly troubled him and Guardini felt especially indebted to him because of this.[60] In discussion with Koch, and two friends, Guardini was able to clarify the inductive method of working that was to distinguish his work. However, in 1916 Koch was pressured into withdrawing from the faculty by the seminary's rector who believed he had "modernist" tendencies.[61] After fulfilling his military service, Koch returned and hoped to retrieve his position but was unable to do so and lived out his vocation as a pastor in the Diocese of Rottenburg-Stuttgart.[62] Guardini considered Koch's treatment as "one of the frequent sins of Orthodoxy."[63] Guardini had respected this man, so Koch's experience would also have stood as a warning for Guardini, not to relinquish his theological independence in his choice of refusing to tackle dogmatic themes. Koch was not the only censured Professor who influenced Guardini. We turn now to Herman Schell whom Guardini wanted to study with.

Hermann Schell

Guardini had hoped to study with Schell at Würzburg but he was not accepted by the university and was unable to do so. Nevertheless it would be a mistake to say Schell had no influence over Guardini's theological formation. Guardini's writing shows many similarities to Schell's work and, since he may have had contact with him through the liturgical

---

59. Krieg, *Romano Guardini*, 5.
60. Krieg, *Romano Guardini*, 5.
61. Krieg, *Romano Guardini*, 6.
62. See Seckler, *Theologie vor Gericht*. Karl Rahner noted that the experiences of the esteemed Koch made Guardini cautious with his own work. See Rahner, *I Remember*, 73–75.
63. Guardini, *Berichte über mein Leben*, 83.

renewal movement or the youth groups, Guardini was influenced by him regardless of not having studied with him.[64]

Schell has been referred to as "a forerunner of the Second Vatican Council," "the most important dogmatist of the last century" and "one of the major intellectual and spiritual driving forces associated with the German Liturgical Renewal and the Youth Movements.[65] After being ordained to the Priesthood in 1873, Schell did his doctoral studies in Würzburg under Franz Bretano whose own work influenced Max Scheler. Schell's doctoral thesis on the unity of the spiritual life in Aristotealian philosophy involved the idea of the "living personal life of the soul" which Schell calls, "self-causality or self-actuation."[66]

Schell was indexed by the Vatican in 1898.[67] Speaking of Schell's Trinitarian Theology, Walter Kasper notes the correctness of Schell's way of grounding the speculation in a fundamental appreciation of self-actuating freedom. Kasper writes:

> Schell came far closer not only to the modern intellectual starting point [of conceiving of God as being-in-action, as freedom and life] but also to the biblical understanding of God than did his scholastic adversaries, who managed to have his work put on the Index.... To the detriment of the Christian faith they thus prevented his approach to the problem from bearing fruit in a new synthesis of faith and knowledge that would respond to the intellectual situations of the modern age.[68]

Thus, as Kasper points out, Schell was hampered in his attempts to bring theology into dialogue with modern thought.

---

64. Krieg, *Romano Guardini*, 26.

65. Greiner, "Herman Schell," 427–54.

66. Greiner, "Herman Schell," 435.

67. The reasons, given three months later included: 1) Schell's concept of God as *causa sui* or self actuation and therefore the method by which Schell grounded the Trinity; 2) The exaggeration of resistance to the Holy Spirit as the necessary evil lying at the heart of mortal sin; 3) The expressed danger, in his work, of the eschatological rehabilitation of the universe and the consequent dissolution of hell; 4) Overemphasis of the quasi sacramental character of death and suffering with the resultant danger of relativizing the necessity of Baptism and the anointing of the sick. See Greiner, "Herman Schell," 440.

68. Greiner quoting Kasper, *The God of Jesus Christ*, 152. See Greiner, "Herman Schell," 440.

Schell was a progressive theologian who had welcomed the "turn to the subject and the re-appropriation of interiority."[69] He wanted God to be seen as personal and not as "depersonalizing Monism."[70] Furthermore, the human person could, "through grace and the power of the Spirit, exist(s) in creative relationship with God."[71] Working towards the (Biblical image) of the Kingdom of God, the human race can be energized and enlivened to contribute to the fulfillment of the cosmos. Writing of Schell's work, Greiner writes:

> The creation of culture and cultural activity are an unfolding of the ongoing creation in which human beings function as special agents linked in grace with the self-actuation life of the triune God. As the universe is ordered and shaped, takes form and direction through the spiritual activity of human beings, culture is promoted and the "kingdom of God" is furthered.[72]

These words, showing Schell's mindset give us a glimpse into Guardini's attraction to Schell's theology. It is not difficult to see how he influenced Guardini's work and actions which will be clearer below.

Collegial Influences

Max Scheler

The phenomenologist Max Scheler (1874–1928) was profoundly important for Guardini's future work. Guardini had been impressed by Scheler's work, and Scheler gave him some scholarly advice. He encouraged him personally to reflect on human biography. Forty years later Guardini recalled:

> In a conversation which was very momentous for me [Scheler] said to me: "You must do what is meant by the word '*Weltanschauung*' [Worldview]: as a responsible, conscious Christian observe the world, things, people, [and their] actions, and then say in a scholarly way what you see.... Investigate, for example, the novels of Dostoyevsky and study their outlook [on life] from your Christian standpoint, in order to illuminate, on the one

---

69. Greiner, "Herman Schell," 451.
70. Greiner, "Herman Schell," 453.
71. Greiner, "Herman Schell," 453.
72. Greiner, "Herman Schell," 454.

hand, the works under consideration and on the other hand, [your] standpoint itself."[73]

Guardini's lectures testify to the way he received this advice. He lectured on "The Catholic Worldview," "God and the World," "Augustine's Religious View of the World and Its Significance for Today," and "Christianity and Culture in View of Søren Kierkegaard's Posing of the Issues."[74] Other lectures he gave were on the works of Plato, Socrates, Augustine, Pascal, Montaigne, Dostoyevsky, Dante, Nietzsche, Höderlin, Sigmund Freud, Rilke, and the Buddha.[75] Guardini contributed significantly to German literary criticism and is discussed in a number of respected German commentaries.[76] This literary involvement enabled him to develop his inductive theology through the phenomenological reflection on the experiences of human persons in literature.[77]

Martin Buber and Martin Heidegger

Significantly, Guardini had regular and professional contact with the philosophers Martin Buber and Martin Heidegger before and after World War II. Ironically, during the war Heidegger was a prominent Nazi supporter while Buber, was forced to flee Germany because he was Jewish.[78] Guardini read and commented on both Buber and Heidegger's work as they did with Guardini's . Buber, who popularized the I-Thou concept,[79] wrote of *relationship* with God rather than *identification*, preferring the distinction between creatures and the Creator. Guardini wrote of the ultimate value of the I-Thou relationship with God in his book the *World and the Person* where he noted that the absolute "Thou" of human persons is God.[80] Yet Guardini's definition of the I-Thou is a little different to Buber's because the God he refers to is the Triune God.[81] This means

---

73. Guardini, *Berichte über mein Leben*, 87, quoted in Krieg, *Romano Guardini*, 91.
74. Krieg, *Romano Guardini*, 91.
75. Krieg, *Romano Guardini*, 91.
76. Krieg, *Romano Guardini*, 92.
77. Krieg, *Romano Guardini*, 2.
78. Paul Mendes-Flohr has recently agued that Buber and Heidegger met after the war for discussion. Mendes-Flohr, "Martin Buber and Martin Heidegger," 2–25.
79. Buber, *I and Thou*.
80. Guardini, *The World and the Person*, 142.
81. He writes, "The real and personal Thou is the Father. He who really says 'Thou'

that the Holy Spirit and Jesus Christ are integral to Guardini's notion of the I-Thou relationship.

In 1922, Buber wrote to the Lutheran Scholar, Friedrich Gogarten, saying that he had met Guardini at a lecture: "[H]e drew close to me, however subsequently withdrew to the distance of [an assured] sense of church."[82] Guardini accepted Buber's invitation to a conference of Christians and Jews, saying he would be honoured to attend. He continued by saying that while at the conference he would like to ask some questions about Buber's recently published book, *I and Thou*. "I am filled with respect, for it is well done . . . however [my questions] are entirely within my positive regard [for your book]."[83] After the war, in 1952, Guardini gave a public lecture at Tubingen, in which he asked the Germans to take responsibility for the Jews.[84] He sent a copy to Buber who was still outside Germany. After reading it, Buber said that he now felt it was possible to speak publically again in Germany.[85] When he did return, Buber visited Guardini in Munich. In 1953, Guardini wrote in his diary:

> Today Martin Buber was here for a cup of tea. He was on his way to receive the German Booksellers Peace Prize. He had spoken in various universities and wanted to rest a little before going on to Frankfurt. It was lovely to be in his company. He is amazingly cultured, wise and worthy of reverence.[86]

Clearly Guardini had respect for his Jewish colleague.

After the war Heidegger visited Guardini as well. Heidegger and Guardini had also exchanged material before the war. In *The World and the Person* Guardini refers to Heidegger's insights on the meeting between persons. "Language," he says, "is not a system of signs by means of which two monads exchange ideas but it is the very realm of consciousness in which every man lives."[87] Guardini continues, noting that Heidegger had

---

to the Father is the Son." Guardini, *The World and the Person*, 156. Guardini goes on to assert that "it is the Spirit who brings man into the intimacy of the personal relation. He inserts him in Christ and . . . so enables him to speak the essential Thou." Guardini, *The World and the Person*, 157.

82. Quoted in Krieg, *Romano Guardini*, 34. See also Gerl-Falkovitz, *Romano Guardini*, 133n38.

83. Quoted in Krieg, *Romano Guardini*, 34.

84. Guardini, *Verantwortung*.

85. Krieg, *Romano Guardini*, 201.

86. Quoted from Guardini's diary by Kobylinsky, *Modernità e Post Modernità*, 239.

87. Guardini, *The World and the Person*, 130.

written, "[Language is] the very first possibility of standing amid the openness of being."[88] Guardini was able to develop this concept further with the assertion that complete speech "tends towards realization of the 'I-Thou' relation."[89] Thus both scholars had been able to contribute to Guardini's notion of the I-Thou relationship which is integral to his notion of Providence.

Scholarly Influences

St. Bonaventure

Guardini wrote both his doctoral and habilitation theses on the work of the medieval Franciscan, St. Bonaventure, and perhaps it could be said that Bonaventure influenced his theology at a time when work on St. Thomas Aquinas held more sway in the Church. Bonaventure, a reformer of his order, was distinguished by his creativity as a philosopher and theologian. J. Guy Bougerol notes that Bonaventure's work is a synthesis of many diverse elements.[90] He writes:

> [Bonaventure's writings] were produced by a great genius, deeply religious, whose ideal was to fuse into one all the truths he could draw from the Scriptures, the Fathers, the masters, and also the philosophers. Here the Neoplatonism of Augustine meets the mysticism of Dionysius, the philosophy of Aristotle, and even the cosmology of Avicenna. Yet the result is not eclectic: everything has been rethought and strongly unified by a powerful mind which places all knowledge at the service of the institution drawn directly from Assisi.[91]

Bonaventure's works provided a rich source for Guardini's own work and style. Guardini did not like the rigid Neo-scholastic type of theology acclaimed by the Vatican at that time[92] and found the fecundity

---

88. Guardini, *The World and the Person*, 131. In a footnote to this assertion, Guardini notes that speech is not a product but a presupposition of human life. See Guardini, *The World and the Person*, 217.

89. Guardini, *The World and the Person*, 131.

90. Schilson, "The Major Theological Themes," 32.

91. Bougerol, *Introduction to the Works of Bonaventure*, 163.

92. For instance, the deductive, inflexible scholastic method was used by Hermann Dieckman, Christian Pesch, Adolphe Tanquery, and Reginald Garrigou-Lagrange. See Krieg, *Romano Guardini*, 17.

of Bonaventure's thought, developed from the life of St. Francis of Assisi which drew out the importance of creation, a useful resource and model for the type of inductive theology he was interested in doing. Bonaventure considered the whole of creation to be important. In his theology, Bonaventure embraces creation while deification of the human person extends to creation with the redeemed human person bringing creation back to God.

Bonaventure, like Guardini, worked from the Scriptures, writing directly on the books of the Bible and using Scripture to illuminate other works. Bougerol notes that for Bonaventure:

> [T]he student must approach the study of the Scriptures in a spirit of deep submission, as a true disciple of Christ, meek and humble of heart. He must also prepare himself to receive the teaching ... with a cleansed mind, so that grace may enlighten his study. Finally he must assent to the teaching with faith and intellectual humility.[93]

Guardini held similar views about the place of Scripture in theology. Furthermore, Bonaventure's employment of the notion of wisdom, not common during Guardini's lifetime, is also an aspect we find in Guardini's work.

John Henry Newman

Guardini had been impressed by Cardinal Newman's works and referred to him in his own book, *Conscience*, written in 1929. As Guardini was to do later, Newman wrote on the Benedictine Order, the Breviary, and the Psalms.[94] Newman also wrote on conscience which was a theme taken up by Guardini later.[95] Newman's work on conscience was distinctive because he emphasized the religious role of conscience and combined it with spiritual advice.[96]

For Newman, conscience was not only a moral sense; it was a sense of duty and God's voice manifested in the heart.[97] Guardini wrote of con-

---

93. Bougerol, *Works of Bonaventure*, 91.

94. See "The Mission of the Benedictine Schools" and "The Benedictine Centuries" in Newman, *The Benedictine Order*.

95. Although Scheler had also written on conscience, it is significant that Guardini cited Newman and not Scheler in his work on conscience.

96. As noted by Guardini in *Conscience*, 79.

97. Terlinden, "The Originality of Newman's Teaching on Conscience," 294–306.

science and response to conscience in a similar way. For both Newman and Guardini, conscience was the voice of God in us.[98] We turn now to the influence of Jean-Pierre de Causade.

Jean-Pierre De Caussade

Guardini's notion of Providence may have been influenced by Jean-Pierre de Caussade's *Abandonment to Divine Providence*. In his early work, Guardini wrote on de Caussade's spirituality in "Die geistliche Lehre Caussades." Caussade was a French Jesuit whose well known book on Providence was originally a series of letters and notes of retreats given to Religious Sisters. Caussade's notion of the importance of the present moment in living with Providence is also advocated by Guardini in his work *The Saints in Daily Life*.

Living with the present moment is also seen in these words of Guardini:

> Where do we see what God wants? . . . [W]e see it in small tasks in complete ordinariness: in a glance at the present . . . . what is noted immediately, what my duty right now is, is God's will. We do that and then we carry God from one task to another. We listen to him and then we will be ready to understand and fulfill the next message. In this way we fulfill our life's work step by step. Therefore: grasp clearly what God wants of you right now.[99]

The importance of trusting God as one lives in the present moment is an integral part of Guardini's Providence writing.

People Guardini Influenced

The creativity of Guardini's thought enabled a fecundity of research in many different areas, spawning a watershed of influence. In his lifetime, Guardini already had considerable influence both in Germany and well beyond and we can only guess at the number of people who came under his influence. Nevertheless there are some things we do know. During the 1950s, priests in seminaries throughout the world were required to read

---

See also Merrigan, *Clear Heads and Holy Hearts*, 38, 107–12, 327.

98. Guardini, *Conscience*, 55.

99. Guardini, "*Von der Freudigkeit des Herzens*," 3.

The Lord[100] as part of their training in the seminary. One of Guardini's students was the well known philosopher, Hanna Arendt. She was so inspired by Guardini's course on Augustine that she decided to do her doctorate on Augustine under the direction of Karl Jaspers.[101] After Vatican II well known theologians such as Karl Rahner, Hans Urs von Balthasar, and Joseph Ratzinger (Pope Benedict XVI) wrote of the importance of Guardini's influence on their work. Guardini gave his chair to Karl Rahner when he retired. Rahner's anthropological approach and "supernatural existential" bear traces of Guardini's anthropology and "presentiment of God" and it may be argued that Rahner took up some of Guardini's ideas and was able to develop them dogmatically. Therefore we can conclude that Guardini's influence was not only great during his life but that the effect of his work will continue to grow and flourish. Krieg draws attention to the fact that three Popes read his work and acknowledged him.[102] In 2015 Pope Francis became the fourth Pope to cite him. Pope Pius XII made him a papal prelate in 1952. In 1962 Pope Paul VI invited him to join the college of cardinals, while Pope John Paul II referred to Guardini as one of the foremost theological scholars in Germany.[103] To those we may add the former Pope, Benedict XVI (Joseph Ratzinger), who wrote on and was inspired by Guardini, before and after he was Pope.[104] Fifthly, in his encyclical letter, *Laudato Si'*, Pope Francis makes numerous references to Guardini's book, *The End of the Modern World*.

Pope Benedict XVI

Pope Benedict was one of the students who heard Guardini preach and teach at the University of Munich as a young man. He was inspired to name his own book on the liturgy with the same title as Guardini's *The Spirit of the Liturgy* and considered Guardini to have had a formative influence on his life, leading Fr. Schall, SJ, to write about Guardini as the "Father of Benedict XVI."[105] Ratzinger's book "is a tribute to and a

---

100. Guardini, *The Lord*.

101. Krieg, *Romano Guardini*, 201. Guardini didn't take doctoral students because of the interdisciplinary nature of his chair.

102. Krieg, *Romano Guardini*, 193.

103. Krieg, *Romano Guardini*, 193.

104. Ratzinger, *The Spirit of the Liturgy*.

105. Schall, "Benedetto XVI Ha un Padre."

carrying on the inspiration of Guardini," he writes.[106] In the preface to *The Spirit of the Liturgy* [the then] Cardinal Ratzinger noted that "[Guardini's] slim volume may rightly be said to have inaugurated the Liturgical Movement in Germany."[107] At the Congress on Romano Guardini which was held in 2010 at the Vatican in Rome, Pope Benedict XVI recalled his youthful student days as one of Guardini's students. Benedict noted that Guardini often repeated the words, "you see?"

> [Y]ou see ... because he wanted to guide us to "seeing" while he himself was in a common inner dialogue with his listeners. This was the innovation in comparison with the rhetoric of the old days; rather that far from seeking rhetoric he talked to us in a totally simple way, and at the same time spoke of truth and led us into dialogue with the truth.[108]

Thus we are able to see the rippling effect of the unique yet faithful teaching of Guardini and the teaching which others bring to the world. The influence of Guardini's work is enormous.

Pope Francis I

Pope Francis as Jorge Mario Bergoglio began a thesis on Guardini early in his vocation and although he didn't finish it, Guardini influenced his work so much that as Pope he cited Guardini numerous times in his encyclical, *Laudato Si: On Care for Our Common Home*. Guardini has in fact been said to have shaped the "Spirit of the Papacy."[109]

Both Karl Rahner and Hans Urs von Balthasar took very different theological paths but because of the creativity, breadth and depth of Guardini's work were able to develop their own path from his original spring.

---

106. Schall, "Guardini."

107. Ratzinger, *Spirit of the Liturgy*, 7. He continues, "It's contribution was decisive. It helped us to discover the liturgy in all its beauty, hidden wealth and time transcending grandeur, to see it as the animating center of the Church the very center of Christian life."

108. Pope Benedict XVI, "A Man of Dialogue."

109. Allen Jr., "How Romano Guardini Helps."

Karl Rahner

When Guardini retired from the University of Munich he gave his Chair to the leading German theologian, Karl Rahner. Rahner, also working with human experience, took up some of Guardini's themes and systematized them as a theologian. Guardini's position of Professor of Christian World View did not carry doctoral students because of the unique nature of the area but that was a source of frustration for Rahner who, to Guardini's disappointment, eventually gave up the Chair in favour of another where he was able to have doctoral students.

Hans Urs von Balthasar

The well known Swiss theologian Hans urs von Balthasar (see above) was very impressed by Guardini and wrote a book on him and his work aiming to give the reader a guide to Guardini's thought.[110]

Relevant Socio-Historical Background: Changes in German Society During the Twentieth Century

Guardini wrote through one of the most interesting and turbulent periods of German history. While we cannot give an exhaustive or even adequate historical overview here, several aspects of the society of that time provide an important context for Guardini's work.

The Period of National Socialism and the Second World War

Germany's experiment with democracy had been far from positive. World War I had seen millions of Germans killed or wounded and the treaty of Versailles had imposed a punishment of hundreds of billions of dollars in war reparations along with losing some of their own territory to France. Extreme right and left movements began to compete for dominance in cities. Guardini lived in Berlin. One of Guardini's students, Heinz Kühn, also living in Berlin at that time, described the situation this way:

---

110. Balthasar, *Romano Guardini*. Balthasar's outline of Guardini's notion of Providence has already been described in this text.

> [T]he war had dealt a devastating blow to a Western world that still rested on an essentially Christian framework of values; the war had ushered in the era of Nihilism, existentialism and relativism. For the people, for us, the political reality of the Weimar Republic became tangible and audible in the streets, in the stores, in offices, schools and universities. The reality was a fanatical, murderous, pitched battle for power.[111]

For Heinz Kühn, and other people living that city, day to day living was very difficult:

> Many were the times when, on my way to school or to a store, I had to duck into a doorway or throw myself to the ground to seek protection from snipers or from a machine gun that begun firing from a roof or window on a column of marchers... whose banners bore the insignia of one or another party... the Swastika or the hammer and sickle... there was inflation and rising unemployment... food riots broke out almost weekly.... I see before me the large cloth shopping bag stuffed with paper money needed to buy one loaf of bread and a quarter pound of margarine.[112]

Clearly, there had been considerable unrest and disorder in the society as we see from this account. Political and social instability reigned supreme and for many people the search for order was central. The National Socialists took up this challenge.

National Socialism as a political ideology had come to prominence after the defeat of Germany in the First World War, although Richard J. Evans argues that the combined forces of nationalism, anti-Semitism, Aryan superiority and mythic Germanic Nordic roots were all gathered together as ideas even before the First World War.[113] With this combined force, Nazism was able to draw on various sections of the society for support. Hitler both articulated the ideals of the National Socialists and provided leadership for them in the context of his own desire to exercise power. He led by articulating a complete identification with the (German) people. In his speeches he claimed his actions were their actions and his victories theirs. Claus-Ekkard Bärsch notes that Hitler had two themes which he constantly repeated. These were "power" and "providence." National Socialism provided the means for his expression of these

---

111. Kühn, "Fires in the Night," 2.
112. Kühn, "Fires in the Night," 3.
113. Evans, *The Coming of the Third Reich*, 41.

two things.[114] Guardini responded with what he already knew about Providence. National Socialism had an important religious dimension which we now consider.

Religious Dimension of National Socialism

National Socialism is commonly identified as a political group, yet, there was a very religious aspect to the Nazi movement.[115] The belief which was held by the National Socialists and so graphically illustrated in the writings of Rosenberg, Hitler and others is the belief in an *ontological difference* in the Aryan Folk which, more explicitly spelt out, argues that the Aryans are a type of Christ figure because of this difference within their soul. They were considered to be naturally virtuous with a direct connection to God. By comparison, the Nazis used the term "untermenschen" (sub-human) to describe the Jews. Hitler presents a similar, although not identical, philosophy in *Mein Kampf* (My Struggle)[116] in which he argues that the Aryan people are the "highest image of the Lord" (*Ebenbild des Herrn*). For him, the Aryan is the prototype (*Urtyp*) of what it means to be human.[117] Hitler was reported as saying that the only real "holy"(*heilig*) person is the Aryan.[118] Furthermore, the Aryan is the incarnation of God or "child of God."[119] This definition according to the National Socialist, Dietrich Eckart, involved the negation of Jews as part of the definition.[120]

In addition to holding a certain worldview with its quasi-philosophical base, the National Socialists were "Hitlercentric." That is to say, Hitler's will and orders, rather than just the ideology and the orders of the

---

114. Bärsch, *Die politische Religion*, 334.

115. The National Socialists were Deists who spoke of "God in us" to refer to themselves as Aryans. Bärsch, *Die politische Religion*, 323.

116. Hitler, *Mein Kampf*, 421.

117. Bärsch, *Die politische Religion*, 334.

118. Bärsch, *Die politische Religion*, 379.

119. Bärsch, *Die politische Religion*, 334.

120. Bärsch, *Die politische Religion*, 73. This is clear when defining the Aryans, because the Jews were always mentioned as the opposite to the Aryans and as the prototype of person from the Devil. Hitler says that the opposite (Gegensatz) of the Aryan makes the Jew, who in his opinion is from Satan and has no God potential. Nevertheless, Hitler stated that he did not believe Jesus Christ was a Jew and makes reference to the fact that Jesus struggled against materialism and the Jews. Hitler referred to Saint Paul and the representatives of Christianity from that time on as Communists. See Jockmann, *Adolf Hitler*, 412.

National Socialist party, were important to them.¹²¹ He was more than just a commander and had quasi-religious status for them. Bärsch draws attention to Hitler's belief that he had a special relationship to God and was, himself, a special link between God and the German people.¹²² The racial aspects of National Socialism were therefore part of a larger picture which was both religious, cultural and psychological.¹²³

Guardini's Theological Response to the Period of National Socialism

Hitler and the National Socialists came to power in 1933. Guardini wrote in his autobiographical notes that he had expected to lose his chair from that year onwards.¹²⁴ Guardini opposed the regime albeit covertly. In his book, *Catholic Theologians under Hitler*, Robert Krieg argues that of the prominent Catholic theologians in Germany only Engelbert Krebs and Guardini really opposed Hitler.¹²⁵ Guardini's opposition could be seen as countercultural as he refused to assent to their claims or support their values. In addition Guardini saw his task as strengthening the faith of the German people and encouraging them to resist the claims of the National Socialists.

In the Preface to the American Edition of *The Faith and Modern Man* (*Glaubenserkenntnis*), Guardini explains to his English speaking readers the reason for writing the twelve essays therein. He says that they were written during World War II "when the Christian life was deeply threatened by hostile doctrines."¹²⁶ He said he wrote them in order to help his readers "elude at least for a time the tightening thought control."¹²⁷ He then goes on to explain that he had been a member of a group of Christian writers who had, covertly, sent material to people by post as they:

---

121. Trevor-Roper, *Final Entries 1945*, 329–32.

122. Bärsch, *Die politische Religion*, 291. Hitler was also afraid that the Jews would triumph and the Aryan people would disappear.

123. Bärsch, *Die politische Religion*, 334 Guardini's writings show his position on this matter to be very different.

124. Guardini, *Berichte über mein Leben*, 51.

125. Krieg, *Catholic Theologians in Nazi Germany*.

126. Guardini, *Faith and Modern Man*, vii.

127. Guardini, *Faith and Modern Man*, vii.

> tried to find ways and means of informing and strengthening the minds of bewildered and harassed people, particularly the young. What was needed, we felt, was a restatement, in terms of contemporary life and experience, of the eternal and spiritual verities.[128]

The Faith and Modern Man is a collection of the twelve essays Guardini originally wrote for his contribution to this series of small booklets covertly sent to people inside letters. Commenting on the essays Guardini writes:

> Each grew out of the urgent questions asked by people in spiritual stress, and is the answer given to hard-pressed Christians in a time of acute physical and spiritual threat. The greater part ... I also delivered as evening lectures in a Berlin church, to an audience of the most varied background, including all denominations, threatened from without by air-raids and from within by the ever-present secret police. I can only hope that the sense of urgency of that time has been imparted to these restatements of some of the fundamental truths of our Faith.[129]

This short passage illustrates Guardini's intention in this period and suggests why his argument became increasingly more Christo-centric in focus.

The different emphasis in Guardini's writing, in this period, may be seen by comparing different editions of certain books. Many of these changes are already evident in 1930. I believe that because Guardini was already addressing the material of National Socialism in 1930, it could equally be argued that the second period in this thesis, that of National Socialism, begins for Guardini in 1930 although Hitler came to power in 1933. The themes, which Guardini drew out and used as covert resistance to the Nazi doctrine, appear in a number of his publications. The most prominent of these points is the immediate mention of Christ in association with Providence. Furthermore, Providence, *as Christ understood it*, is contrasted with the social system and pure "nature." That is to say the concept is completely radical in the sense that Providence here is completely different from nature or the social order. This radical,

---

128. Guardini relates the covert details of the secret writing group and how they made small booklets with the essays in them and sent them within letters by ordinary post to avoid detection. They were able to do this for quite sometime before the Nazis stopped them by suppressing the paper supply.

129. Guardini, *Faith and Modern Man*, vii.

non-determinist aspect is very important for Guardini because he argues that the human spirit in history enables choice which would not have been possible with something such as pure "nature."[130] Already in this time, then, Guardini shows how Providence in Jesus Christ's meaning is the work of the Holy Spirit and is not an impersonal force as Hitler believed, cannot be equated with that which is mere order, and does not carry benefits for some and not others. Providence is neither social nor physical but refers to fulfillment of the person in their life and work.

In arguing for making the Kingdom of God and God's justice the primary concern, Guardini is identifying a disjunction with the immediate social environment, which we know from historical hindsight, was developing defectively. He continues by saying a person must think, judge and act with Christ and the person's existence will change. In this the "new heaven and new earth" will come into play around the person. This point, spelt out well, will be repeated in his future writings. The prominence Guardini gives to human action in this period reflects a double agency and Guardini's belief, that a person can influence their environment, positively or negatively. This belief enables Guardini to argue that Providence is not a fixed pattern and when a person changes their attitude and mode of existence, their destiny will also change. We have said that Guardini's writing was used in covert opposition to the regime of this period.

The White Rose

Guardini's writings on Providence and other writings in this time, not only proved to be the means by which Guardini was able, covertly, to express his opposition to this regime, they were also the way in which he was able to influence others to resist as well. In this period Guardini successfully used his writing to strengthen people in their faith and help them to look to the Lord as their true source of life and happiness. For instance, we know from the diary of a member of the "White Rose"[131] resistance group who, along with others of that group, was beheaded for

---

130. Guardini, "Aus der Biblischen Gotteslehrer," 1–15.

131. "The White Rose" was a name given to a resistance group which was opposed to Hitler. This group was composed of students and intellectuals who formed the group from mutual acquaintances. See *The White Rose*, exhibition catalogue supported by a grant from the Alfried Krupp von Bohlen und Halbach Foundation and produced regularly with a friend of the leaders of the White Rose.

his opposition to Hitler, that Guardini's writings were very important to him and to others in the group at that time.[132]

The White Rose (*Die Weisse Rose*) was a name given to a resistance group which was opposed to Hitler. This group was composed of students and intellectuals who formed the group from mutual acquaintances.[133] Two of these students, Hans and Sophie Scholl, who were later martyred for their opposition, belonged to the group in the city of Ulm. This group was influenced by Romano Guardini, whose works many members were reading although Guardini himself was not a part of the group and didn't have personal contact with their members until 1943 when he moved from Berlin to the small village of Moosehausen near Ulm. There, until the end of the war he had contact with friends of the leaders of the White Rose.[134]

On the twelfth of October 1943, a small number of students, including the Scholl brother and sister, and a professor associated with the German resistance movement, distributed leaflets against Hitler and were beheaded for their action. Among them, Willi Graf had written to his sister. His sentiments were clear. "You know that I haven't been gentle in my action but I have pushed the issue from its depths from the awareness of the gravity of the situation."[135] In numerous diary entries Graf made reference to Guardini. For example his diary records, "18.9.1942. It has stopped raining. In addition today I managed to read Guardini in the tranquility of the hour at Midday."[136]

Then in November he talked of going for a walk with others and talking with them about Guardini.[137] A few days later he wrote:

> In the evening others arrived and we read Guardini and talked about prayer. We returned home during the night. I had walked a good way in the clarity, coldness and purity of the moonlit night.[138]

And again:

---

132. Guardini, *La Rosa Bianca*, 69–70; Guardini, "Es Lebe die Freiheit."
133. Guardini, *La Rosa Bianca*, 2.
134. Guardini, *La Rosa Bianca*, 8 (my translation).
135. Guardini, *La Rosa Bianca*, 65.
136. Guardini, *La Rosa Bianca*, 69.
137. Guardini, *La Rosa Bianca*, 69.
138. Guardini, *La Rosa Bianca*, 69.

> I continue to study the dogmatics of Schmaus and also I often read and re-read Guardini, which has so much to explain and say. This in effect, is the work that seems to me, in this moment, to be important.[139]

While visiting Bonn in order to try and win more support for the resistance, Graf's diary entry of 17 November 1942 recorded:

> On the first afternoon I took the icon to Marita. We looked at this lovely representation and Marita was very happy. While walking through the city with Marita and Heinz, we compared Jünger and Guardini, as grasping the whole world from within and then reflecting on it.[140]

From these examples we can see the importance of Guardini's writings to young people at that time and more particularly those who eventually gave their lives in showing opposition to the National Socialist regime.[141]

Providence Understood in Opposition to Hitler's Understanding

The themes, which Guardini drew out and used as covert resistance to the Nazi doctrine, appear in a number of his publications. The most prominent of these points is the immediate mention of Christ in association with Providence. At a time when Hitler often talked about providence, Guardini focused his attention on Christ's understanding of Providence with the intention of helping his readers identify the important discerning element of Christ in their lives.[142] Furthermore, Providence, *as Christ understood it*, is contrasted with the social system and pure "nature." That is to say the concept is completely radical in the sense that Providence here is completely different from nature or the social order. This radical, non-determinist aspect is very important for Guardini because he argues

---

139. Guardini, *La Rosa Bianca*, 70.

140. Guardini, *La Rosa Bianca*, 69.

141. While I was researching Guardini's work in Munich, about 2002, there was a Neo-Nazi rally and march through the city. Many people turned out to watch and there were many people holding banners or signs of resistance to the Neo-Nazis. A large number of people wore an artificial white rose on their lapel.

142. Kreig notes that in *Der Herr*, Guardini developed a Christology to strengthen the integrity and spiritual life of those Germans living in the Third Reich who believed that they had to accept everything which was being done there. See Kreig, *Romano Guardini*, 160. In the Preface to the English version of *The Faith and Modern Man*, cited above, Guardini amplifies this point.

that the human spirit in history enables choice which would not have been possible with something such as pure "nature."[143] Already in this time, then, Guardini shows how Providence in Jesus Christ's meaning is the work of the Holy Spirit and is not an impersonal force as Hitler believed, cannot be equated with that which is mere order, and does not carry benefits for some and not others. Providence is neither social nor physical alone but refers to the care of God for the individual person and the "whole" along with fulfillment of the person in his or her own life.

Guardini's criticism of National Socialism, reflected his opposition to all forms of Totalitarianism. Guardini believed that totalitarian regimes are essentially religious movements and that they serve religious needs albeit, often, in an unsatisfactorily way. For instance In his article, "Zur Totalitarismuskritik von Romano Guardini,"[144] Hans Meier argues that Guardini's criticism of all totalitarianism reflects his belief that the political leaders in totalitarian regimes are able to tap into an inner religious desire which people have and in this way the leaders need to be seen as mythological leaders rather than politicians as such. In other words, they are quasi-religious leaders who play into the natural yearning for the infinite which God has placed in human persons. The National Socialist ideology had a definite mythological aspect which served a quasi-religious purpose and a number of writers recognise Guardini as an example of one who offered covert resistance to these mythological beliefs.[145]

An example of Guardini's engagement with the socio-political climate of the time was the publication of "Der Heiland" (The Savior) in 1935. Guardini criticized the National Socialists for their view that Jesus Christ was mythological. In this book Guardini tried to bring out the Jewishness of Jesus before comparing Jesus Christ to mythological "saviour" figures. He shows how Jesus Christ was very different to these mythological figures, and completely unlike a person who could be identified as Hitler although he was not explicitly named. Guardini was called to the Reich's Office to explain himself and thereafter the National Socialists sent an official along to listen to his lectures and followed Guardini's

---

143. Guardini, "Aus der Biblischen Gotteslehrer," 1–15.

144. Meier, "Zur Totalitarianismuskritik," 7–10. We should nevertheless note that Guardini did not believe that "democracy" as such was the panacea for all ills either. Krieg notes that Guardini was distrustful of democracy. See Krieg, *Romano Guardini*, 135.

145. See Krieg, *Romano Guardini*, 121; Krieg, *Catholic Theologians in Nazi Germany*. 116; Bärsch, *Die politische Religion*, 145, 327; Knoll, *Glaube und Kultur*, 384.

movements. In his autobiographical notes Guardini states that from 1933 onwards he expected his professorial chair (Chair of Catholic Worldview) to be abolished but it did not happen until 1939.[146] In 1937 Guardini had written *The Lord* (*Der Herr*). In this book Guardini was able to show that Jesus was not a power figure but a person whose manifestation of God led him to act as God shows his own omnipotence and power, that is, through love and service. Krieg notes that *The Lord*, read in many German households throughout the war, had been reprinted four times by 1942.[147]

Although they initially tried to use Christianity and the idea of a national church as a vehicle for their doctrine, the National Socialists who were not atheists, as such, were Deists who called themselves *Gottglaübigen* (believers in God). In saying that they were "believers in God," they distinguished themselves from Christians by being "not Christian," which is to say that they believed in God but not in Jesus Christ as God. In light of the prejudice against the Jewish race, it is interesting to note that Adolf Hitler did not believe that Jesus Christ was a Jew. He was quoted as saying, "Jesus Christ was certainly not a Jew. The Jews would never have handed one of their own people to the Roman courts; they would have condemned Him themselves."[148] Hitler often used the term Providence. For instance, he announced, "When I learned that Schuschnigg had broken our treaty, I felt that now the call of providence had come to me. And that which took place in three days was only conceivable as the fulfilment of the wish and the will of this providence."[149]

Guardini held a different view of Providence. Having developed his notion of Providence earlier from the Biblical view, Guardini's focus, in this period, on Christ's understanding, enabled an understanding of Jesus' teaching on Providence which has further developed his own doctrine of Providence. To understand Guardini's intention further, we turn, first, to specific differences in the texts themselves.

---

146. Guardini, *Berichte über mein Leben*, 51. See also Krieg, *Catholic Theologians in Nazi Germany*.

147. Krieg, *Romano Guardini*, 133.

148. In this conversation, Hitler went on to add that, "His mother may well have been a Jewess." Night of 29th–30th November 1944, in Hitler, *Hitler's Table Talk*, 721. In 1920, Friedrich Andersen argued that Jesus, the "Heiland" [Bringer of Blessings], was not a Jew but an Indo–European who possessed Nordic traits. See Krieg, *Romano Guardini*, 122. Krieg also notes that the radical proponents of the Volk religion were anti-Christian. Krieg, *Romano Guardini*, 122.

149. Speech reported in "Le Temps," April 1938. Hitler, *My New Order*, 483.

Specific Differences in Guardini's Providence Writings in the National Socialist Period

In this period Guardini's work was not only more Christocentric but he clarified and stated his Christian position on Providence more forcefully. *Das Wesen des Christentum* (first written as a journal article in 1929) and *The Lord's Prayer*, written in 1932, show Guardini's orientation well. The first book deals with the character of Christianity and, unlike Adolf Harnack's book of the same name, Guardini draws the conclusion that the essence of Christianity is irreducibly Jesus Christ.[150] *The Lord's Prayer* treats the main themes from Christ's prayer, the "Lord's Prayer," and the major reference to Providence occurs in the fourth petition, "Give us this day, our daily bread." Here in this book, we are able to detect a slight but important change of focus. Although the National Socialists were yet to be in power, Guardini had already adopted a way of speaking about Providence according to a pattern much more in keeping with 1933–1945, the period of National Socialism, than we find in his earlier work. In particular, although Jesus Christ was by no means absent in his earlier writings, the work of this period draws out the centrality of Christ in living with Providence in a way that was not done earlier. In the 1939 publication of the article, "Was JESUS unter der Vorsehung Versteht" ("What JESUS Understood about Providence") (later published in *The Faith and Modern Man* as "Providence"), Guardini made a clear point, with large print for the word Jesus (JESUS), that Providence, in his text, referred to Jesus' understanding as distinct from that of "anyone" else.[151] In the 1944 edition of *The Faith and Modern Man*, Guardini repeats the title and material of the monograph with the same large print for the word Jesus, showing the clear reference to Jesus' understanding, but in the post-war 1949 version of the same work, he simply called the same chapter "Providence." Furthermore, where the 1944 version, covertly, refers implicitly to Hitler, the 1949 version is explicit and names Hitler as the person in error. Through Guardini's writings in this period, we are able to see Guardini's focus on the Biblically based idea of Providence as an attempt to re-orientate his readers in the understanding of God's Providence. He wants to show that Providence for Christ is not a "power model." This was especially important because although Hitler often used the term Providence, in his public speeches and private conversations, he used the term to mean

---

150. Guardini, *Das Wesen des Christentums*, 14.
151. On this point, see also Reber, *Romano Guardini Begegnen*, 158.

a special force which brought benefits. In particular Hitler uses the term repeatedly. He believed he had been chosen by "Providence" to effect things in the world. Guardini did not consider such beliefs to be commensurate with Christian doctrine.

In the early period, presented in the next chapter, I will argue that Guardini's theology of Providence is based on the theology of God the Creator and sustainer of this universe and loving Father of mankind as found in the Hebrew and Christian Scriptures. I argue that this image of God in whom the human person can trust is one of absolute goodness, immeasurability, ineffability and incomprehensibility. In short beyond anything the human person can imagine. In the center of this image is the Trinitarian image of God the Father of light and love; God the Son who has lived our human life and is really the Lord of life; God the Holy Spirit who pervades creation and everything in this world and who guides everyone who lives the life of faith. To live with Providence the person lives from the wisdom of God who guides everyone who lives the life of faith. God guides both the world and the human person to a holy redeemed world.

Guardini's Writing on Providence after 1945

The time of World War Two had seen the perpetration of unthinkable atrocities in Germany.[152] In the wake of the holocaust, to say nothing of the overall cost of the war in other ways, what does a theologian who has written so much about the Providence of God have to say? The awareness of what had been done in the name of being German must have been horrifying for many Germans and it certainly was for Guardini.[153] Furthermore, in his autobiographical notes Guardini noted that with the removal of his university chair[154] in 1939 and the closing of Burg Rothenfels, where he did his work with youth, he lost the two major points of deep involvement with people. Like many Germans at that time he must

---

152. I refer primarily to the holocaust here.

153. Krieg, *Spiritual Writings*, 27. Krieg notes that after the war Guardini reneged on what he had then perceived to be a negative depiction of the Jews in his book *The Lord*.

154. Although Guardini had expected to be put out of his position in 1933, it did not occur until 1939. Guardini, *Berichte über mein Leben*, 51. Guardini was instrumental in establishing the Catholic Academy of Bavaria, which was endowed with his estate on his death.

have faced questions of his own identity and the meaning of existence. Post war Germany was a different society with the presence of a large number of American service people and their families. Guardini's earlier writing with its breadth of understanding on many issues including questions of identity, reflections on culture and society and the human person gave him a unique position in the new society. At this time together with issues of Providence where he was dealing with negative aspects of the war, there were issues relating to the new society which were also being addressed. Guardini's writing on Providence, at this time, shows a clear link between living with the Providence of God and personal responsibility.[155] He will assert that Providence is ultimately eschatological and ends in judgement and justice.

---

155. Simply and negatively put, it could be summarized in the statement that one cannot live both a completely Providential Christian life and be irresponsible at the same time.

3

Romano Guardini's Writing in His Early Life and Analysis

Introduction

IN THE FIRST CHAPTER, I considered Guardini's overall theology and gave the rationale for this thesis. In chapter 2, I considered the socio-cultural background and influences which helped to form Guardini. I turn now to his writing on Providence, moving chronologically, through three major periods of his life, in order to note the development of his thought. As we look at Guardini's rich thought on Providence over the three periods outlined in chapter 1, it will be helpful to group it under four major themes he referred to when writing about Providence throughout his life, and to note the continuity and development within each theme as we move though his life's work. These four themes are: 1) Jesus Christ and Providence; 2) Providence is understood in Relationship with God; 3) The Individual Person is Important to God; 4) New Creation and New Existence.

Here we cover the first period from 1916 when the First World War was in progress, to 1930, on the eve of the National Socialist period in Germany. We find Guardini already establishing his four key themes which will re-emerge in the other two periods. There are four major works, dealing with Providence, which mark this period. At one end, we have a sermon he preached, published in 1916 as an article, "Seventh

Sunday after Pentecost: Divine Providence."[1] In the middle of this period, 1922, *The Church and the Catholic* was written. At the other end are two major works both published in 1929, *Conscience* and *The Living God*. Before turning to the four particular themes, let us look at the first work in this early period since it sets forth the theological underpinnings of all that Guardini will write on Providence throughout his life, especially his view of the nature of God.

The First Text on Providence

The first text on Providence, written long before Guardini's other works on Providence, stands alone and deserves a special mention at the outset. It was published in 1916, during the First World War, and seven years before further texts explicitly dealing with Providence. The article, "Seventh Sunday after Pentecost: Divine Providence," was published in a journal called *Chrysologus*. Like many of Guardini's written works it was, first, preached before a congregation before being submitted for publication. The date on the liturgical calendar was the Seventh Sunday after Pentecost and the First World War was in progress. It was published under Guardini's pseudonym "Dr. Wacht."[2] The points which Guardini makes here lay the groundwork for much of his later work. Along with other themes which emerged in this early period it can be seen in this text that Providence for him is grounded in the theology of God the Creator and is orientated towards helping people to have the understanding and capacity to repeatedly trust God and live as a Christian in the world.[3] In this text Guardini demonstrates the importance of each individual person in God's view. Each person has a part to play in God's plan while God has the same love and care for each individual in his heart as for the whole. This truth enables the individual Christian not to despair in the long

---

1. Guardini, "Siebter Sonntag nach Pfingsten." The quotations are from my translation of the German. It is fitting that Guardini's first major work on Providence should have been a sermon when we consider how important he was as a preacher and how many hundreds of people flocked to his sermons every Sunday.

2. Guardini's pseudonym is mentioned in chapter 1.

3. In Guardini's later work he does not specifically refer to Providence as "Divine Providence." This enables him to juxtapose his notion of Providence with that of others, especially Hitler, without the charge that his notion belongs only to theology. Yet the basis of his concept is clear here.

on-going test in days of tribulation but, conversely to trust, trust, and trust again in the God of Providence.⁴

The Grounding of Guardini's Writings on Providence: The Nature of God

Guardini's Doctrine of God is absolutely foundational to his understanding of Providence because it indicates the way in which God acts. In other words Guardini is able to show what type of God he refers to in his Providence texts and why God can be trusted. He refers to God in relational terms. In the later periods Guardini's thought is Christocentric and increasingly more Trinitarian. The nature of God is not repeated as explicitly in the later periods but must be understood as the background to them. Right throughout his work Guardini refers to God's love which can be considered an ever-present understanding. Although I have also used metaphysical terms such as omnipotent or omnipresent Guardini has chosen to use the Biblical language of relationship.

God Knows: The Omniscience of God

In the first text on Providence in 1916, Guardini presents God as a Creator God: "He is the Creator of all beings."⁵ This Creator has complete foreknowledge of future events rather than taking risks and leaving the future open in such a way that God in Godself does not know the outcome.⁶ In this first text Guardini uses a military image to refer to God's omniscience.⁷ Guardini holds that God's providential work is possible because of God's omniscience. This Creator God has a world plan which will only be completely made known to us in the judgement.⁸ Guardini states that

---

4. Guardini, "Siebter Sonntag nach Pfingsten," 543.
5. Guardini, "Siebter Sonntag nach Pfingsten," 541.
6. The debate in Openness Theology where some theologians believe that God takes risks and doesn't know the outcome in the future is referred to here. Guardini believes God allows for creaturely freedom and includes the free action of human persons in Providence, but he also believes that God knows the outcome for the future.
7. Guardini, "Siebter Sonntag nach Pfingsten," 540.
8. Guardini develops this aspect of judgement in *Freedom, Grace, and Destiny*, which was written more than thirty years later. Writing for educated laity, Guardini uses the term "All-Knowing" for God's Omniscience.

the will of the Lord guides everything in his plan and guides each person's destiny simultaneously with his guidance of the whole world:[9]

> He knows trees, grass and animals. And us ourselves! He knows us completely. No thought from him is passed over. He knows what once was, and what will be once again in the dark future, lies before him in bright light.[10]

The all-knowing God not only has a world plan, known only to God's-self from eternity but God has moved the stars, seas, animals and trees to fulfill the laws of nature[11]—everything serves God's will and is at God's service. Theologically, Guardini's description of God shows that our Provident God is ineffable and incomprehensible. That is to say, God knows each human person very well, and may reveal God's-self in Providential action. Yet paradoxically God cannot be completely known and our knowledge of God is limited although a person may comprehend the enormity of God as their "vision" becomes clearer. "His Providence is overwhelming. . . . But we have a certain comprehension of it."[12]

God the Creator Has Infinite Wisdom, Power, and Patience

Guardini's God of Providence has much more knowledge of future events than we have and we have argued for God's omniscience but in guiding the human person God uses wisdom and patience in order to allow the human person to act with initiative and err on life's path. I will argue, below, that Guardini, considers each human person to be important to God, yet he also asserts that human persons are insignificant in the light of the enormity of God. On the face of it these two aspects would seem to be a contradiction. Guardini is able to reconcile these two points because he expresses God's omnipotence as loving Father. Furthermore, the omniscience of God enables God to guide a person with wisdom and patience. In the overall situation God is God.[13] Guardini puts the under-

---

9. Guardini, "Siebter Sonntag nach Pfingsten," 543. This aspect underpins the importance of human action in the world.

10. Guardini, "Siebter Sonntag nach Pfingsten," 541.

11. In the next period of time to be considered, the National Socialist period, Guardini will show how the laws of nature are important but the human person is much more than these and cannot be reduced to "the natural" as such.

12. Guardini, "Siebter Sonntag nach Pfingsten," 542.

13. Guardini, *The Living God*, 59.

standing of a person's sinfulness with the same noesis and contextualizes it in God's patience which is the power with which God achieves God's purposes over time.[14] When Guardini says that God is all-wise he is also able to elaborate his statement further. Wisdom is the knowledge of time that belongs to things.[15] God's patience, which may be needed to enable Providence to occur, belongs here. Although God's mode of existence is eternity, God has created time to have one-after-anotherness of things. The works of human persons continue the work of God in the world and God's will is that we bring moral and social values to fruition.[16] In order to consider God's will and other aspects of God's nature we now turn to insights gleaned from texts in the second half of Guardini's early writing.

Our Relational God is Simplicity, Fullness, and Absolute Love

Guardini argues that God is as simple as light while containing all possibilities.[17] God who is a God of endless possibilities is also love and holds the nature of human persons in God's love.[18] The God of Providence has not left human persons alone to work everything out for themselves. God's attention to the human person arises out of God's loving patience, which enables God to hold infinite possibilities of grace and love open to life. Guardini's understanding of how we know God and God's will is holistic. In a manner similar to Rousselot's understanding,[19] Guardini argues that when the heart is ready the spiritual "eye" discerns the presence of the "great other" in things. In other words, one may intuit from the heart and discern a sense of being pointed to God. Furthermore, life itself experiences the living God but the mind organizes and assimilates the experience. Thus a person could enhance or limit the awareness because of prior experiences, knowledge or expectation. Guardini holds that God's will and Providence in each individual human person's life is known in relationship. The will of God guides everything in God's plan.

14. Guardini, *The Living God*, 63.
15. Guardini, *The Living God*, 64.
16. Guardini, *The Living God*, 67. Guardini would like to have seen the social world learn from and conform to the Gospel and Christian message rather than the other way around. Although his work deals with the social world, he clearly shows that the context is the enormity yet incomprehensibility of God.
17. Guardini, *The Living God*, 64.
18. Guardini, *The Living God*, 69.
19. See MacDermott, *Love and Understanding*.

God's Will

The will of God is not a force that denies a human person capacity for self determination. Guardini writes:

> The will of God is what ought to happen in the world He has created, what ought to emerge from man's work, from the freedom of the human spirit, so that the world may come to be what God intended it to be. The will of God is the consummation of the divine creation of which man, with his freedom is part.[20]

The will of God is not a power forcing a person to comply but is an active force, within a person, which helps a person to fulfill God's demands. The human person is a contributor to the consummation of the world. Guardini equates this power with grace.[21] Guardini writes that when the will of God is done by a person it is the work of that person but work done through God. "His will acting in me, the whole process being a mysterious unity."[22] Guardini believes that God's will is not ready made but is constantly being renewed. "When I confront a duty and fail to fulfil it, the will of God has not been done."[23] In such a situation a person takes the consequence of not responding to the will of God (it is sin in the eyes of God) but God will give the person a new opportunity to act with God.[24] The will of God is not an impersonal act but the love of the Father which as a power within a person, encourages and sustains.

Yet we could argue that the will of God could be seen as the "power" which limits a person's self determination so that the person is little more than a pawn or string puppet. Guardini mentions freedom of the human person. Is the person really free? The question revolves around the traditional freedom and human will axis. Guardini answers that question in this early period by linking a person's freedom to the power of grace saying that "the stronger the power of grace, the more freedom belongs to itself."[25] Here he contextualizes human freedom in God's patience by saying that:

---

20. Guardini, *The Living God*, 49.
21. Guardini, *The Living God*, 50.
22. Guardini, *The Living God*, 50.
23. Guardini, *The Living God*, 50.
24. Guardini, *The Living God*, 51.
25. Guardini, *The Living God*, 52.

God accompanies everything that happens, cooperating with human freedom. This is the ineffable mystery of His patience, which is possible only because He is the truly living God and the almighty living God.[26]

Grace enables a person to be more free. Without grace a person may be locked in a natural, albeit human, determinism. Yet, God will not abandon a person, even if they depart from God's will, because God is patiently waiting for them to act in accordance with God's will. It is God's power and love that enables God to act with patience in such a situation and enables a person to be really authentic.[27]

Arguing for personal authenticity and freedom, Guardini says that human persons are most unique and themselves when they act out of the ground of their being which is God. That means that when a person acts "independently" it is not from an isolated position but from that which is sustained from an inner relationship with the ground of (his or) her being. The person knows she is not God and is able to completely "be" herself, while still knowing that the ground of all being sustains her. "[W]hen God alone is acting, only then are we really ourselves. And that is Providence."[28] In other words, the unity-in-difference between the human person and God enables a freedom from and for God in the spiritually grounded person.

God's Nature and the Human Person

Guardini is opposed to an abstract intellectual idea of God and chooses to remain with the personal language of the Scriptures. He says that the "Living God" of the Bible can eventually replace the "God of philosophers and the poets."[29] In later texts of the early period, relationship with God is essential to understanding God's Providence and the way God is. In *Conscience*, first written in 1929 (nearly fifteen years after the 1916 article), Guardini focuses on the anthropological aspect while grounding

---

26. Guardini, *The Living God*, 52.

27. Authenticity in some existentialist terminology refers to a quality of existence in which the existent has become genuinely himself or herself. Consequently they do not necessarily follow social norms or take refuge in rules or ready made ideals but accept themselves as unique persons who have to realize the possibilities that belong to them. "Authenticity," in *A New Dictionary of Christian Ethics*, 49.

28. Guardini, *The Living God*, 31.

29. Guardini, *The Living God*, 19.

Providence in the Good (*Das Gute*) Conscience (*Das Gewissen*) and relationship with God as it is borne out in living practice (*die Sammlung*). The Good is named by Guardini as the Holiness of God. Fundamental questions underlie this writing. For instance one may ask if a person is essentially good, as some Roman Catholic theology has traditionally suggested or fundamentally bad as some Protestant theology would say. Guardini's answer, in *Conscience*, would be that the Good touches a person from within and wants the Good to be done while a person has an internal faculty (conscience) which is able to respond to it. It may also be asked if Guardini is presenting a type of natural theology here but the volition of the person is invoked with the need to respond to the Good. In order to further consider the character of the God of Providence who calls us to relationship, we turn to the Good.

The Good: God's Holiness

Guardini understands the holiness of God to be "the Good."[30] He argues that the Good is a quality of the living God; it is God's Holiness.[31] God is relational and the Good works with human conscience. The Good, is more than a concept. When a person has contact with the Good, God is experienced interiorly and God's guidance is not merely cold control but a gentle loving offer of guidance for someone who is already supported by God. We have said that Providence, for Guardini, involves the guidance of the world by God simultaneously with guidance of the person. God's presence in the world is not always apparent and must be disclosed in each situation. An internal dynamism exists. Guardini believes that disclosure happens in normal daily life. Working existentially from life and human actions Guardini argues that God comes to a person as the Good which touches them from within. "This Good does not hover vaguely somewhere in remote and inaccessible space. It is in contact with me; it touches me."[32] The human response to the Good is conscience which will be discussed below. We make reference to Jesus Christ first.

---

30. Guardini, *Conscience*, 53.
31. Guardini, *Conscience*, 53.
32. Guardini, *Conscience*, 24.

Theme 1: Jesus Christ and Providence

We move now beyond the foundational concept of the Doctrine of God which Guardini sets down in this period. We turn to what he says about the particular four themes we are presenting as a framework for understanding his theology of Providence. In relation to Providence there is little emphasis in the writings of this early period on the subject of the first theme, namely the understanding of Jesus Christ about Providence. Although Guardini refers to Christ as central in the Liturgy the theme of Christ and Providence come into prominence in the second period, the period of National Socialism, for reasons we shall note in the next chapter. For the time being, since there is so little to consider on this first theme in this period, let us move immediately to the second theme.

Theme 2: Providence Is Understood in Relationship with God

Guardini understands Providence as occurring in relationship with God. The relationship itself makes the guidance of God possible in the communion of a reciprocal relationship. The human person dwells in God and God dwells in the human person. In this early period Guardini grounds his argument for the possibility of relationship with God by referring to two ways that God is available to human persons as interior dispositions. These are: the "presentiment" of God and conscience. He also addresses the following aspects of the theme: 1) Mutual understanding and assent to God; 2) Mutual relationship; 3) Personal and social integration; 4) The human person in the world; 5) Christian practice in living with Providence; and 6) Creative tension between the person and world. Guardini uses a number of different terms to refer to the relationship with God, so the concept is nuanced by the use of these words. In the texts of this time Guardini uses the words "agreement" (*Ein-Verstehen*); "assent to" (*Einverständnis*) and "together [or mutual] understanding" (*Zusammenverstehen*) to refer to the togetherness-with-God and harmony (*Einvernehmen*). Agreement is the predominant term Guardini uses for assent to God and one's assent is needed for the decision to allow oneself to be opened to eternity; to be opened to God in this way. Although God's initiative is important in the relationship with God, human volition is important too especially as "fate" is countered by the guidance, not force, of God. One important effect of the relationship with God lies in the possibility of being able to discern God's intention or "will." Sensitivity to God is learnt from experience such as a presentiment of God. We turn to that aspect now.

Presentiment of God

In *The Living God*, Guardini wrote of a "presentiment" [*Ahnung*] of God within a person.[33] Presentiment is understood as a yearning for the Infinite and for the experience of love enabling these things to engender a search for eternal truth.[34] The presentiment of God, experienced initially in the young, will assist the orientation to God which living with Providence requires. The notion of presentiment enables Guardini to overcome arguments regarding the alienation of human persons with the other, the world or God.[35] Moreover it indicates a universality in Guardini's theology that is in the realm of natural theology. This is the anthropological aspect of "God as background." Guardini argues for both an ontological and more spiritual aspect to presentiment. He argues that each individual person can sense spiritual realities.[36] More specifically, human persons, when young, have an ontological drive towards the source of these "spiritual realities":[37]

> He has a sense of spiritual realities, of the supreme importance, and his responsibility for them. The place where he senses the reality of the spiritual and passionately experiences its absoluteness is the very place where he senses the reality of his own personality.[38]

---

33. Guardini, *The Living God*, 94. Later, on a similar point, in *Jesus Christus*, Guardini writes, "It is part of our very nature to be hungry, hungry for that which will satisfy us for eternity." Guardini, *Jesus Christus*, 53. Guardini's position is conservative and he argues that presentiment indicates merely a *pre*-sentiment and not actual knowledge.

34. Guardini, *The Living God*, 16. We recall the words of St. Augustine here, "You have made us for yourself, O Lord, and our hearts are restless until they rest in you."

35. On this point Guardini will argue against Kant. Kant's notion of autonomy of the self can, according to Guardini, herald an alienation from others. Kant was wrong, Guardini argues, because he put morality only with the subject; that is to say with "self."

36. Guardini, *The Living God*, 15.

37. Guardini, *The Living God*, 15.

38. Guardini, *The Living God*, 15.

From the anthropological point of view, Guardini's argument, here, presents an epistemological-ontological context for human experience and the real knowledge that Revelation will bring. Thus the historical aspect of presentiment can enable an implicit awareness to be made explicit. In this context, Guardini holds that all of our awareness must be a presentiment, and not actual knowledge, since only Revelation can lead to a full reality of God.[39] Guardini's argument concerning presentiment or premonition indicates a universality and suggests a common basis for the assertion, made in his book, *The Church and the Catholic*, that all people are created equal.[40] This aspect will be important in the discussions arising in the second period.[41] Guardini wants to understand the things that assist the interior movement to God. The notion of presentiment is complemented by Guardini's assertion in his books, *The Living God* and also in *Conscience*, that a person acting with conscience is open to the eternal. We have already adverted to conscience in association with the Good. We turn now to a more detailed understanding of conscience itself.

Conscience, the Good, and Providence

The Good and the conscience are an essential part of living with Providence. In *Conscience* Guardini says:

> Here is Providence – the way in which the life of the individual, as a member together with many other members, builds up the whole . . . and the way in which the happenings of this whole are ever directed towards the life of the individual . . . in order to inform the demand that confronts him, and to be his foundation, task and test. And the living tension of these two forces

---

39. Guardini, *The Living God*, 19.

40. By focusing on the anthropological aspect and indicating a universality in "presentiment," Guardini is able to avoid serious difficulties with the prevailing theology of the time. The Scholastics had made a distinction between created and uncreated Grace. Uncreated grace was God in Godself touching human persons within while created grace grew as grace in human nature through the habitual presence of uncreated grace.

41. It is in this context also that Guardini raises the question of Providence and answers it in a Christological way, saying that the examples of Providence which are given in the New Testament suggest the essence of Christ's gift.

perpetually renews itself in the situation. This is Providence continually consummating itself.[42]

Guardini goes on to argue that in it the whole becomes the expression of the will of God in that moment and the individual is shown how to be a member in the will of God of the whole. He argues that God speaks in both. From within "in the urging of conscience; from without in the arrangement of things."[43] Guardini considers conscience to be an ordinance of God's Providence.[44]

Conscience and the Good work together as the temporal and eternal, proceeding in tandem. The human person's faculty of response to the Good and a type of knowing is the conscience. The conscience is an essential part of Providence.[45] "[S]omething which responds to the Good, as an eye responds to light—[is] *Conscience*."[46] A gift of grace is given with clarity of conscience. When a person draws near to God, that person will be given the correct way of looking at things and have the capacity for correct choice. Although the conscience acts in accordance with nature, clarity of conscience is supernatural and is the result of grace and a movement towards and into God.

The relational aspect of conscience, as developed in relationship with the dynamic, fulfilling Good means that the moral authority is not an inanimate law. Rather, the human person becomes a loving-being-drawn to acting with Good and therefore moral. Since the Good occurs in the overall reality of life it cannot be confined to one section of it such as "moral life." Consonantly, morals must be formed in every situation.[47] Morality arising from the Good is borne out in moral deeds that can give the earthly paradigm an eternal quality. In this way the truth of God can be lived out in the world. Moreover, a well-lived moral life can engender meaning and values. In this way a concrete world constructed from the

---

42. Guardini, *Conscience*, 58.
43. Guardini, *Conscience*, 60.
44. Guardini, *Conscience*, 61.
45. Further explication of Guardini's notion of conscience follows below.
46. Guardini, *Conscience*, 24. Guardini believes the real knowledge is revelation and all other knowing is pre-sentiment. Nevertheless, I will argue below that, as with the Hebrew Scriptures, Guardini considers the heart (where conscience is perceived) to be the same as mind. Thus, conscience is also known in the mind in a way that is not dualistic.
47. We do not take this to mean that the morals themselves change according to the situation as such.

neutrality of nature can become a beautiful world moved from an internal dynamic of the Good. Providence is revealed in the ability to move with the Good.

In living with Providence, the conscience of each individual person is extremely important because in this early period Guardini argues that through acting with conscience a person is open to God and God's guidance. Guardini links the notion of conscience with "the Good" (*Das Gute*) which he first defines as the "holiness of God." By working from the anthropological position, Guardini is able to show conscience and moral actions as intrinsic to the relationship with God and integral to life in the world.[48] Conscience is seen by Guardini as the nexus between the temporal and the eternal. The nature and effect of conscience is twofold. Firstly there is the Spiritual aspect. A spiritual openness to God can occur through conscience. Conversely, openness to God can enable conscience to be perceived. Furthermore, in acting with conscience one can perceive and follow the will of God for one's life. Secondly there is the Moral aspect. Moral actions can open one to the eternal or, alternatively, openness to God can enable moral action to be carried out. Guardini considers conscience to be the place of the eternal in time.[49] It is an essential part of living with Providence.[50] Conscience is able to enable a person to experience the surety and rightness of that which comes from God because conscience opens a person to the eternal and moral:

> Conscience, therefore, is the point where the Eternal enters time. It is the birthplace of history. 'History,' which means something very different from a natural process, is kindled in the conscience. History means that through a free act on the part of a human being, the Eternal comes to pass in time.[51]

The concrete existence of the human person enables the eternal actions to be grounded and seen in the concrete world. Through moral actions a person is open to eternity whilst still in time. Guardini holds, moreover, that acting with conscience gives a capacity for openness to God.[52] In other words conscience is not only better when a person is

---

48. In later work Guardini shows how each individual human person can contribute to God's work in this world.

49. Guardini, *Conscience*, 39.

50. Guardini, *Conscience*, 60.

51. Guardini, *Conscience*, 39.

52. Guardini, *Conscience*, 43.

open to God but in the exercise of conscience that same openness can be enhanced. Furthermore, since free human deeds imply human volition, there is some human decision and action required rather than a passive natural movement of energy involved or blind following of a command. In this way, conscience is able to be a volitional act made in communion with God rather than just a natural act.

Conscience, in Guardini's view, is therefore, the organ of the everlasting demand of the Good, which insists upon fulfillment. By means of his conscience man is thrown open to eternity. Yet not withstanding, he is adjusted to time, to daily events and happenings. Conscience is the organ which indicates the eternal and ever-new demand of the Good, by means of concrete happenings; which continually enables us to recognise afresh in what manner the eternal and infinite Good is to be directed and realized by time. It is at once obedience and fresh creation; understanding and judgement; penetration and decision.[53]

Acting with the conscience, therefore, is obedience in response to the Good and at the same time is new creation since the person is able to initiate action. We noted, above, that a decision to act morally is a movement into God. The relationship with God reveals moral actions to be more than a set of abstract moral prescriptions. Rather, conscience as a response to "the Good" is a dynamic human response to the guidance of a loving, Providential God. In this way the human person can be a loving being drawn to being moral and drawn to God.

Guardini considers that at its lowest level the ethical conscience is the ground of the soul but is as its highest level the apex or edge of the soul.[54] The Good is an "ordinance of God's Providence."[55] That is to say the Good is God's providential gift to the human person for conscience. Since the conscience enables moral deeds to be carried out, Guardini would define the moral as beyond what is merely earthly; the secret of the conscience is the *"Agreement with God"*[56] and one's agreement with

---

53. Guardini, *Conscience*, 43.
54. Guardini, *Conscience*, 55.
55. Guardini, *Conscience*, 61.

56. Here Guardini uses the German word *Das Einverständnis* which the English translator terms "agreement." This word has the meaning of "giving assent" to something. Guardini, *Conscience*, 61. Although the translator uses the word "mystery" for *Geheimnis*, I have translated it secret, which I think is closer to the original meaning. Guardini's idea of a secret, within, for the Christian, had special significance in the next period, that of National Socialism, because the Nazis talked of secrecy and made a virtue of secrecy to cover their deeds.

God, involves a moral aspect as well. There is a volitional aspect to acting with conscience. The actual choice for Good is left to the person to decide as a response to conscience. Guardini believes that in this way the person is both able to understand another dimension of conscience, namely the will of God, and to carry that out. Guardini considers the ability to carry out the will of God as the "deep and valuable gift of conscience."[57] The initial awareness of "God-within" is God given. Ultimately, to live with Providence a person lives in communion with God. We have said that Guardini puts this type of communion with the notion of relationship and agreement with God. The more one is with God, the more one may know what the Good is with the clarity which comes from God.[58] Guardini's concept of conscience, the Good and his notion of a "presentiment" of God go hand in hand.

Mutual Understanding and Assent to God

We have said that Providence is understood, indeed made possible, in relationship with God and refers to the act of choice after a decision to orient one's being to God. The assent to God is very important for living with Providence. It is important to note that the assent to God is not a natural process *per se*. The assent to God is volitional and Guardini understands the assent as needing prior repentance especially because of the human person's possible need to control everything in their environment and to "play God" despite their imperfection and finiteness.[59] The act of choice requires a heart-felt "yes" to God's claim and the assent must come from within a person and be an act that is more than knowing. Rather, it constitutes an "agreement" or mutual understanding and is therefore not one-sided. The "mutual understanding" is the working relationship with God which holds the secret of Providence.[60] Furthermore, in this mutual relationship the human person is able to develop personal integrity.

Mutual understanding with God is the way God guides a person. This position involving relationship as the mode of living with

---

57. Guardini, *Conscience*, 62.
58. Guardini, *Conscience*, 57.
59. This assent, which is not a natural process and also involves repentance, will be important in the next period, of National Socialism, where the "natural," and Aryan ethnicity, was seen as a perfect path to God.
60. Guardini, *Conscience*, 61.

Providence, rather than acceptance of fate, which some people, wrongly, see as Providence, enables Guardini to cater for human free will because the notion of the "guidance of God" may raise the question of how Guardini understands human integrity. The person is not a marionette. Therefore in living with Providence, the "direction" of God is better expressed as an "agreement" or "together—understanding." This agreement has given the human person the capacity for knowing what the Good is through the understanding with God. But the understanding is not "out there." Rather, the person is touched, from within, by "the Good," (which I have argued, above, Guardini considers to be the holiness of God). This "together-understanding" is an integral part of that person's life and therefore not external to that person. Choice is involved and the person has the capacity to co-operate with God in God's on-going creation and presence in this world. The initiative for relationship lies with God and comes from God's wisdom and love.

Mutual Relationship

Guardini wants to understand the things that assist the interior movement to God. Consonant with the assertion of God's initiative is Guardini's belief that a positive response to the experience of the Good is necessary for the relationship between God and human persons and subsequently for Providence to occur. When the human person is invited to share in God's life and creative act by participating in a relationship[61] with God, Guardini doesn't envision a detachment from the world, an aesthetic retreat or flight to the desert of disembodied spirituality. Rather, he asserts that the individual person's destiny is woven into the life of the community at large and that is God's secret work-place. A person understands God's purposes in the context of community.

I have written, above, that central to Guardini's notion of Providence is the type of reciprocal relations where the human person dwells in God and God dwells in the human person. The basis for this relationship, with God, is the relationship between God the Father and his Son. Some theologians have used the Greek term *Perichoresis* for this type of relationship. We have noted that Guardini wrote his graduate work on

---

61. The relationship is a "covenant style" relationship. These are the words I use here to describe Guardini's concept. Guardini uses the same words in a later book (*The Life of Faith*).

Bonaventure and Guardini's concept here is akin to the Bonaventurian principle for Trinitarian relations. Bonaventure uses the Latin term *Circumincessio*, which implies dynamic movement of interpersonal relations, within the Trinity, entailing a type of dance around each other. In Guardini's argument, human persons could be seen as being invited to this mutuality which is possible because each person already exists in the heart of God. In Providence-living God guides the individual human person simultaneously with guidance of the world, and fulfillment for each is able to occur within the other.[62] The world itself is not finished but in process yet is held and guided by God:

> God embraces us, surrounds us, penetrates us. He stands within our inmost being; there where our being inwardly borders on nothingness, is God's hand upholding us. Then he speaks to us; not as a universal Force, nor as a mere Law; not as an 'It,' but as a 'He,' to whom a 'you' is possible. It is thus that God speaks within us. Yet this same God is the Creator and Lord of the world; from eternity the world and its events have lain in the hollow of His Hand. The world is not a finished piece of machinery which functions automatically, but is always held and directed by Him. Whatever happens, happens *through* God-even if it happens in accordance with the laws and powers of Nature, for these are God's instruments.[63]

Here Guardini is refuting any Deist possibility. God did not just create the world, and human persons, then turn his back on them or remain distant. Rather God is present, immanent, and continues to be involved with the world in a guiding and caring sense. God is personal and wants a personal relationship with human persons. In *Conscience*, Guardini builds an argument for relationship with God and others in the world

---

62. In the manner of Bonaventure, Christ is the exemplar for Guardini (Lat. *Exemplum*, meaning a pattern of model). "The exemplarity of God refers to the notion that God, besides being the efficient and final cause of creation, is also exemplar. An exemplary cause is the model according to which something is made. Bonaventure, for instance, believed that the exemplar of all reality, is Christ himself." T. Kondoleon argues in the *New Catholic Encyclopedia* for a preconceived form of a work (as an intentional idea) which exerts an influence upon the will of the agent. See "Exemplary Causality," in *New Catholic Encyclopedia*, 5:528; "Exemplarism," in *New Catholic Encyclopedia*, 5:524. Like other theologians writing in the period of National Socialism, such as Karl Barth, Guardini's theology in that period moves from being Christological to Christocentric. See Lindsay, *Covenanted Solidarity*, 199. Guardini, *Conscience*, 71. Nothing is forced upon a person, all occurs in mutual agreement. Guardini, *Conscience*, 60.

63. Guardini, *Conscience*, 58.

by showing the way personal integrity is established. We now turn to a further consideration of this aspect.

Personal and Social Integrity

In order to live Providentially, a person needs to have personal integrity. Guardini uses the notions of *Autonom* and *Heteronom* to show what integrity means in this context, arguing for a type of *Theonom* instead. If morality is "self-enslaved" one becomes an *Autonom*.[64] Guardini considers Kant to have advocated this position.[65] This situation, contrary to Kant's assertion, is devoid of real morality because one is no longer related to the absolute source of one's being. On the other hand, the other possible extreme is just as dangerous. If one binds morality to a reality outside oneself, one becomes foreign to oneself and a *Heteronom* and therefore there is a loss of personal integrity and, consequently, morality. Guardini believes that if one is too much of an *Autonom*, one is open to the possibility of, reactively, slipping into being a *Heteronom* very quickly and therefore being unable to maintain one's real integrity.[66] Likewise, if one moves to "self" one is already alienated; outside oneself so to speak because the real self is grounded in God not in the individual person as such. On the other hand, if the movement is to away from self and to God, God is still "another" and one is foreign.[67] In order to live with the integrity and responsibility that Providential living demands, one must change his or her basic idea. God is not "me" as such, yet God is the ground of my being and my Creator.[68] This point enables Guardini to argue that in this situation, one is more than one would be if one were oneself alone. Because of the relationship with God, personal integrity is grounded and established in the source of life which knows no end.[69] Yet,

---

64. Guardini, *Conscience*, 63.

65. Guardini, *Conscience*, 64.

66. Thus the movement, into heteronomy during the Hitler period may indeed have been a result of extreme autonomy in the Weimar period.

67. Guardini, *Conscience*, 65.

68. Guardini, *Conscience*, 65. In relationship with God, the person is then a *Theonom*.

69. Furthermore, since the Good is the Holiness of God, the more a person acts in accordance with that Good, and indeed the will of God, the more that person growing-in-integrity, from the source of life itself, actually becomes more uniquely themselves.

in their relationship to God human persons also grow in a social context and it is to this we now turn.

The Human Person in the World—Social Reality

Guardini deals with Providence from the anthropological aspect.[70] This approach enables Guardini to place Providence more clearly in a social context as well as divine. Social reality and the world as such are important for living with Providence and God can guide one in one's own life, simultaneously with the guidance of God for the larger "whole." We have said that Providence in Guardini's schema involves guidance of the human person and the whole towards God's holy kingdom. Guardini uses the notion of "poles" to refer to two different spatial areas. One can understand the inner and outer life of a person by the assertion that one pole is within a person and the other is in the environment at large. A tension and movement between two poles enables conscience, internally, and the Providential arrangement of things, externally, to mutually complement and influence each other. Furthermore, the life of the individual contributes to the whole and vice versa. This is made possible because the life of the individual is "over there" in the whole.[71] In other words, social interaction with others brings the influence of an individual person into the society at large. This aspect will be very important for Guardini's later argument that the Christian is a door for God in the world and thus in the relationship with God the influence of God is brought into society. Conceptually, Guardini understands the life of the individual to be complementary with the life of the whole. Since Guardini believes that individual Providence and the Providence of history are complementary not mutually exclusive, they can also be mutually conditioning.[72] The living tension, he asserts, builds every situation from the two poles and

---

70. Guardini was apparently able to live with the integrity he espoused. Robert Krieg develops each of these points well in Krieg, "Romano Guardini's Theology of the Human Person."

71. Guardini, *Conscience*, 59. This aspect will enable Guardini to argue later that when a person, in relationship with God, opens his or her heart in loving trustful obedience to God, this person can be a door of God's creative love and someone who brings God's creative action into the world.

72. In this context I employ this term to refer to the mutual exchange and conditioning effect of Providence both in the life of the individual and Providence in the life of the whole.

God's Providence is revealed in this tension. The spatial aspect of Providence is important here (we recall Guardini's concept of the opposites) because Guardini sees God as a type of artist whose action is revealed in the incarnational world. Guardini believes the individual person can participate in God's will while that action can be appropriate for the whole. God speaks in both. God speaks interiorly to the individual human person in conscience and, in the external, environmental world of the same person, in Providence (arrangement of things). We can understand this aspect from daily events and reflection on events. The moral life of human persons extends from the new impulse of this relationship. Guardini believes that energy is derived from the interaction between the two.[73]

Christian Practice in Living with Providence

Certain actions and practices may assist the possibility of living with Providence. We have already referred to the importance of acting with conscience and being a *Theonom*, living in relationship with God. Guardini also addresses this important area by dealing with the inner and outer aspects of a person. The interiority of a person, a result of the grace of God may be nurtured by a constancy, by allowing oneself to "be," by Prayer and meditation, by patience, readiness and reflection on each day's activities, by understanding oneself and by the Sacrament of Confirmation. The outer life grows as the person interacts with others in the world, pays attention to their duty and the present moment in everyday activities, and allows the grace of God to guide. Grace is essential to growth in faith because while inner vigilance and external experience build on each other, grace is important for real sanctity. Grace grows in relationship with God.

Guardini refers to the inner life as a life growing from the depths in God and the outer life as that which grows through contact with things in the world. In this context he draws attention to the importance of things which nurture a person's faith. The assent (consent) to God means that the whole of human life can be lived out of the relationship, which is human and divine. When the Good is done in a certain situation it is the guidance of God who moves the heart.[74] We have argued that Guardini believes the "Good" touches conscience and in this context he

---

73. Guardini, *Conscience*, 60.
74. Guardini, *Conscience*, 74.

draws attention to the importance of human action in co-operating with grace. Conscience develops as a result of recognition of the Good as an ordinance of God's Providence and develops in agreement with God as a result of response to the Good in each daily situation.[75] A person's conscience, developed in faith, can become the way it was meant it to be: the Holy God's living voice in us.[76]

On a personal level, prayer and meditation can help the movement of the heart to God. With a focus on God, Guardini suggests Newman's prayer for the clarity of conscience.[77] This understanding, well developed in Newman's thought, is shared by Guardini. Guardini argues that a deeper understanding of conscience means:

> Knowledge-of oneself and before God-of the Good, as the demand of God's holiness; it means the understanding, - of oneself, and before God, in the light of each situation as it occurs - of the Good, as an ordinance of God's Providence.[78]

Reflection on daily events is important as the assent to God develops conscience. Guardini links Providence with duty and interiority of the present moment in action and reflection on the work of God's grace to enable learning from life itself.[79]

The grace of God is active and Guardini says that when the Spirit is strong the inner space, the depth, and the focus are all signs of its effect.[80] This can imply that sometimes a person must simply "be" rather than do.[81] Silence and patience belong in this practice as a person allows God to move the heart. Yet in this very individual and personal account Guardini still assigns a place to the Church. The Sacrament of Confirmation is important. Guardini believes Confirmation is the "sacrament of

---

75. Guardini, *Conscience*, 61.

76. Guardini, *Conscience*, 101.

77. "But I need Thee to teach me day by day, according to each day's opportunities and needs. Give me, O my Lord, that purity of conscience which alone can receive.... My ears are dull, so that I cannot hear thy voice. My eyes are dim, so that I cannot see Thy tokens. Thou alone canst quicken my hearing, and purge my sight, and cleanse and renew my heart. Teach me ... to sit at Thy feet, and to hear thy word." Newman, *Meditations and Devotions*, 520, quoted by Guardini in *Conscience*, 79.

78. Guardini, *Conscience*, 60.

79. Guardini, *Conscience*, 78.

80. Guardini, *Conscience*, 85.

81. Guardini, *Conscience*, 94.

conscience."[82] In this sense Guardini links the work of the Holy Spirit to the growth of conscience and the capacity to do good in this world. It could be said that there is a creative tension between the human person and the world.

Creative Tension between Person and World

Guardini holds that the world is eternal and from the beginning the "whole" and individual have been built together. The relationship with the world is such that there is a focus in the person and one in the collective that is the world. In this creative tension between the person and the world God's wisdom and love occur. Providence is to be seen in many situations which occur in the world along with the unending wisdom of God and when a person lives with Providence, conscience is not a finished product but living, and the fulfillment of conscience occurs when the natural conscience is touched by grace from faith and belief and the person is able to act from conscience. Inner vigilance and outward experience are important natural things for growth of the conscience but grace is essential to it. Guardini holds that patience, readiness and prayer are important, along with a number of other things including repentance which he calls inner cleansing. The interior life must have depth, the development of different dimensions and vigilance. The result will be fullness and clarity about what is right. Reality and worth are a part of this clarity.[83] We have said that, in this early period, Guardini expresses his idea of the heart as centered on conscience and there is a link with the moral life of a person.[84] The practice which is important for the interior life includes regular solitude and silence. Life must have a rhythm incorporating these things and it is important to follow the "middle way" or moderation.[85] Perhaps, prophetically, Guardini laments that the middle way was not seen in the German society of that time.[86] Thus Guardini

---

82. Guardini, *Conscience*, 79.

83. Guardini, *Conscience*, 83.

84. Brüske, "Epilogo." Brüske rightly notes that Guardini was foreshadowing the later work of Karl Rahner and his notion of Anonymous Christianity with this argument.

85. Guardini, *Conscience*, 84. Here we could see the influence of St. Benedict who advocated these things in his rule.

86. 1929, when Guardini wrote this, was already the eve of the National Socialist period.

is able to show the dynamic nature of God-in-relationship who touches creation and Providentially allows disclosure of God's-self and purposes while guiding a person's life and the world at large.

To summarize this section it may be said that, contemplation, prayer and adoration of God are all necessary for development of the relationship with God and living with Providence which is known externally from the arrangement of things in a particular situation.[87] In the article of 1916 attention was given to Guardini's argument that as Providence is developed in relationship with God, human choice in the context of mutual agreement is important. Later, he writes that the play between the Good and the human response of conscience is combined with the capacity for receiving grace. Christian commitment and practice, including the Sacraments, are shown to be important for the growth in holiness that we might associate with wholeness rather than anything resembling a rarefied distance from the world and things in it. Providence living occurs in such a context. In part two we will begin with the theme of the importance of the individual to God.

Theme 3: The Individual Person Is Important to God[88]

We have said that Providence occurs in relationship with God and now we will consider a further refinement of that statement as an essential part of living with Providence, namely, the assertion that the individual person is important to God. I use the term "individual"[89] to show that, in Guardini's view, the human person is not a collective or dispensable.[90] I

---

87. By "a particular situation," Guardini means one in which the particular person finds significance in relationship with other persons or things. In this sense, a general law may not speak for that certain person who finds personal significance that another does not. "The Good which requires to be realized, develops clearly from what on each occasion has to be done." Guardini, *Conscience*, 29.

88. The word Guardini uses to refer to the individual person in *Conscience* is *Mensch* (human). In later works, to be considered below, he nuances the word by saying a person is more than *Individuum* or *Mensch* (individual or human) and is *Person* (which is clarified further in chapter 4). In that light, I refer to *Mensch* in this article as human person, individual person, or person.

89. Guardini often uses the terms *Einzeln* (individual) and *Mensch* (human person) in this period, which in German can be nuanced further and on page sixty-five of the book, *Conscience*, he clarifies that these terms do not mean only *Individuum* (separate individual) but *Person* ("not one chance in a dozen but unique").

90. This will be contrasted with Hitler's view in the next chapter. Hitler believed

have said that Guardini believes individual Providence can be in harmony with general Providence; Providence of the person and Providence of the world can go together so that each contributes to the fulfillment of the other.[91] In this early period, in an argument never rescinded, Guardini shows why the individual is important to God. In Guardini's mind, the importance of the individual is understood in the context of God's love. Furthermore the personal, life-transforming Providential nature of God is given to the person, already linked to God by existence, when that person responds to God. We turn now to a further nuancing of that assertion.

God's Mark

In 1916, Guardini had addressed the subject of the individual person's importance to God by comparing God with a human military commander. Reflecting on a newspaper article written, as it was, during World War One, he comments on the reports of a "successful" battle in which only a "few" lives were reported to have been lost, Guardini writes:

> "Only a few men!" Haven't we already clarified how shameful that word "only" is for us. How poor is the strength of our small minds that over a great success we can forget how irreplaceable each human life is?[92]

Each—human—life, the words carry the sense of significance consonant with Guardini's understanding. He maintains that in God's view the person is irreplaceable and of infinite value. Furthermore, and interestingly, he asserts that each person lies in the heart of God in God's interior self.[93] In this context he is able to argue for another difference from the earthly military commander:

> God's wisdom is something else! God makes it possible for each person to rise above the earthbound state; each is Christ's brother, each is the eternal Father's child. Each person is in God's heart and written with *indelible* letters; each is of value to him,

---

that the individual was dispensable as long as there were others to replace him (see chapter 3).

91. Guardini, "Siebter Sonntag nach Pfingsten," 542.
92. Guardini, "Siebter Sonntag nach Pfingsten," 542.
93. Later, Guardini will argue that the ground of each person's being is God which leads to questions about God's heart.

to an endless degree because he paid with the blood of his Son. ... He carries every person's destiny with the same endless love in his heart because he is not only the Lord and Regent of the world but our Father who loves us and therefore it is not hard to understand why He cares for each hair of our head.[94]

In this statement, Guardini states that transcendence is possible for the human person as he argues that God will lift a person up.[95] In Guardini's mind, the person is in the care of God, but is not only in God's "hands." Rather, he or she is in God's loving *heart* with their names written in *indelible letters*.[96] In indicating the human person's existence and image in God's heart as written here, and also understood from his argument for Theonomy, Guardini is able to show how Providence need not be an imposition of something in a person's life over which he or she has little control.[97] A relationship with God already exists and based on reciprocal love can develop even more. In *Conscience*, Guardini notes that the word 'conscience' and its meaning are "connected with the ultimate layers of religious consciousness with the 'Ground of the soul' and the 'spiritual spark.'"[98]

Further, Guardini writes of the uniqueness of each human person:

> I am not a 'case,' one among a dozen others, but I am unique.
> I am not only an individual but a personality; I not only bear

---

94. Guardini, "Siebter Sonntag nach Pfingsten," 542.

95. In the manner of his "theological father," Bonaventure. The Franciscan scholar Zachary Hayes notes that Bonaventure's theology has been perceptively elucidated for other scholars by Guardini who understands Bonaventure as writing that "God appears in personal terms, seeking the creature and lifting it up so as to lead it back to Himself." See Hayes, *The Hidden Centre*.

96. We may put this argument with the passage referred to earlier but written in 1964, where Guardini recounts a dream in which he understood that each person is given a word uttered from God into his or her being at the beginning of life. That person's life is to be an elucidation and a fulfillment of the divine word, which can come into harmony with the person and will be the basis of God's judgement at the end of his or her life. See Guardini, *Berichte über mein Leben*, 20. Pope Benedict XVI, speaking about Guardini's work, argues that "the truth of man is authenticity – conforming to one's nature." He argues further that the obedience of being is adoration which is the obedience of our being to the being of God. See Ratzinger, *Fundamental Speeches from Five Decades*, 247.

97. "Covenant Style" relationship is my term for Guardini's concept, but in a later work he himself uses the term "covenant" for our relationship to God in Providential living where God's justice must prevail. See Guardini, *The Virtues*, 154.

98. Guardini, *Conscience*, 72.

within me the universal essence, but one which derives its characteristic stamp from this unique quality of mine—from my name. I hold this name from God. I am in this world, but do not become absorbed by it. With my inmost being I come directly from God and face Him directly. He has created me as this particular individual. The name he has given me does not fit at all into the universal genus 'Man,' nor does it fit at all into the structure of the world. Only God knows it. Therefore I can become familiar with my name (my most intimate possession) and master it only where it is stored up—in God . . . that which is final and supreme only comes about really in my encounter with God. This knowledge of God, this knowledge of what lies between Him and myself alone, this process by which I become intelligible to myself before Him, is conscience in its supreme religious depth. I, as he whom God has named, have my own task to perform in His world. And I shall only become that particular individual by doing God's Will in my regard. I am however constantly meeting this Will afresh in the situation.[99]

This statement on what must be called vocation is a statement about every human being. An individual person with his or her humanity, given by God, is unique. In relationship with God, that person can grow and develop at the level of being and become the person he or she has been created to be and share in the life of God while retaining individual difference.

Sharing in the Life of God

When, in the earlier quotation Guardini says that God makes it possible for a person to rise above the earthbound state he refers to transcendence and a type of participation in God that already reveals the beginnings of the mature Trinitarian thought which will be evident in Guardini's later work. The idea refers to deification of the human person through participation in the divine life. The person becomes like God yet is not God as such, nor as God is in God's innermost being. Guardini understands both the person and the world to be in the same process of deification. Deification here would refer to the process of a person becoming sacred or holy rather than becoming God as such. Yet this statement does not mean that humanity is raised to a purely spiritual level. Rather, human persons, it

---

99. Guardini, *Conscience*, 74.

will be argued later, are liberated, while in the world, to a new and holy existence.[100] Such is Guardini's notion of redemption which in chapters 3 and 4 will be shown to be through Jesus Christ who brings human persons into his own relationship with the Father. In fact, Providence, as will be shown later, in Guardini's writing is the process of a person, becoming redeemed, in a world also in the process of being redeemed. The human person can contribute to this process by allowing God to be active in his or her life, making the person more Godly and enabling the person to be a door for God in the world. Guardini will argue that Godly people can help the world to be a Godly world. If this were to occur, in the sense of ongoing creation by God, the human person could be viewed as a type of co-creator.[101] Furthermore the person is able to live from the eternal while still in time.

Repentance

Yet the individual person has a personal responsibility. The assent to God involves repentance. Guardini believes that human repentance, God's forgiveness and God's creative power is important in forming the Christian. The more profoundly the person has become a Christian, the more that person will be aware of the preciousness of it and want to do what God wants. The person must persevere, watch and wait and pray for the patience of God in order to do so. What happens if the will of God is not done? Guardini writes that grace within a person helps them to fulfill God's plan but when it is not done, God will re-create although someone has to bear the pain of the mistake. (God's intention for a person may not be carried out or may be blocked by another.) Guardini's position is severe because Guardini believes God's holy will has been violated. He writes that God forgives but the person must have an awareness of the moral law and their own shortcomings in order to open to that forgiveness. Repentance rather than superficial relief is the appropriate response of the appeal to God.

Forgiveness is a serious matter for Guardini. Forgiveness occurs in the heart and he recalls God's words to Moses before the burning bush

---

100. Guardini, *The Church of the Lord*, 75.

101. This is asserted in the context that Guardini considers God in God's innermost self, inaccessible and incomprehensible to human persons. Human persons are not God as such and when human persons create they are not prime creators as God is.

"put off your shoes for the place where you now stand is holy ground."[102] "Repentance wants truth and belongs to God's sphere."[103] Repentance is not the act which "covers up"[104] This is a coming before God, on God's own territory and with "cap in hand." The condemnation (*der Anklage*) from the heart is deep-seated because God himself condemns.[105] Guardini writes that "God doesn't ask us to 'cheer-up', because the situation is serious. Creative life has been lost."[106] Guardini holds that God asks us to see the full gravity of what we have done and then he will come to us with creative love.[107] It is an appeal to the "deepest mystery of the creative power of God"[108] because only God has the power to recreate the personality burdened and defiled by sin. Repentance is associated with being "born again." What does he mean by this term?

Born Again

Guardini understands that for the fullness of one's relationship with God one must be "born again." Conversion (*metanoia*) would be an appropriate way to express this process. His vision, as we see elsewhere, is often mystical. Although this situation could be called conversion, Guardini refers to a process which begins early in life or in Baptism although the potential is there from the first (biological) birth and develops with grace. This "second" birth is from God the Father in Christ through the Holy Spirit to community of "godly life." One becomes a "child of God."[109] In other words one is able to participate in the life of the Triune God. The

---

102. Guardini, *The Living God*, 46.

103. Guardini, *The Living God*, 52.

104. Guardini, *The Living God*, 53.

105. Guardini, *The Living God*, 56. The German reads, "Der eigentlich anklagt in der Anklage des Herzens, ist Gott selbst." The translator uses the word condemnation for the German word Anklagt which can also be accurately translated as accusation, indictment or charge.

106. Guardini, *The Living God*, 58. We recall that for Guardini, one should responsibly attend to one's duty and do whatever the present moment requires, in order to carry out God's will.

107. Guardini, *The Living God*, 59.

108. Guardini, *The Living God*, 52.

109. Although Guardini uses the word *Gotteskindschaft* (child of God), one of his female English translators uses the word Sonship, bringing a gender issue to the text that Guardini did not bring.

'Our Father' is the content of the person's prayer"[110] That is to say, the person acts with Christ and relates to God as God's son or daughter. Therefore repentance, conversion, the assent to God, the agreement and the mutual understanding are Christological and found the relationship in which the born again person has been born again to the community of "Godly life." Sharing in Trinitarian life is ultimately to share in the life of God and be guided by God's wisdom. It is to be with the persons of the Trinity as they dynamically relate, in and through each other; a unity in difference. The Trinity is the context for understanding the way God relates to human persons. Guardini's argument for Providence and the importance of each individual person to God, as studied in this section, shows the fullness of human potential.

Theme 4: New Creation and New Existence[111]

Creation can be renewed through God's love and can also be renewed through the actions, especially moral actions of human persons. God's divine guidance of individual human persons, in mutual agreement with that person, occurs simultaneously with God's guidance of history. Providence for both takes place one through the other and is directed towards the holy kingdom.[112] Both the new creation and new existence are mutually reinforcing because the material world and the spiritual world proceed in tandem. A person living according to God's Providence can help to transform the created world. In this section, then, I will show Guardini's argument, to be taken up in later periods as well, for an ontological, (as well as ethical) transformation of the world and everything in it. This transformation is not a natural process but a radically different move through God's grace present in the world. We turn now to a further explication of that notion.

---

110. Guardini, *Conscience*, 63.

111. In the initial pages of this thesis we quoted Guardini as writing, "Jesus' message about Providence also does not mean something like the Hellenistic world order, but rather the divine guidance of history which is directed toward the realization of the holy kingdom, but at the same time the guidance of the destiny of every individual so that the one takes place in and through the other. 'Seek ye therefore first the kingdom of God and his justice, and all these things [necessary for life] shall be added unto you. (Matt. 6:33)'." Guardini, *The Virtues*.

112. In Guardini's mind, repentance is integral to this process.

Grace in Creation

The material world is not just a material world but also a world brimming with the grace of God. Creation is permeated with and sustained by grace. Guardini illustrates this point by reflecting on the life of St. Francis. He writes that in St. Francis' life some of this awareness of grace is released. Furthermore, Guardini notes that in studying Francis' life we are able to see the relationship between things. In the relationship between things the divine center of the world is revealed. Guardini believes this center is shown in the resurrection. "The Lamb," Christ, is at the world's innermost center.[113] This aspect of the divine in the world enables Guardini to argue for spirituality "in the world" and is opposed to any life-denying type of spirituality that advocates remaining in the "desert." For him, creation is important and every aspect of our lives happens in God. He asserts that only an "inferior piety" wants to "enhance the things of God by disparaging the things of the world."[114] The mystery of God also applies to nature, which is not just a material reality.[115] Guardini believes that those who come to creation devoutly, and with a purified heart, understand that the world speaks of its creator because God's transformation has an unfailing beauty. Yet, this *new* world is both here and now and also in the future (already and not yet). The world of the new creation has an undeniable eschatological aspect to it. He writes, "One day, the light of God's heart will break forth from all things and they will be radiant and the meaning of God's love for his creation will be revealed to us"[116] In other words the grace inherent in creation will be more clearly seen.

Freedom in Grace

Grace brings freedom and Guardini believes that the human person is responsible for using their freedom for God's world. He holds that the human person must use their own freedom to stand within the newness of the freedom of God's activity.[117] In this way God's freedom can become the person's freedom and God's intention can be done in the world

---

113. Guardini, *The Living God*, 106.
114. Guardini, *The Living God*, 86.
115. Guardini, *The Living God*, 105.
116. Guardini, *The Living God*, 112.
117. Guardini, *The Living God*, 25.

through human persons. The world can "become" through us.[118] That is, through human action, the world can grow in grace and move towards fulfillment and completion. Guardini asserts, further, that we are most ourselves when God is acting in us. In other words when a person lives from the fullness of their own being, which is grounded in God's Being, they act out of their real nature which is free from external social constraints, and that action in itself is Providence.[119] Furthermore, "The stronger the power of grace, the more freely freedom belongs to itself."[120] That is to say, human freedom in its fullness arises proportionally in the context of grace.[121] Moral deeds are contextualized in the freedom of grace.

Moral Deeds in the World

In *The Living God*, Guardini argues that God has a dynamic quality which makes it possible for God to renew everything in the world from God's love.[122] Yet, in living with Providence, there is responsibility for the human person. Guardini believes that the world is not finished and, in cooperating with the Good or with God, human persons are able to make the world finished from within, through moral deeds.[123] He argues that, a concrete world constructed from the neutrality of nature exists but that world can be a morally bad world or a beautiful and moral world moved from an internal dynamic of Good and all that the word entails. Thirdly, Good is evidenced by deeds, judgements and choice. Moral deeds bring another dimension to human actions and can give the earthly form an eternal dimension.[124] In this way the reality of being can be taken at the

118. Guardini, *The Living God*, 25.

119. Guardini, *The Living God*, 27.

120. Guardini, *The Living God*, 42.

121. This assertion will be re-visited in chapter 4 when the notion of freedom is studied, inquired about, and developed in the aftermath of the National Socialist terror. Although we will see that Guardini has much more to say, we will also note that Guardini's position is not very different from this early argument, demonstrating that his early work is the basis for development of his later theology.

122. Guardini, *The Living God*, 28.

123. Guardini, *Conscience*, 34.

124. Guardini, *Conscience*, 33. We note the similarity of Guardini's thought to that of John Henry Newman (whom Guardini cites) here, who argued for the perception of God while acting with conscience. See Newman, *Apologia Pro Vita Sua*; Ledek, *The Nature of Conscience*; Amico, *The Natural Knowability of God*. In *Conscience*, Guardini

heart because with it one is opened to eternity while still in time.[125] Guardini's approach is existential. This action occurs in the overall reality of life rather than a part of it; the morality and wholeness inherent in the Good, are not to be separated from the whole of life but rather should be incorporated in it as in a wholeness that progressively brings other aspects to fulfillment. Morals must be formed in every situation:

> Morality is not one particular concern beside others. The whole of reality forms its material; all that exists forms its content. Saint Thomas Aquinas says: "The Good must be done. . . ." What is 'on each occasion essential,' . . . is the situation with its whole fullness of content; the life which is always meeting me afresh in the situation, with everything which it holds.[126]

Good is action done in a living concrete world, not just a principle or something abstracted from the real world. This action of acting morally in each situation, enables the Good to develop meaning for the person.[127] The actions which a human person does in the world are important and in this next section we will develop a further refinement to an earlier reference to the heart and trust.

The Heart and Trust: Repentance and the Redeemed Existence

In order to have a redeemed existence, a person must first turn to God and realize he or she is finite and limited. The human person is not God, with God's Goodness, enormity, incomprehensibility and all that the understanding of God implies. We argued, above, that Guardini believes redemption for the human person occurs as a result of the act of repentance. Guardini, portrays the act of real repentance as the transformative action living with Providence requires. Repentance leads to changes in

---

argues that conscience is the voice of God within us, and here in this book we note the similarity to Newman's words, "I see Thee not in the material world but I recognise Thy voice in my own intimate consciousness." Newman, *Meditations and Devotions*, 496. Nevertheless, Guardini does see creation as evidence of God's work. Furthermore, while arguing that the conscience opens a person to the eternal, Guardini still preserves God's omnipotence by his assertion that the Good is a characteristic of God and not all there is to God.

125. Guardini, *Conscience*, 44.

126. Guardini, *Conscience*, 35.

127. Andrzej Kobyliński writes that, in Guardini's mind, the conscience is like a bridge between the person and God. Kobyliński, *Modernità e Postmodernità*, 317.

the person in the process of conversion to God. To elaborate further on another dimension of "choice" (the act of repentance) it may be said that real repentance in the light of the depth of God speaking to a human person, along with awareness of the will of God, is to be perceived in the non-conceptual source of the heart. This is not an intellectual action, nor is it corporate as such. Rather, for Guardini the heart of each individual is very important because this organ holds the possibility of perceiving God's will and intention. This organ, rightly understood, holds the key to the requirements of Providence. A relationship with God which can enable God's guidance implies trust in God. Guardini's argument for God's omniscience and omnipotence presents God in a way in which shows that a person may have that trust. Guardini relates trust to the heart. We can say that, for him, Providence revolves around the heart because it is in the heart that one is able to perceive the rightness of an action or sense of God's presence that leads to confidence in one's actions and trust in God.[128] In chapter 2, we noted that Guardini places heart with mind not the emotions. Here in this chapter, we see the practical application of this. God's providence may be understood in the created world.

Providence in Creation

Guardini argues from classical theology that there is significance in everything that happens in this world because a greater heart and power is in control.[129] He adds, "Providence means that everything in the world retains its own nature and reality, but these serve a supreme purpose which transcend the world: the loving purpose of God. Furthermore the human person will understand God's Providence from the experience of things in his or her life in the world. God, who is personal, has a dynamic quality and it is this dynamism that enables God to continually renew everything from God's love.[130] Guardini notes that trust in God's Providence is not always easy or understood and must be known out of every experience.[131]

---

128. Guardini, "Siebter Sonntag nach Pfingsten," 543. We have noted Guardini's assertion that when a person experiences a movement of their conscience, they are experiencing the eternal in time.

129. Guardini, *The Living God*, 23.

130. Guardini, *The Living God*, 24.

131. What Guardini means by this "out of every experience" will be clearer below where Guardini says, "Good continually becomes apparent and in different ways . . . from what is right in the situation – the Good is determined step by step through the

As a philosopher of existence, Guardini is concerned with human experience and he notes that the truth of continued human existence is very different from God's holy truth. The way that people can learn about God's truth is initially as Providence in their human experience. Yet a person not only experiences joy and happiness in his or her life but also discouragement and darkness. These things are perceived in the human heart. Therefore, focus on God and God's nature is important because a good and loving God does not incite negativity in the heart. Guardini, asking for trust in God, writes:

> Now it is valid to pray, I believe in you Father in Heaven and I trust in you. Also when I don't understand and also when my heart is apathetic and cold. I trust while I believe. . . . On you O Lord have I set my trust. In eternity will I not be put to shame.[132]

When one places trust only in oneself despair can eventuate but in this situation trust must show that it is a virtue or even godly. Guardini asserts that a person's heart must pluck up courage and say, "Lord I believe that you guide everything. Lord, you guide my life, you guide this evil time. I trust in you."[133] God can be trusted because God is omnipresent. Therefore one can repeatedly affirm trust in God rather than looking to oneself or to others. One can say:

> I trust in God's providence. I don't know how he will help me or when but I want to trust and I must. Trust must be put down like a rock and left there . . . until it is light again and that trust is won. In such a test it will be completely strongly established and, with the saints, [one] can in holy triumph sing the Ambrosian song of praise, On you O Lord have I set my trust; it will not be violated, now or in eternity.[134]

Here we see an important aspect of Guardini's notion of Providence. Evil exists, human weakness exists, but to live providentially one must place their trust in God, over and over again, no matter what the circumstances,

---

course of my life." See Guardini, *Conscience*, 47. Guardini's intention here is to show the Christian life as a path rather than a completed achievement.

132. Words from the *Te Deum* in the Breviary. Guardini, "Siebter Sonntag nach Pfingsten," 543.

133. Guardini, "Siebter Sonntag nach Pfingsten," 544. The citation refers to a passage used in the Ambrosian breviary often used in Northern Italy.

134. Guardini, "Seibter Sonntag nach Pfingsten," 544.

until the person has learnt to live out of that trust which will stand the person in good stead for eternity.[135]

Guardini was to return to the aspect of trust time and time again along with trust's sister-concept, faith. For him the organ which perceives feels and experiences both positive and negative emotions, is the heart and thus the person lives out of the dynamism which drives the spirit from within. The Spirit of God which mixes with the human spirit in the heart moves the heart in an increasingly God directed way. The human person can have a redeemed existence. We have adverted to Guardini's assertion of mutual relations between the human person and God. In later chapters this relationship will be shown to be inextricably linked to the relationship which occurs through Christ. This relationship of trust in the living God occurs in the world.

Holiness of Existence

The relationship with the living God in the world means that Providence is moulded by the materials of human life. It could be said that Guardini is able to present a more organic notion than one in which a dry abstract theory is given. The "heart" which is an integral part of the person's awareness and response to what is right and good is therefore important to Providence. Guardini refers to intuition which perceives in action and reflects the reality of the spiritual touch from within:

> Underlying [conscience] is a depth which stands revealed in the phrase, 'I know *of myself*, that it is right in this way'; something inward, therefore something connected with the old concepts of the 'spiritual spark' and 'ground of the soul'.[136]

Accordingly, in living with Providence and in order to apply the awareness in a practical way Guardini links the Good and conscience, and the practice of Recollection.[137] In this way morality, human integrity and re-

---

135. Guardini's position here is that which could be called a "submission theodicy." See Plantinga et al., *An Introduction to Christian Theology*, 218. They argue that the difficulty with this approach is that for a proponent of this view evil can be justified at the expense of humanity. In later work Guardini was concerned to clearly put human actions and responsibility, and not passivity, forward as an important accompaniment to trust in God.

136. Guardini, *Conscience*, 25.

137. It will be shown below that daily prayerful reflection on one's own experience, is an essential part of living with Providence.

sponsibility can be associated with Providence. Providence in Guardini's writing refers to ultimate fulfillment and consummation rather than benefits in this world as such.

Guardini relates holiness and freedom in a move which will be developed further in the later period of his writing. He believes that holiness can only grow in freedom and says that God asks us to give him room to grow in freedom. Later Guardini argues that God makes the space in which he wants to dwell. While living one's life, therefore, one can expect it to reveal a pattern and a Providence.[138] Consonant with this aspect, is Guardini's assertion that one can listen for the gentle tokens of God's presence in one's dealings with people and things.[139] God's holiness is an important aspect of our life as well, since for Guardini God's holiness, as the real aliveness of God, is that which moves the soul. In other words, that which comes from God's utterly incomprehensible and holy interior, is not only constant and unchangeable but dynamic as well. Guardini's argument for holiness of existence is thus, in this early period, based on trust, and attention to conscience.

From 1930 onwards, Guardini explicitly refers to the passage in Matthew 6, the traditionally understood passage of Jesus' words about Providence, in which Jesus exhorts his listeners to first "seek the Kingdom of God." Guardini understands Christ's words about the Kingdom pivotal for talking about Providence. Indeed in Guardini's definition of Providence used on the first page of this thesis, Guardini says that in Providence living, the individual and whole are guided by God towards God's holy Kingdom. Guardini used more than one way of speaking about the Kingdom in his later work but in his early work, foundational for some of his later ideas, his view of the Kingdom is personal and very mystical. We turn to a consideration of this early view now.

The Kingdom of God

A person who lives with the divine guidance which directs Providence, will move towards God's holy kingdom. It will be shown in later chapters that the Kingdom of God is a central vision which Guardini intends as inextricably linked to Providence; new creation perfused with God's dynamic and vibrant love, and the individual person in communion

---

138. Guardini, *The Living God*, 83.
139. Guardini, *The Living God*, 83.

with God and all of creation. Since the Kingdom of God is an important aspect of Guardini's concept of Providence, and he will increasingly tell his readers, in the words of Jesus, to "seek first the Kingdom of God and his righteousness." It may be instructive to state, at this point, how he expresses the concept in his early writings. Here, in the understanding which links Providence with the Kingdom of God, we are able to see Guardini's Pneumatology very clearly and Guardini identifies the experience of the Holy Spirit as axiomatic in forming this Kingdom. Guardini holds that when the Holy Spirit is alive and active in people's hearts, the kingdom of God is growing. His vision in his early work is somewhat mystical. He develops the idea further by saying that when the Holy Spirit is active in individuals, the Church is active in people's hearts, and this is the kingdom of God in mankind. Guardini names the kingdom of God, here, as the Church.[140] What Guardini means by the kingdom of God may be understood from a passage in *The Church and the Catholic*, which he wrote in 1922:

> The kingdom of God means that the Creator takes possession of his creature, penetrates it with his light; he fills its will and heart with his own burning love and the root of its being with His own divine peace, and moulds the entire spirit by his creative power which imposes a new form on it. The kingdom of God means that God draws his creature to Himself, and makes it capable of receiving his own fullness; and that He bestows upon it the longing and power to possess him. It means ... that the boundless fecundity of the divine Love seizes the creature and brings it to that second birth whereby it shares God's own nature and lives with a new life which springs from himself. In that re-birth the Father makes it his child in Christ Jesus through the Holy Ghost.... This union of man with God is God's kingdom. In it man belongs to His Creator, and his Creator belongs to Him.[141]

From this passage, we can see that the Kingdom of God is the capacity of the creature to live a life from the fullness of a heart filled with the Holy Spirit. A change in being is possible. How does this occur? Guardini tells us that the human spirit is moulded by the Spirit of God as God fills the heart and will with God's own burning love and peace. A new form of being then comes into existence. Furthermore, the person is seized by the longing, power and love of God and brought in renewed spirit to the

---

140. Guardini, *The Church and the Catholic*, 33.
141. Guardini, *The Church and the Catholic*, 33.

second birth to share God's own nature through the interaction of Christ and the Spirit. This new life springs from God in Godself and the union of the human person and God in this way is the Kingdom of God.

Furthermore, while these readings may give an impression that Guardini is orientated towards individual experience, alone, mystical or otherwise, we must note that Guardini regarded the community of the Church to be important and the objective referent that gave validity to the experience and indeed made that possible. He writes:

> The Church is the Kingdom in its supra-personal aspect; the human community reborn into God's Kingdom. . . . The Kingdom of God has a subjective side as well. That is the individual soul, as God's grace takes possession of it in that private and unique individuality by which it exists for itself.[142]

He says, "In the Church we become one with the Holy Ghost; He unites us with the Son, and . . . in Christ we come back to the Father."[143] Guardini believes that since God is the goal, one's concerns must be God's concerns and one's vision must be focused on the Trinitarian God:

> He is the sublimest, and all - embracing sovereign power, and the wisdom which pervades the world, the sublimity which lifts us from our narrow ways. The Son is the way . . . as we become one with Christ we approach the Father more closely. And the Holy Ghost, the Spirit of Jesus, is the Leader, and shows us the way. He bestows Christ's grace, teaches Christ's truth, and makes Christ's ordinances operative.[144]

Thus the Trinity is central to the vision of a new existence which Providence living brings.

We have argued that Guardini believes human persons can affect their environment and, since that is the case, can be a grace-filled door for God in the world. For Guardini the kingdom of God in mankind is the Church[145] and from these passages we can see how he can conceive of it as both individual and community. Community is more than "herds or human ant heaps; community is a mutual relationship of personalities."[146] Furthermore, it is specifically Christian, for:

142. Guardini, *The Church and the Catholic*, 35.
143. Guardini, *The Church and the Catholic*, 25.
144. Guardini, *The Church and the Catholic*, 24.
145. Guardini, *The Church and the Catholic*, 33.
146. Guardini, *The Church and the Catholic*, 38.

> This elevation of the creature is not a natural event but God's free act. It is bound up with the historical personality of Jesus of Nazareth, and with the work which He accomplished at a particular period of history. Nor is it a natural process, but an operation of grace, exceeding all forces of nature. [As collective, it is] . . . the mysterious unity which, though composed entirely of individuals, is more than their sum total . . . It is sufficient that God's grace should take hold of the community as such, that something which transcends the individual. This however can be accomplished in a small representative group.[147]

Guardini is keen to show that the spiritual elevation of a person is not a natural event. There is no natural procession as we find, for instance, in Avicenna's scheme of thinking. Rather, God freely acts in order to bring this about. In some of his later writings Guardini concentrates on the more collective image of the Kingdom of God and the base would be the insights presented here. In this early period, Guardini's presentation of the Church (and Kingdom of God) is therefore very Trinitarian, linked through Christ to God in the Holy Spirit and showing a God who is both transcendent and immanent. Furthermore, in this experience a person's existence is transformed by the presence of God who in immanence touches a person's heart. We are reminded that in Guardini's understanding of Christ's awareness, Providence is not from the world, nor the mind, but from God.

Schilson notes that in Guardini's overall work on the Kingdom of God the "Pneuma" in this world is so completely through Christ that it could be called a Christocentric pneumatology.[148] Nevertheless, with regard to this point, Guardini's early work on the Kingdom of God was more Theocentric than some of his later work. In Guardini's 1926 work, *Thoughts on the Relationship of Christianity and Culture*,[149] Guardini's notion of the Kingdom of God understood from Pentecost[150] as having opened up in or through Christ, means that a person "living as Christ," does so through the Spirit with Christ's actual being.[151] Trusting obedi-

---

147. Guardini, *The Church and the Catholic*, 34.
148. Schilson, *Perspectiven Theologischer Erneuerung*, 232–34.
149. Guardini, "Gedanken über das Verhältnis," 385–91.
150. Later in 1949, Guardini expressed the situation this way, "the disciples are gripped by the power of the Spirit; they experience an interior transformation; the fullness of the reality of Christ becomes clear to them; the glory of Christ overwhelms them." Guardini, *The Word of God*, 82.
151. This aspect is developed in Guardini's 1939 work, *The World and the Person*.

ence with Christ to the Father occurs in this way.[152] Guardini had earlier asserted that the Kingdom of God occurs when Christ lives in a person. Guardini sees the sacrifice of Christ as the foundation for this. As Christ lives and has effect in a person new creation occurs and that is where holiness is to be found.[153]

In human existence Guardini's notion of *Pneuma* refers to a quality of difference in the "spiritual" as different to the "natural," not the spirit as different to the body.[154] By taking such a position Guardini is able to retain the wholeness of body and spirit that he uses to distinguish his concept from Kant's dualism and show the relationship to God in a way which also involves human volition. Knoll notes that the hidden character of the new changed reality, revealed in Christ, is developed from the movement to faith, hope and love while enabling a person to participate in Godly life. It is a new orientation.[155] In a liturgical sense, what is done in the Spirit is called the Kingdom of God.[156] "Hope is the Kingdom of God which is in a state of becoming."[157] This "becoming" is also a developed "living form" of Christ."[158] Working from Guardini's writing on Faith and Culture written in 1926, Knoll notes that Guardini understands the concept of the Mystical Body of Christ (Corpus Christi Mysticum) as occurring through the *Pneuma*. In fact "The Mystical Body of Christ" is already here, not in a historical sense, but in the "hope" therein. Knoll argues that the Kingdom of God as a state of becoming has three foundations for Guardini: Firstly, it is to be seized continually on a new basis by human persons. Secondly, it occurs through the free grace of God and thirdly, it understands that the world will be brought to its end when the result is accomplished.[159] As such it is the *Parousia* and therefore a religious category which will be built historically from the present. Furthermore the Kingdom of God is not only to be developed but some of the present earthly form of the world as it is now will go at the same

---

152. Knoll, *Glaube und Kultur*, 256.
153. Guardini, "Heilige Gestalt."
154. Knoll, *Glaube und Kultur*, 255.
155. Knoll, *Glaube und Kultur*, 255.
156. Knoll, *Glaube und Kultur*, 256.
157. Knoll, *Glaube und Kultur*, 256.
158. Knoll, *Glaube und Kultur*, 256.
159. Knoll, *Glaube und Kultur*, 257.

time.¹⁶⁰ Here then in this passage the eschatological nature of Providence is presented as a world in and through God and which, in this time and space, in contemporary expression already but not yet: already starting, but not yet completely fulfilled. Guardini's presentation of the Church (and Kingdom of God) is therefore very Trinitarian, linked through Christ to God in the Holy Spirit and both transcendent and immanent.

Conclusion to Chapter 3

In his 1916 work, Guardini developed the notion of a covenant—style relationship with God as the way in which God has invited an individual to participate in his plan for the world. Themes which emerge in this early text are repeated and developed throughout Guardini's life in his writing on Providence. We have argued that his notion of Providence is Biblically based and commensurate with mainstream Christian theology. In these early texts it is possible to appreciate the assertion that his notion of Providence is grounded in God the Creator who is also the Loving Father of the Scriptures. Guardini's Providence thinking is a type of concurrence and his view is that human action occurs in relationship and not independently with just a glance at God. In other words, to be a type of "co-creator" is to respond to God the Father as Christ did. There is a double agency in Guardini's work and it will be developed further in the next period with a focus on anthropological issues. In this way Guardini is able to show how God's loving guidance in and through Christ in the Holy Spirit can become God's way of guiding a person who is completely free to choose how he or she will live. Guardini believes that, contrary to what one might expect, grace can increase the freedom of a person. Later he argues that when a person receives the grace of God, that person experiences the expanded awareness that one might associate with the wisdom of God.¹⁶¹ Such an experience will allow a person to potentially "let go" certain conceptions and ideas and become open to a wider range of possibilities. Furthermore, in association with God, that individual can become a type of "co-creator" with God as they cooperate to bring God's love into the world. Since Guardini believes that God is incomprehensible and omnipotent, the person, the creature, knows him or herself as

---

160. Knoll, *Glaube und Kultur*, 257.

161. See "Aus der Biblischen Gotteslehrer," 8, where Guardini declares that "Providence is the guidance of every person's life through God's loving wisdom."

infinitely loved by God, yet not God, who transcendently remains God above all. We have argued that Guardini is able to declare that the world can "become" through human persons.

Conscience enables the person to experience the surety and rightness of that which comes from God. Acting with the conscience gives a capacity for openness to God. Likewise, obedience to God is assisted by this action. Morality is an important aspect of living in a Providential way. The interior conscience is balanced by the exterior condition in the world, which brings the Providence of things[162] with a conscious awareness. A person must put concern for the kingdom of God as foremost in their interests and when the relationship with God occurs, it is called a Theonomy. That is to say, the person does not act completely alone but in association with the ground of their being, which is God; the being of that person acts in accordance with the "being" of God. Therefore, the authority, which is developed in a covenant-style relationship, is God. Grace is an important aspect of this relationship because the person doesn't act or respond alone as such. In *The Living God*, Guardini says that God gives human persons a "pre-sentiment" of himself which enables them to sense spiritual realities. A person must hear God speaking to her in the depths of her heart, repent and assent (say yes) to it. God is not an abstracted principle, but dynamic; alive and ever new. The human person must use his or her own freedom to stand in the freedom of God's activity to contribute by helping the world to "become"; to develop, from God's freedom. The person is a co-creator in that situation. We note that although the human person can co-create, the context is that of the loving covenant-style relationship with God and therefore one in which a person continuously has the opportunity to live as God wills in each situation. As the "prime Creator" God is always above and beyond anything which we might create from created things. Creative life may be lost if a person doesn't do the will of God and the person should feel deep repentance for such an action. This type of co-creation, in which God is always God should be distinguished from God's creation which is the original creation. Human persons create with created things.

Guardini's early work therefore, was a clear foundation for his later work on Providence, yet as will be shown, there is development and change in Guardini's overall concept of Providence; as a concept it is dynamic. His early formation formed an awareness of the importance of the

---

162. The Providence of things can be understood as the arrangement of things since Guardini's argument for Providence is spatial rather than temporal as such.

world, of prayer and Sacred Scripture. Each of these things are important to his notion of Providence developed initially from Scripture, furthered in association with theology, especially from his doctoral work on Bonaventure, and nourished by his own Christian practice as an educator, secular priest and Benedictine Oblate. The notion of God as Omnipotent, Omnipresent, and Omniscient is an important indicator of God's capacity to guide the world. The argument of the importance of each individual person to God was, along with Guardini's other theology on this early period, the basis of his later writing which was to serve him well in the period which followed, that of National Socialism.

4

Guardini's Writing on Christian Providence in the Time of National Socialism

Introduction: Guardini's Providence Texts in this Period[1]

IN CHAPTER 3, I argued that Guardini's early work was foundational for his later work on Providence.[2] In this chapter, I consider how his

1. Guardini's books or articles from this period relevant to this thesis are:
    1) "Aus der Biblischen Gotteslehrer" ["From the Biblical Doctrine of God"]
    2) *The Art of Praying*
    3) "Der Heiland" ["The Saviour"] (Reprinted in *Unterscheidung des Christlichen*, 362–88)
    4) *The Lord*
    5) *The Lord's Prayer*
    6) *Pascal for Our Time*
    7) "Was JESUS unter die Vorsehung Versteht" ["What JESUS Understood about Providence"]
    8) *Das Wesen des Christentums* [The Essence of Christianity]
    9) *Wille und Wahrheit* [Will and Truth]
    10) *The World and the Person*

    The *World and the Person* is the major anthropological work and will be used extensively in this chapter.

2. As argued previously, Guardini has a basic Providence paradigm (*Gestalt*) which is dynamic. In this sense whilst there is certainly development in his work, it is also possible to speak of a dynamic paradigm (*Gestalt*) to show that the design or pattern was essentially there in the beginning and certain aspects of it have been brought to the fore at certain times. Guardini's insistence on living with Providence in a real sense makes such a form necessary and possible because the society in which a person is living is also dynamic.

understanding of Providence developed during the period of National Socialism. Guardini's writing on Providence provided a covert means of opposing the National Socialist doctrine. Although the National Socialist period, in a strict sense, covers the years 1933–1945, by 1930 Guardini's publications were already showing the changes which characterized his work in the National Socialist period.[3] Therefore this chapter will cover his writings from 1930 to 1945 and will show that while Guardini engages with the society in which Hitler and the National Socialists dominated, he covertly opposes their doctrine and therefore presents a counter-cultural theology as he highlights the difference between Jesus Christ and Hitler and draws attention to the world as God's creation rather than just nature, as such.[4]

In the main anthropological text of this period, *The World and the Person*, Guardini situates the chapter on Providence after the section dealing with the human person, integrity and strength. Some of this information is a basis for acting with Providence. In this chapter, I will again follow the themes drawn out in the previous chapter: 1) Jesus Christ and Providence; 2) Providence is understood in relationship with God; 3) The individual person is important to God; 4) Providence brings new creation and new existence. We will show that Guardini's notion of Providence was *developed* and *clarified* in very significant ways during this period,[5] and in particular, that his Christology and his notion of Providence became much more Christocentric.[6] We will argue, once again, that Providence is not hindered,[7] and belief in Providence is made possible as the human person lives in relationship with God. As a result of that intimate relationship, the person's being changes and

3. For instance, see Guardini, *The Lord's Prayer*.

4. Guardini covertly opposed the National Socialists in his writings and was engaged in covert activities against them (see chapter 2). An example of Guardini's engagement with the socio-political climate of the time was the publication of "Der Heiland" (The Savior) in 1935.

5. See chapter 2 for a comparison of features of Guardini's books written in the National Socialist period and later.

6. The movement to a very Christocentric position was not unique to Guardini. Mark R. Lindsay, for example, writes of a similar move by Karl Barth at that time. See Lindsay, *Covenanted Solidarity*.

7. By the person themselves. In *The World and the Person*, Guardini argues that we are artisans of our own fortune. That statement would have to be nuanced because, despite the double agency he argues for, ultimately Guardini does believe God is in control.

he or she lives differently in the world. In this period Guardini argues that the person's being changes as a result of the indwelling Christ. Here, also, the themed emphasis changes, with a slight but important shift, to the way Jesus understood Providence. Jesus may also be understood as embracing the other themes as well. For instance his relationship with God the Father was important for him. Guardini shows the necessity of discipleship; that following Jesus in all things is important for living with Providence at this time. Before turning to our first theme, of how Jesus understood Providence, we briefly note Guardini's insistence on the importance of the heart, and the connection with mind in responding to God's Providence.

Guardini's Notion of the Unity of Heart and Mind

In chapter 2, we noted that the heart was important for Guardini because God could be intuited there and a person's own disposition and actions could flow from the heart. Guardini refers to the heart in a number of his Providence texts. In this period Guardini once again uses the notion of heart and develops it from the work of Blaise Pascal.[8] For Guardini the heart is the same as spirit with the spirit moving the heart towards clarity of vision.[9] The heart is important in Providence living because it is in the heart that the human person will have inner certainty as he or she places their trust in God. Interpreting Pascal in this period of National Socialism (1935), Guardini says of the heart that:

> It is not the expression of the emotional in opposition to the logical, not feeling in opposition to the intellect, not "soul" in opposition to "mind." "Coeur" is itself mind: a manifestation of the mind. The act of the heart is an act productive for knowledge, certain objects only become given in the act of the heart. But they do not remain there in a-rational intuition, but are accessible to intellectual and rational penetration . . . the phenomenon depends on the interrelationship between knowledge and will, apprehension of truth and love—objectively expressed, between essence and value. "Value" is the character of preciousness of things which makes them worthy of being . . . Heart is the mind rendered ardent and sensitive by the blood, but which at the same time ascends into the clarity of contemplation, the

---

8. Guardini, *Pascal for Our Time*.
9. Guardini, *Pascal for Our Time*, 129.

> distinctiveness of form, the precision of judgement . . . Heart is the organ of love—namely the relationship of the centre of man's desires and feelings to the idea; the movement from the blood to the mind, from the presence of the body to the eternity of the mind. It is what is experienced in the heart.[10]

For Guardini heart and mind constitute a unity.[11] As such, what is known can be known from the heart.[12] In the same work Guardini asserts that the force of the heart is natural and it therefore stands "in the state of fall, in ambiguity. . . . [I]n it too is chaos, illusion, quasi-nothingness."[13] It is important in his view for the person to respond to the call of God so the heart will change and the person can share in God's nature.[14] Then they are able to give up the point of reference of themselves and to have the genuine center which is:

> the counterpart of the divine centre which is calling. For the first time awakens the genuine, God intended self, the real self. . . . And in it awakens a new love, a new faculty of appreciation, with a new inner certainty and freedom. It is what theology calls "divine virtue" of love, which consists in a sharing in the love of God, and is thus a grace.[15]

The real self is awakened by God's call, calling forth a new love from the human person which in Guardini's view is caring love (charity). We will see further evidence of this argument below and now turn to the first theme.

---

10. Guardini, *Pascal for Our Time*, 120.

11. This is the biblical view of heart and mind.

12. Contemplation gives clarity and the opportunity for connatural knowing, that is knowing from sharing in the life of God in Godself. Andrew Tallon writing of the notion of heart illuminates this point further. He says, "the natural development of the ethical is the mystical (the core of the Person - centred theology) . . . connaturality is the normal way, the saint . . . exists and acts as an embodied spirit, more highly actualised by virtues affectable and affected by God and then responding." As such he argues that connatural knowing and loving are the normal ways of discerning the spirits rather than discursive conceptual knowledge. Tallon, "The Heart in Rahner's Philosophy of Mysticism," 700–28.

13. Guardini, *Pascal for Our Time*, 136.

14. Guardini, *Pascal for Our Time*, 137. As in other points in this thesis, we refer to participation in God.

15. Guardini, *Pascal for Our Time*, 136.

Theme 1: Jesus Christ and Providence:
How Jesus Understood Providence[16]

In chapter 3, I referred to the qualities of God which were the basis for Guardini's early writings. I said that he shows how God is shown to be trustworthy. In this period of time Guardini shows how Jesus, unlike the National Socialists, does not speak of an 'order to things' but indicates the care of God. For Jesus Providence was a work of the Holy Spirit and is understood from the heart. Heart and mind work in tandem and the appropriate attitude to have is faith. Furthermore, God is a God of love. Jesus shows how the person living with Providence is not the "superior"[17] person but the God-loving person. Such a person would be open to the work of the Holy Spirit. We now turn to that pivotal insight.

Providence is a Work of the Holy Spirit

In the article, *What JESUS Understood about Providence*, Guardini argues his position from the Lord's Prayer and the Sermon on the Mount, that Jesus speaks out of an urgency of the heart about Providence. In the Lord's Prayer, Jesus advocates trust in God and deep prayer which will give a person a quiet and confident heart and the practice of faith. Guardini puts the classical scripture passage for Providence (Matt 6:25–34), with the "Our Father" and Jesus' teaching in the Providence passage. Guardini notes the simplicity and profundity of the Lord's Prayer which "expresses this teaching not only by the ideas contained in it, but by the fervent trust which pervades it."[18]

In this period, Guardini reinforces the assertion of his early writings, that God can be trusted and Providence does not arise from nature, nor from an energy nor from world order.[19] Providence is beyond worldly

---

16. Guardini, "Was JESUS." In this article Guardini uses upper case letters for the word JESUS to make a distinction between Jesus' understanding and that of Hitler.

17. Guardini, "Was JESUS," 6. The National Socialists promoted the idea of the "superior person."

18. Guardini, "Was JESUS," 1.

19. Guardini, *The Lord's Prayer*, 74; Guardini, "Was JESUS," 5. The search for order was central for many people at that time. Heinz Kuehn who lived in Germany notes that National Socialism followed the Weimar Republic which had been Germany's attempt at democracy, but by many accounts, had been characterized by unemployment, inflation, unrest and a violent struggle for power by competing groups who often used firearms in public places. See Kuehn, "Fires in the Night," 2. In contrast to this type of

conception. Christ, himself is radically different to the social order and the laws of pure nature which the Nazis absolutized at that time.[20] In Christ's meaning Providence is the creative work of the Spirit in which God's care comes to be joined with the history of the individual person. Guardini argues that Holy history comes upon the history of the human person.[21] Christ has shown that because of the presence of the Spirit, there is a creative, unpredictable and radical element to Providence. For this reason Providence may entail some risk on the part of the human person.[22] Conversely, addressing the social striving for order, Guardini, writes:

> What Jesus meant by "Providence" is something absolutely different – something daring, unprecedented; something which simply does not belong to the world and its rational ideas, but comes from heaven.[23]

Providence in Jesus' understanding is a different way to live with Providence. Guardini rejects a child-like faith or one built on scientific principles[24] or one which comes through a "superior man."[25] Human persons can live with faith and trust in God precisely because Providence is a work of the Holy Spirit and God, who holds all people within God's-self, and can be trusted to care for the human person. In other words, the predictability and order purported to be essential according to the Nazis, could be replaced by trust in God who may be surprising and creatively unpredictable yet never relinquishes care. Since Providence is a work of the Holy Spirit, the heart is inextricably connected with this possibility. Order will still occur but it is different type of order. It is God's order

---

insecurity, National Socialism clearly represented order and control to many people.

20. The National Socialists had a concrete determinist world view in which they had elevated the idea of the "natural" to the point of idolatry. Adolf Hitler announced, "Our worship is exclusively the cultivation of the natural and for that reason, because natural, God willed." Hitler, "Speech September 6th Nürenburg," in *My New Order*, 501. Hitler linked the will of God to what is "natural."

21. That is to say, the Holy Spirit comes upon the human person.

22. Guardini, "Was JESUS," 5.

23. Guardini, *The Lord's Prayer*, 73. Guardini advocated trust in God which was beyond human control.

24. Not science but belief. Guardini, "Was JESUS," 4.

25. Guardini, "Was JESUS," 6.

which comes from trusting God and living a life of faith that is focused on the Kingdom of God.[26] We turn now to the notion of the care of God.

The Care of God

Guardini writes that Jesus' teaching about Providence wasn't answering the question of *whether there is an order to things* but rather it was speaking to the question of the living person and whether anyone cares.[27] The individual *care* of God, along with the importance of each human person, brings the assertion that Jesus Christ is the *person* in whom God gives the answer to the question in men's hearts. The Providence that Jesus taught should not only be in a person's thoughts but also in their interior attitude of a quiet and confident heart.[28] Christ's teaching about Providence revolves around the question of a person's existence, where the person's destiny comes from, in what hand and power that person finds himself and how he can understand and come into contact with it.[29] The appropriate attitude to have is faith. Yet, as argued earlier, Guardini believes in a double agency, and along with the importance of faith Guardini asserts that a number of associated things, including the love of God, are also important for living with Providence. Providence of the individual proceeds with that of the whole. Thus in addition to having faith and quiet confidence in God, the human person must be God-loving. We now turn to Guardini's argument for the God loving person.

The God-loving Person

Guardini writes that the teaching of Christ does not refer to the superior person but the God-loving person whether their life appeared to be great or obscure.[30] This statement may be seen as a response to the National Socialist challenge whose adherents believed that the Aryan was a

26. Guardini, "Was JESUS," 9. In a post war version of this text published as a chapter in *Faith and Modern Man* with the title "Providence," Guardini names Hitler as a person who thought Providence had identified him to carry out its work. Guardini writes that for Hitler identification with the masses was mixed with a tormenting sense of inferiority. See Guardini, *Faith and Modern Man*, 58.

27. Guardini, "Was JESUS," 5.
28. Guardini, "Was JESUS," 2.
29. Guardini, "Was JESUS," 2.
30. Guardini, "Was JESUS," 6.

superior person. At that time, people with disabilities were being executed for their deficiencies.[31] Guardini states, with courage, that he is not writing about the "superior person" since a person cannot be defined by biological or social qualities alone.[32] Fulfillment which transcends these qualities is promised from the fullness of grace itself.[33] Grace, Guardini writes, means Providence must refer to the condition of the world as a whole and the place of the human person and his or her birth into such a world. The events which touch a person or form around that person can be seen in that light. Thus in living with Providence, the human person must be as Jesus was and taught, that is, God-loving. A God-loving person will live in relationship with God.

Seek First the Kingdom of God

In the Scripture passage about God's providence, Matthew 6, Jesus urges the human person to "strive for the kingdom of God" and focus on the kingdom allowing the new orientation to form his or her life. The drive is collaborative as the person surrenders to God. Guardini relates the experience to inner transformation:

> The kingdom of God means that God rules directly and powerfully; that God, in the freedom of His love has forgiven sin, and that man sanctified by the holiness of Christ, belongs entirely to God. . . . The kingdom of God means that His truth illumines the mind. . . . The Kingdom of God means that He the Father the Brother, the Friend, is near, in the depths of the spirit, in the core of the heart; that love rules perceptibly in our goings and our comings . . . that the whole of existence is transfigured by it, and that while everything is transmuted into this one thing, the essential beauty and character of each blossoms forth . . . that God becomes distinct to us in His reality and fullness; that He rules in all things and that the creature is in Him, one with Him, and for this reason is free to be himself.[34]

---

31. Post, "Alzheimer's and Grace," 12–14.
32. Guardini, *The World and the Person*, 174.
33. Guardini, *The World and the Person*, 174.
34. Guardini, *The Lord's Prayer*, 53.

A new paradigm and a new orientation of being is brought into existence when the person focuses on the kingdom of God and allows God to direct his or her actions:

> If God's creative love is taken up by the loving solicitude and trust of the Christian, if man's freewill is opened to it and gives it scope, then a new form of reality emerges from it. A new "order" originating from God comes into being, an order applied to the salvation of the new being.... He receives what he needs in the sight of God even if it is by means by darkness and sorrow. In the measure that a person puts the quest for the kingdom of God first ... will he be one with God in love. Then, by God's Will, a new, all embracing unity will arise. Events will co-ordinate themselves around such a person, and all that happens will be from God's love. Providence means ... that structure of existence which comes into being around the person who makes God's concern his own.[35]

When a person focuses on the Kingdom of God, he or she will be one with God in love. By God's Will, made possible in the Holy Spirit,[36] a unity will arise. We now turn to Guardini's argument for the relationship, with God, in this period.

Theme 2: Providence Is Understood in Relationship with God

In this section in chapter 2, we argued that God invites the human person to relationship in mutual agreement between the human person and God. Furthermore, Guardini believes human freewill can be used to make a choice to respond positively to God. In the relationship with God, the Good touches a person interiorly while the conscience enables a person to respond. Now in this chapter, I show how Guardini developed his idea of Providence by 1) focusing on the importance of the indwelling Christ and 2) juxtaposing that notion with the I-Thou relationship as developed by the Jewish philosopher Martin Buber.

The human person is a child of God and relationship to God occurs through the indwelling Christ who brings freedom.[37] Guardini

---

35. Guardini, *The Lord's Prayer*, 75–76.

36. "The Holy Spirit is in essence the fulfillment of the Will of God." Guardini, *The Lord's Prayer*, 64.

37. This freedom is the freedom of grace.

shows how personal integrity can develop and grow under the guidance of God. The Spirit and Being of God, in relationship and co-operation with a human person, transform the being of the human person, moving towards transformation of the world through that person. In these writings, Guardini shows how a person can move from passive acceptance of destiny and fate in order to be strong, active and living with Providence. How then does that occur? We turn first to the importance of the indwelling Christ.

Providence Is lived with Jesus Christ—Indwelling—Real

Guardini asserts that Jesus is not just one savior among many others but historical, pre-existent, and eternal.[38] As such Jesus Christ is directly relevant to the sanctity of personal existence. Importantly, for the development of his notion of Providence, Guardini focuses on the centrality of the *real* (Jesus) Christ and Christ's existence as a *historical*, Jewish person who is also eternal (as God is) yet *immanent* as Christ within. Guardini, showed that Jesus Christ,[39] must live within a person in order for that person to be like God.[40] In *Wille und Wahrheit*[41] (Will and Truth), Guardini clarified the way a person could live with God's Providence in relationship with Christ. Guardini contextualizes the relationship with Christ in the love of God affirming personal experience as the way of understanding that dynamism and love. The words of Scripture saying, "The Lord comes to me," refer to reality and not an image.[42] Furthermore,

---

38. Guardini, "Der Heiland," 374.

39. Identified in some of his writings, such as *The Lord*, as Jewish. We recall that Hitler did not regard Jesus as Jewish.

40. In chapter 2 we noted that Hitler and the National Socialists, on the other hand, believed the Aryan, unlike people of other races, had God within, that Aryans were naturally Godlike, and the God-likeness was both in the soul and in the blood. The National Socialists considered it a natural racial, characteristic. See Bärsch, *Die politische Religion*, 336.

41. Significantly, the Nazis had a magazine called *Will and Power*.

42. Guardini links the reality of God, present everywhere in the world to another point, important to his understanding and development of Providence, namely, that the being of creation is not already finished and closed but, rather, remains in movement. Creation is such that God, who dwells in inaccessible light will come and, in love, give the gift of God's-self as the love-goal for human persons. Guardini, *Wille und Wahrheit*, 140.

the "more intensively one engages with reality, the more intense will the Godly movement be"[43]

Guardini's theology is incarnational and redemptive. He believes Christ is redemptive for a humanity which has fallen deeper and deeper into unreality since the "fall." God has come to his creation, first with the prophets and then with Christ who was able to heal the destiny of humanity by his atonement. Guardini holds that the key point here can be understood by going back to the words of St. Paul where he refers to the perichoretic mutual indwelling of Christ, "Christ is in me" – "I am in Christ."[44] For Guardini this indwelling is not an image or idea but a reality:

> [The indwelling of Christ] is no parable, it means not only that my welfare is with Christ in meaning; or that he brings a form of how I must be in a caring heart; or his Truth is efficacious in me, or his example; or his way of thinking. Here the living reality is meant.[45]

The actual Spirit of Christ in his reality enters into the heart of the human person. The death and resurrection of Christ and the strength of the Holy Spirit makes it possible for Christ to be within a person in this way which belongs to the character of the soul. Therefore, the task of love is to "be Christ" which will be "developed in being a human person, remodelled with Christ included as inner model, as efficacious power, as remodelled creation."[46] In this way the person is able to live as God meant human persons to be and the person really is able to become "God's child" and truly a child of humanity. Thus kinship with Christ and the state of being "God's child" is established with Christ within a person.

How does Christ come into a person?

> He comes into one through faith, through baptism, through the Eucharist. Through baptism he comes once and for all. Through faith and the Eucharist he comes time and time again, always new. And always new through every elevation of the heart through prayer and obedience through everything that

---

43. Guardini, *Wille und Wahrheit*, 140. Guardini is not advocating a movement away from anything here.

44. Guardini. *Wille und Wahrheit*, 142. These words are also to be found in John 14:20.

45. Guardini, *Wille und Wahrheit*, 142.

46. Guardini, *Wille und Wahrheit*, 142.

providence a task and skill carries.... When I now believe and trust I am not he who effects things but Christ who works in me. He is in me with the blaze of his Holiness. He penetrates my heart and my will so that he can let in inner freedom and with that from there form my complete being.[47]

Christ, who dwells within the human person, penetrates the heart and will of a person, and enables the growth of grace which gives the freedom for new being to form the person from within. Guardini argues that the beginning of this process is to believe and become a "child of God." One's "Christ being" is a secret that one only knows in faith.[48] Christ is able to go deeper and work throughout the complete person so that growth in Christ may continue. Guardini links the work of Christ to love, which, he asserts, enlarges the soul.[49] He believes that the character of love can grow when Christ has awoken it and the more one loves, the more Christ can grow. This is the love without end.[50] Yet human persons act in a world of people and things. It is important that Christ is not just an instrumental principle within a person where he could arguably be "used" (in the worst sense of the word). The personal relationship with Christ is important. In Guardini's interactive world openness and communication with others are important aspects of the relationship with God and the context for the relationship with Christ. In this period of National Socialism Guardini develops his notion of the I-Thou relationship with a personal turn.

The I-Thou Relationship and Development of Person

Guardini develops the relationship with God further as he moves from the more instrumental notion of the Good or conscience of the earlier period to the loving notion of the I-Thou relation which is integral to faith and living with Providence. The I-Thou relationship occurs within the world and it may be said that the created world is a necessary part of this experience because according to Guardini the world speaks of its

---

47. Guardini, *Wille und Wahrheit*, 143.

48. It should be noted here that the German word which Guardini used (Glauben) takes on two meanings in English, namely belief and faith. While the German word is used for both, one could argue that the word "belief," in English, carries a little more surety or assent to something than the word faith does.

49. Guardini, *Wille und Wahrheit*, 145.

50. Guardini, *Wille und Wahrheit*, 146.

Creator. Guardini argues that meaning for the person is dependent on the possibility of an encounter. Not only speech but language, *per se*, is an important sequel to encounter. Within the notion of encounter Guardini has made his own caveats. He takes issue with actualistic personalism, which insists on self-activity for the realization of personhood. Likewise, he refutes the view that equates person only with individual, "taking it only as an object."[51] Guardini is critical of the discussion about the dual nature of the subject–object relation and the dichotomy which often exists in such a notion. Subjectivity, a negative term for Guardini, refers, in his mind to the individual as a "closed" entity who relates to the other from their own closed center. Therefore, in subjectivity's extreme form, the other person can be considered to be "over there," and is a type of tool in the accomplishment of that individual's own purposes. We could argue further that in regarding the other as "object" one may "hold onto" the other. The other would therefore be attached to the subject for use in the subject's purposes. Yet Guardini rejects this type of likely dualism that is inherent in the subject-object relation. The ontological openness of the human person is important and developed further in human interaction. Guardini holds that in order for the personal relation to proceed, the subject–object relation must cease. In order for this to occur, one first turns to oneself. He writes:

> In the measure in which I first release the being which at first I regarded only as an object, and consider it as a self meeting me from its own centre, permitting it to become my "Thou," I pass from the attitude of using or fighting subject into that of the "I."[52]

In other words, the "other" must be freed to enable the true "Thou" to meet one, from one's centre. In this way one becomes ontologically open and the protection of objectivity falls away on the part of the other as well. Guardini believes that personal destiny springs from the openness of the "I–Thou" relation or the denial of it. For him such a relation may occur at various depths from, "the respect shown by a greeting, in a stirring of sympathy, and then as trust, comradeship, love."[53] He even extends this possibility to a *quasi* "I–Thou" which involves inanimate objects such as a landscape, or the world itself, in the attitude of a personality,

---

51. Guardini, *The World and the Person*, 129.
52. Guardini, *The World and the Person*, 127.
53. Guardini, *The World and the Person*, 128.

as may occur in the mythical or poetic attitude.[54] The regard for one's neighbor and the possibility of charitable love as one's self begins with such an opening to the being of another. Since Guardini even extends this possibility to a quasi "I-Thou" in an object such as a tree or landscape, and even mythical beings, he is also able hold the world as one. All of life is important for the possibility of ontological openness which in its most profound form involves the relationship between the human person and God as the true Thou of the human person. Providence is experienced in this context. Language is important to the development of the I-Thou relation.

Language in the I-Thou Relationship

Guardini's view is human and personal. For him, person is both dynamis and being, act and form. Importantly, he holds that language is not the expression of conclusions but occurs simultaneously with thought:

> Thought is not a pre-verbal act of the mind which only later, as a result of some decision or for some particular purpose, is formulated in words, but it takes place from the first moment in the form of interior speech. Language is not a system of signs by means of which two monads exchange ideas but it is the very realm of consciousness in which every man lives. It is a connected whole.[55]

Since language can occur simultaneously with thought, it can convey the direct and open being of one's inner self. Guardini notes agreement with Heidegger who wrote that language offers "the very first possibility of standing amid the openness of being."[56] In this sense he is able to argue that speech has an ontological aspect to it. In support of this aspect he argues:

> [C]omplete speech which is carried on in the common responsibility for truth and the common bond of human destiny, tends toward the realisation of the "I-Thou" relation. In this way

---

54. Guardini, *The World and the Person*, 129.
55. Guardini, *The World and the Person*, 130.
56. Guardini, *The World and the Person*, 131. At the same time silence comes into its own as the counterpart to speech. Guardini, *The World and the Person*, 215.

speech becomes the objective plan for the construction of the "I-Thou" encounter.[57]

Thus, speech is axiomatic for the "I-Thou" relationship and the encounter with the other. In the contact with another human being, one is able to attain the freedom which frees one from the bonds of oneself.[58] In loving another person, regardless of who that person is, and in seeing their structure of value, the other person's validity is perceived.[59] Expressed differently, Guardini says that in confrontation with the "Thou" a person loses the objective quality and therefore separateness of the situation. This "I-Thou" must be reciprocal and genuine and therefore Guardini argues that personal destiny either springs from the openness of the "I-Thou" relation, or cannot happen because of the closed-ness of the same when fulfillment has been denied on the part of the "Thou."[60] That is, destiny will take a different turn when the "I-Thou" relation is closed because the person is made to be ontologically open and linguistic. The human person is relational and holistic.

To consider Guardini's notion of inter-subjectivity, in the context of a biological, social, psychological, spiritual and historical life in the world, is essential to an understanding of Guardini's intention. A person is in a state of becoming and is not fixed. This corresponds to Guardini's notion that Providence, which reflects a person's decisions, is not fixed but "in-progress." Guardini presents us with a dynamic person in a dynamic world yet does not see the human person, alone, as complete in the "I-Thou" relation toward another person. For him the notion of the world or person is incomplete without referring to the ground of the world's existence, which is God.

The Person's True "Thou"

In Guardini's ontologically contingent world the person exists primarily in relation to the infinite God who is the person's true "Thou." The person's true "Thou" implies a relationship in which the human person not only stands opposite God as a created being but actively shares in a

---

57. Guardini, *The World and the Person*, 131.
58. Guardini, *The World and the Person*, 118.
59. Guardini, *The World and the Person*, 118. In addition, in the relationship with God in Christ, a person is able to see the world from Christ's perspective.
60. Guardini, *The World and the Person*, 128.

relationship of being as the "Thou" of God. In this sense the person is also open to the being and wisdom of God. Earlier we have said that Providence is the loving guidance of the human person through the wisdom of God. Providence is most completely experienced in relation to God. The finite person's "absolute dignity" and authenticity comes from God. Guardini, who has argued that God is the ground of each person's being, posits the beginning of this relationship as a "call," which addresses the question of human integrity. God is not presented as an autocratic bully and therefore a person does not lose the capacity for decision-making or volition in that call. The call is not a command.

The created world, as a context for Providence and the relationship with God, is important. Guardini believes the world itself communicates its maker—God. He uses the term, "world-word," (*Welt-Wort*) to indicate that the world which could be understood to be a type of "creation-concert" is actually a "word" directed to human persons and designed to elicit an answer from each person.[61] Guardini expresses this idea by saying:

> Man is the one who is meant to be the hearer of the world-word. He is also meant to be the one who answers. Through him all things should return to God in the form of an answer.[62]

In other words, when one observes the world as creation one is meant to perceive the Creator behind such handiwork and respond accordingly. The world is an integral part of Providence:

> God is the absolute "Thou" of man. The created personality subsists in the fact that this is so. If it were possible for man to step out of this relation to God, that means, not only to forsake God but to bring it about that he no longer stood ontologically in this 'Thou'-relation but only in a relation of a created being to its creator as the norm and realisation of its existence, then man would cease to be a person.[63]

Having said that, complete fulfillment of the human person lies in that person's relation to God, Guardini writes that he is not referring to a "religious encounter" which "takes place in the world and history."[64]

61. Guardini, *The World and the Person*, 143.
62. Guardini, *The World and the Person*, 143.
63. Guardini, *The World and the Person*, 142.
64. Guardini, *The World and the Person*, 143. Again, it is possible to see a refutation of the type of pattern being put forward by the National Socialists.

Rather, the human person's relationship to God is based on Christ.[65] It is Christ who brings the possibility of the "Christian's personal consciousness" to the human person. Guardini sees the relationship to Christ as essential for the conversion to a Christian existence. To be a Christian is to live from the existentiality of Christ because in our Trinitarian faith we can come before God with Christ-within-us enabling Christ to bring us into the fabric of his own relationship with God. This Christian Theonomy also entails looking to the historical life of Christ as the objective of moral behavior.[66] Although God remains hidden, the relationship with God which occurs in interiority is referred to by Guardini as inwardness.

Interiority and God's Inwardness

In living with Providence Christian inwardness is important because God's grace is revealed in interiority. Christian inwardness is not a space into which God comes but is, rather, the gift which God brings. God "Himself creates the interior depth and breadth in which God wishes to dwell. It depends on God and can only be received from God."[67] God has the initiative. Guardini takes the view that God's whole being consists of act and exists in pure activity.[68] In such a view God is, simultaneously, both stable and dynamic. God possesses God's-self in act and it is this self-possession that shows God's unique absolute inapproachability, and power of action which God alone has. In other words, God is omnipotent and incomprehensible:

> God's own inwardness is His place and also His hiddenness. The very thing that makes him wholly manifest to Himself, His absolute brightness, conceals Him from all that is not Himself. 'He dwells in light which no created being can approach' (1 Tim 6:16).[69]

While God is stable and complete in Godself, God is also incomprehensible, for this light is so deep and full that a human person can never

---

65. Guardini, *The World and the Person*, 143.
66. Brüske, "Epilogo," 234.
67. Guardini, *The World and the Person*, 45.
68. Guardini, *The World and the Person*, 46. Here we can see concurrence, in Guardini's thought, with the thought of St. Thomas Aquinas who held that God is pure act. See Caputo, *Heidegger and Aquinas*, 137.
69. Guardini, *The World and the Person*, 46.

comprehend or perceive it in its entirety. Yet, it is this same God who comes to the believer in Christ. Furthermore, God is God's own inwardness, and it is this inwardness that the believer receives:

> If God comes in Christ to the believer, God's inwardness comes to him, for God is Himself His inwardness. If he gives man the privilege of participating in his nature, he also permits him to share His own Holy inwardness. It becomes the believers own. In the form of grace he is to share in its life.[70] This finally and essentially is Christian inwardness.[71]

Christian inwardness denotes the grace of Christ and the Holy Spirit. In other words it is Trinitarian. Believers are able to share in the grace of Christ. Here then is a restatement, in this period, of a theosis similar to that expressed during Guardini's earlier period but now Guardini shows the importance of Christ in participating in God.[72]

Sharing in the Life of God through Christ

Guardini writes that God allows the believer to share God's own holy inwardness which in the form of grace becomes the way the believer shares in God's life. As he argues for a type of participation in God, Guardini's position here accords with St. Thomas Aquinas' understanding of God. This view is worth discussion because it touches upon Guardini's notion of Providence.

We have already considered Guardini's argument that the Good, which touches a person from within, is not static but changing and alive. It will become increasingly clear that Guardini believes in a dynamic empowerment, from within, for the person living with Providence. Therefore it may be instructive to note one line of Christian thought in

---

70. Guardini uses the word *"mitvollzeihen"* here which has the sense of carrying out something with somebody. The word *"lebendig"* used for life means lively and active life.

71. Guardini, *The World and the Person*, 46.

72. In a post war book, Guardini will say, "Once a man believes in Christ, Providence takes the place of destiny in directing his existence. This brings him by means of grace into the relation existing between the Father and the incarnate Son. "To the degree 'the old man is put off' and 'the new man put on'—and this happens in every genuine act of the Christian life—the notion of destiny is changed into Providence.... [T]he whole character of existence is now changed." Guardini, *Freedom, Grace, and Destiny*, 207.

this direction. As a Christian philosopher, Aquinas, departing from Aristotle's position, used the concept of Beingness in a different way to Aristotle. Beingness was "act" (*actus*) for Aquinas and not just "something" as it had been with Aristotle. In other words there is a dynamic quality to it. This act or actuation of existence can be conceived of as the "inner doing" whereby something *is* at all.[73] The philosopher Thomas Sheehan notes that for Aquinas, the world, created by the freewill of the creator, is radically contingent and God is supernaturally supreme while God's essence is "to be."[74] In this scheme, since God created *ex nihilo*, beingness can be understood as a "radical insurrection against nothingness"[75] In Aquinas' understanding, God, as the act of beingness, makes creatures to be and preserves them, as radically contingent in their beingness.[76] In this understanding, seen already in Guardini's notion of Providence, creatures can participate in the dynamism and beingness of God which is pure act. Sheehan also notes, that this type of creationist metaphysics involves the concept of "the finite or infinite 'doing'[77] of beingness entailing the causal doing of beingness to others."[78] That is to say, the beingness of others can be as God's own beingness is.[79] This is an important point, and shows an understanding which can underpin Guardini's notion of the human person as a possible door for God to the world.[80] Guardini's concept is not just that of 'beingness' but of the human person participating in the Being of God, which is Trinitarian and radically Christological. Furthermore, as open and acting with the Being of God through Christ within, the Christian can live with Providence and their destiny in the world can change. The presence of the indwelling Christ enables the human person to participate in the divine life.

Guardini refers to participation in God as a mystery in Christian existence that can only be grasped in faith. That is to say, it is not gained by grasping after knowledge but by giving oneself without reserve to God. The person is changed by faith. When he or she:

73. Sheehan, *Karl Rahner*, 143.
74. Sheehan, *Karl Rahner*, 144.
75. Sheehan, *Karl Rahner*, 143.
76. We note, at the same time, that God is more than Being, as such.
77. Sheehan translates, Aquinas' word *actus* as "doing." Sheehan, *Karl Rahner*, 144.
78. Sheehan, *Karl Rahner*, 144.
79. Sheehan, *Karl Rahner*, 145.
80. It would be congruent with the understanding of John 7:38–39a, espoused by Christ and recorded by St. John, which is quoted on the first page.

steps into this relationship, believing, loving, hoping, then there awakens within him a life that does not come from himself. But it is realised in him and so he becomes the man his Creator intended him to be. Faith, love and hope are the divine and "infused" virtues, by means of which man shares in the divine life. Beneath them lies the inexpressible unity of the Christian existence of which St. Paul speaks in his epistles.[81]

Human persons need to act boldly in faith and give themselves to the Creator. Guardini doesn't believe that human interiority, of itself, is able to produce the same effect. Yet, the "infused" virtues of faith love and hope are necessary for this participation in God. How does a person get these virtues?

Christian interiority and Christian abandonment to God occur through faith, becoming a "child of God" and *"going where Christ stands."*[82] Christ is "in" the believer.[83] Furthermore, the submission to the life changing "spirit of the living God"[84] enables human persons to become free of themselves because a real paradigm shift occurs in one's life, and the person attains Christian self-knowledge. He writes, "Christian self-knowledge in a man is the grace given participation in God's view of him."[85] In Christian self-knowledge, one doesn't understand from one's subjectivity but, rather, from God's view of that person. In this context we may also place Guardini's view of the necessity of quiet times of prayer, openness to the spirit of God and daily reflection on experience, as an essential part of this self-knowledge.

Guardini believes the world of time rightfully belongs to the world of the eternal, supporting the notion of overall unity in this world. This unity of the human and divine is formed in loving union with God. Guardini writes that the world of being has a new order in this relationship, for Divine Providence is:

> not the order of nature, which exists in itself, but that order which exists between God and those who give themselves to him in true faith. To the extent that man recognises God as his Father, that he places his trust in him and makes the kingdom the primary concern of his heart, to precisely that extent, a new

---

81. Guardini, *The World and the Person*, 47.
82. Guardini, *The World and the Person*, 47.
83. Guardini, *The World and the Person*, 53.
84. Guardini, *The World and the Person*, 48.
85. Guardini, *The World and the Person*, 49.

order of being enfolds about him, one in which "for those who love God all things work together unto good (Rom. 8:28)."[86]

The person may still have pain or misfortune but God provides for the person's needs and everything serves the true end of his or her life. God's care is for his or her particular good. Providence in this situation is both individual and communal. In Providence-living there is a new arrangement of being for the human person. This is the order which comes from participating in the love of God and living the eternal—in—time made possible when the person entrusts him or herself to God.[87] In that relationship self-knowledge is imparted as God's view of that person. "Christian self knowledge in a man is the grace-given participation in God's view of him."[88] Living the eternal in time as Jesus taught, enables one to be more complete. A person's being is continually renewed in relationship to God the Father. Guardini believes we are more complete the closer we come to God, and when our essential nature exists "in God" everything is able to enter God's vitality.[89] In other words the human person becomes more vital and 'alive' in the relationship with God.

The Creative Power of God out of Human Hearts

In *The World and the Person*, Guardini links the relational understanding of Providence to revelation by the grace of God. Rather than being pre-occupied with gaining God's Providence, he believes the appropriate way for one to proceed is by making God's concern one's own concern, because conversion and repentance of the person must occur first, and in this way the person will want God's kingdom and his justice to come about. Guardini argues that Christ said the course of events will fall into place around the faithful and will form wholeness in the world of the individual.[90] That wholeness will differ according to the mentality and character of the person and how much sway God has in their lives.

---

86. Guardini, *The Lord*, 178. This statement is further affirmation of Guardini's argument that the order of Providence does not reflect the "superior man" but the God-loving one.

87. Guardini, *The World and the Person*, 49.

88. Guardini, *The World and the Person*, 49.

89. Guardini, "Die christliche Innerlichkeit," 465–72. We note here that God is presented as dynamic alive and flexible.

90. Guardini, *The World and the Person*, 194.

Guardini holds that the course of events is not predetermined but fluid and full of potential. Submission to the will of God can change a person's destiny. Furthermore the world is in the hands of God and the laws of nature are God's servants. This understanding enables Guardini to say that when a person lives with Providence, and a new being forms around him or her and the course of the world is ordered first in individual lives and then in the world out of human hearts:

> A man with the faith of which we have spoken forms as it were a portal of entrance for the creative power of God which is directed towards the world.[91]

The lives of individual Christians are important for allowing good or evil to be brought into the world through them. In this way, through the human heart, the person can share care for God's holy kingdom.

Theme 3: The Individual Person Is Important to God

In chapter 3, I argued that Guardini's notion of the importance of the individual person in God's eyes, was a central predicate of his notion of Providence. I argued that each individual person was irreplaceable and of infinite value to God. God enabled transcendence and yet repentance and assent to God were necessary. The person must also be 'born again' and can share in the Trinitarian life of God. Here, in this period, and in the context of earlier writing Guardini develops the notion of "person" to argue the way such a person can live with integrity, assured of God's care. Guardini reminds his readers that they are "called," wanted by God, yet the response by the persons themselves must be of their own volition. We turn to the notion of person.

The Notion of Person

Guardini holds that the person living in God's Providence is a person who is able to stand with self possession and integrity. Guardini links the notion of person with self-possession, relations with another and the relationship with God. He does not hold the view which Hitler had advanced, that the individual was not important nor does he equate the notion of person with the "perfect person" as they did. Gunda Brüske

---

91. Guardini, *The World and the Person*, 194.

notes that in this period 1933/4 Guardini developed his Winter semester lectures with focus on the human person because he was aware of the challenges of National Socialism and wanted, in opposition, to give the Christian position.[92] Despite his argument for the importance of each individual person, Guardini believes that a way of misunderstanding Providence is to place the emphasis on human persons themselves. This is no place for hedonism. The emphasis should be on God and the things of God. Nevertheless, in that context he wants to understand what the human person is like and how that person, so important in God's eyes, can develop in a way commensurate with Christian doctrine. In order to understand his position a little more closely we turn to his in-depth study of human persons and statement concerning the nature of "person" which he undertook in order to analyze the assertion that human persons are irreplaceable and of infinite value to God.[93]

Called

In chapter 3, I argued that Guardini believes the human person is grounded in God. Here Guardini affirms that the concept of creation, which expresses God's relation to man, comes from God's grace.[94] "Subjects" are not subjects as such but have a "call" (*Anruf*) from God, which indicates freedom of choice in the acceptance of God and a different status in relation to God. Corresponding to God's act of creation, human persons have the capacity for decision. There is no necessity, no determinism. Human persons are free to decide for or against God. Furthermore, Guardini clarifies his position in response to God's "otherness." He acknowledges that the term "other" is useful, but only as a way of distinguishing the human person from God. He argues that the religious consciousness is able to apprehend that "God is not I" and God is not another either:

> God is not "I" . . . but He is not another either . . . [God is] beyond conceptual thought. But this inexpressible something can be immediately apprehended by the religious consciousness.[95]

---

92. Brüske, *Anruf der Freiheit*, 99.

93. We have already adverted to the fact that Hitler believed the individual human person was unimportant and replaceable.

94. Guardini, *The World and the Person*, 21.

95. Guardini, *The World and the Person*, 31.

In this way Guardini hopes to overcome a dualism whilst retaining a theistic position. He doesn't equate human persons with God nor does he promote over-subjectivity or an unreal sense of self.[96] There is balance here in this position. Furthermore, he argues, the love and creative energy of God, make the human person become themselves and enables them to exist as themselves. He writes:

> The creative energy of his act makes me to be myself. My special character is rooted in Him not myself. . . . The concept of the "other" has no meaning here. . . . The concept of creation which expresses God's relation to man signifies two things. First that man is really given his own existence, and then, at the same time, that God is not "another" beside him, but the absolute source of his being, and closer to him than he is to himself.[97]

There is unity in difference in this act, of which Guardini speaks. It is the basis for the "I-Thou" relationship which we have considered. Guardini writes that:

> Only because man originated in answer to the call of God and is maintained by that call, because he is the "Thou" called forth by Him who gives his name as the "I am," does man have the possibility to know himself as an autonomous being.[98]

In other words, God created human persons and "calls" them to that personal relationship with God's self in a relation in which the a priori principle is God-in-God's-self who sustains the life and being of that person. This is a relationship of mutual respect. Furthermore, in the same context, human persons have a special type of responsibility to other created beings.

Providence proceeds with the awareness that the "call" of God has the attitude of respect or esteem[99] (*achtung*) which God is able to give the human person. Consonant with this attitude, is the "naming" (*bennante*) of the person.[100] On the one hand honouring God emphasizes a distance

---

96. Guardini, *The World and the Person*, 132.

97. Guardini, *The World and the Person*, 30.

98. Once again, we draw attention to the Neo-scholastic notion of efficient causality as distinct from formal causality, and that which Karl Rahner refers to as quasi-formal causality.

99. Guardini, *The World and the Person*, 32.

100. In chapter 3, we adverted to Guardini's belief that each human person is held in the heart of God, and God has given each person a name commensurate with his or her calling.

between God and human persons, but on the other hand, the mode of creation and notion of "call" (*anruf*) annuls it. God shows his love for the human person by "giving him all, being and nature."[101] The capacity for being and loving comes from God. "He makes him into that which alone can really be loved, a person. God, who is the absolute Person, makes man His 'Thou.'"

Guardini's use of a double agency in Providence may be understood here as a Theonomy in which the I-Thou relationship gives the human person the capacity for acting with God in the context of their own person. Furthermore, "Only because the creating God really placed the created world in man's hand, can the latter come upon the idea that he must create an autonomous culture."[102] In this sense Guardini is referring to the fact that human persons are created in a way which is qualitatively different from birds and trees because human persons are decision making self-determined creatures whom, as we argued above, have the capacity to share in the life of God. The danger would be extreme autonomy which wants separation from God.

A cautionary word must also be said against this particular argument of Guardini concerning the difference between human persons and animals. To be fair to Guardini, he has considered the example of St. Francis and certainly admits of God's grace in creation and the recognition of the grace the birds and animals probably experienced when they were near St. Francis. Yet, in his attempt to address the uniqueness, and need for responsibility, of the human person in God's eyes and embrace the view of the Christian and Hebrew Scriptures with regard to the place of the human person *vis a vis* God's other creatures, he could put himself with those people whom ecologists and animal theologians argue against because they see the earth as their own dominion to use or destroy at will. This aspect will be referred to below as the context for human responsibility in this world.

The Human Person and Love

In the post war period, Guardini will argue that the person who lives with God's Providence must be a person who loves. The notion of what a loving person is, can be understood from this period written in the period

---

101. Guardini, *The World and the Person*, 31.
102. Guardini, *The World and the Person*, 24.

of National Socialism. Guardini holds that it is important for the whole person to be able to love. For Guardini that refers to the ability to:

> behold the structure of value in another being, above all in a personal being, to perceive its validity, to feel that it is important that this should exist and develop; to be moved by concern about this realization as if it were one's own. He who loves moves forth into freedom, freedom from his real bonds – himself. And by the very fact that he banishes himself from his own sight and feeling, he fulfils himself.[103]

When one loves, one perceives the value in another and is able to feel a sense of identity with this other. In that way, complete empathy is possible, and at the same time, a person becomes free because freed, from the bonds of self, that person is fulfilled. Guardini believes that only in "departing from oneself" in the perception of another's value, is one enabled to have the:

> openness in which the self is realised and everything flourishes. It is in this space that true creation and the pure act also take place, all that bears witness that the world is worthy of existence.[104]

This is the context in which Guardini is able to assert that someone who renounces love is diseased.[105] A healthy individual has the capacity for interiority, the capacity for decision and the capacity for justice and love. A person possesses the capacity to belong to oneself in a way which can enable integrity, and has an ontological openness with the capacity to love. The human will is also associated with these other aspects of a human person and Providence itself.

Human Will

Guardini believes the concrete reality of the individual mind, with its center of activity in a particular organism, is the center of individual historical responsibility. The interiority of the person is also an interiority of the will. He argues:

---

103. Guardini, *The World and the Person*, 118.
104. Guardini, *The World and the Person*, 118.
105. Guardini, *The World and the Person*, 118.

> A true will is found only when an organ of evaluation is affected by the character of value possessed by the object or by the meaning of the situation and when it grasps this value as something valid in itself, and takes up an attitude in relation to it . . . from that point proceeds the action.[106]

An attitude towards something which becomes action occurs when a person evaluates something as having value, validity and meaning in a given situation. This formation, as will be shown, works towards the development of integrity and responsibility.

In his understanding of the human person Guardini links a capacity of ontological openness of the human person with mind and the capacity for meaning. Person is, "the structured, interior spiritually creative being, insofar as it stands in itself and is self-determined."[107] Self determined in this context means that one is unique in one's "being," and I "cannot ultimately be possessed any other authority, but belong to myself. . . . I cannot be replaced by anyone else, but stand on my own, that no-one can substitute for me, but I am unique."[108] "Person" means that one belongs to oneself and therefore cannot be used or possessed by anyone or any other authority. As one's "own purpose" one stands alone and is unique.[109] It may be said that a person must have the capacity to stand as an entity in oneself. This quality is an important prerequisite for human integrity. Responsibility of the human person stems from this aspect. Guardini states that in order for a person to grow and survive, truth and justice are necessary and since the 'person' issues forth from the spiritually creative being, the person can also be damaged if these things are renounced.[110]

---

106. Guardini, *The World and the Person*, 109.
107. Guardini, *The World and the Person*, 114.
108. Guardini, *The World and the Person*, 114.
109. We may argue that Guardini is speaking for authenticity of the person here. In the previous chapter, we argued that the truth of a person's authenticity is the conformity to one's nature. Authenticity, in the terminology of many existentialists refers to a quality of existence in which the existent has become genuinely himself or herself. Consequently, authentic people do not necessarily follow social norms or take refuge in rules or ready-made ideals but accept themselves as unique persons who have to realize the possibilities that belong uniquely to them. See "Authenticity," in *A New Dictionary of Christian Ethics*, 49. We should distinguish this type of autonomy from subjectivity and autonomy as such. Guardini is critical of pure autonomy and extreme individuality and advocates Theonomy. This definition of authenticity would be compatible with his concept of Theonomy.
110. Guardini, *The World and the Person*, 16.

In order to consider these aspects we turn to each of these points individually, beginning with the aspect of mind. Firstly then, the person is a living individual, with the capacity for interiority. In the animal, as opposed to plants, interiority is formed primarily by the mind. The concrete reality of the mind grasps meaning. Guardini believes that the interiority of man is one of action and creation which work together to reveal and express meaning. An example of how this operates occurs in a work of art which comes forth from the interiority of a person and the art-work displays the interiority of mind and meaning which is experienced. For Guardini, these activities distinguish man from mere animal-hood. Nevertheless, human action is less certain than spiritual certainty because spiritual certainty, which the human person also has, finds its certainty in meaning, not immediate existence. This is an important point for Guardini's notion of Providence because Guardini will ultimately argue that one may not have complete fulfillment in this life or, as in the case of Jesus Christ, everything may not go well in terms of immediate existence, but nevertheless God's purposes may be fulfilled and this greater meaning prevails.

Person as Determined by Mind

Guardini holds that an important aspect of the person is the personality which, for him, is the individuality of the person as determined by mind.[111] A human person is able to live with Providence because of his or her capacity to grasp meaning. Meaning directed by mind, is made possible by the spirit, since the spirit by nature is immeasurable and indomitable. Guardini explains it this way:

> Through the spirit that determines it, personal interiority becomes, on principle, unmeasurable. Only its expressions are measurable, and these depend upon conditions which are also measurable. But the interiority cannot be measured.... Because of the spirit this interiority also escapes all domination. Its expressions can be governed, but only those processes which are accessible for habit, suggestion, etc. The spiritual core remains free.[112]

---

111. Guardini, *The World and the Person*, 107.
112. Guardini, *The World and the Person*, 109.

Ultimately the spirit must remain free because spirit is determined by the true and the good.[113]

Guardini links meaning with consciousness. He says, "True consciousness is found only when the process of perception is penetrated by the spirit and leads to the grasping of the meaning."[114] True consciousness enabling understanding leads to meaning but is determined by the value of truth not biological interiority. According to Guardini, "this interiority perceives the claim of existence to be grasped for its own sake to be understood."[115]

Guardini adds:

> [T]he doctrine of Divine Providence must be combined with another: that there is a consummation of meaning even for such destinies which appear meaningless from the point of view of the world as it is. Important as talent, health, hereditary, education, social environment and one's role in the world may be – the ultimate for man cannot be confined to these. A fulfillment is promised which transcends all of the immediate possibilities—without and in spite of these—from the pure creativity of grace which is beyond the reach of any judgement.[116]

The person, then, is concerned with the capacity for decision and meaning directed by mind. The spiritual core of a person being free, is that which can protect the person from ultimate domination by another. Yet the grace which a person may have surpasses any of the person's gifts or qualities. As Guardini wrote, domination of the human person was well in progress by the Nationalist Socialist regime and disabled people were being executed.

An intrinsic part of human nature is the capacity for justice. In order to remain whole and in harmony with oneself, one cannot turn from the true and the Good or renounce justice, without becoming diseased and out of intrinsic harmony with oneself because, according to Guardini, these things are essential to one's life work. Furthermore, the order of truth is revealed by the Good and justice. In this period, Guardini writes of justice, as the "acknowledgement that things have their intrinsic character and a readiness to preserve the right of this character and the

---

113. Guardini, *The World and the Person*, 116.
114. Guardini, *The World and the Person*, 108.
115. Guardini, *The World and the Person*, 109.
116. Guardini, *The World and the Person*, 174.

laws that spring from it."¹¹⁷ In order to explain the importance of justice in one's life, he writes:

> As a person, man has been set free to stand on his own feet and to act from his own initiative, without being God. The condition for the reasonableness of this manner of being is that he should take his place in that order which is based upon truth, namely in justice, and that he should even make justice his real life-work. The finite person is significant only if he is orientated towards justice. In forsaking justice the person becomes endangered and dangerous – a power without order. And by this very fact the person becomes diseased. He is no longer in harmony with himself.¹¹⁸

This notion of justice is therefore *intrinsic* to a person's humanity and reveals the order of truth. One cannot play God and be orientated towards justice at the same time. The orientation towards justice must be primary. Nevertheless, it must be argued that while this notion is very insightful, such an argument for justice could seem to be unbelievably weak when we consider the number of innocent people already being interned at that time in Germany. Appropriately, the concept of justice was addressed more fully after the war in *Freedom, Grace, and Destiny* where Guardini links it with Providence and the justice of God.

Providence in Guardini's view presupposes the possibility of personal authenticity and integrity. In Guardini's early writings, we have been able to appreciate his own understanding of the importance of the individual in this world and to God. Yet, while Guardini had already adverted to the importance of the individual to God in his early writings he continued to present the same thing in this period. In *The World and the Person*, he intensified his inquiry into the nature of persons even more. Writing in the period of National Socialism, Guardini shows that he considered the Nazi policies to be dehumanizing, and to be destructive of the quality of human existence.¹¹⁹

It is well-documented that Hitler did not regard the individual to be important, and he was recorded as saying:

> [As a soldier] I learned that life was a cruel struggle, and has no other object than preservation of the species. The individual

---

117. Guardini, *The World and the Person*, 117.
118. Guardini, *The World and the Person*, 117.
119. Krieg, *Romano Guardini*, 133.

> can disappear, provided that there are other people to replace him.[120]

And again:

> I have been Europe's last hope. She proved incapable of re-fashioning herself by means of voluntary reform. . . . [T]o take her I had to use violence. . . . Europe must be re-fashioned in the common interests of all and without regard for individuals.[121]

Thus, Hitler did not consider the individual person to be important. Yet when a person spoke to Hitler, he or she called him *"Mein Führer"* (My Leader). By comparison, in the book written in this period, *The Lord's Prayer*, Guardini notes that God cares for each person as an individual and is "absolutely there for each one."[122] Yet, he asserts, Jesus does not ask us to call God "My" Father but "Our" Father. In other words there is a social dimension to the prayer:

> The 'Our Father' replies with a warning. It reminds us that consciousness of oneself and one's uniqueness can be pagan. . . .
> I am a man among men; but by Grace I am Christian 'among many brethren.' . . . The only sovereign person is God.[123]

Guardini's belief that each individual is important to God, who alone is sovereign, is an important predicate of his work and notion of Providence.

Guardini clearly presents a different view to that which was that presented in the society of the time. In 1923 he had written that all people are equal. He said, "Catholicism regards every human being as the child of God. In this respect all are fundamentally equal."[124] In his book, *The Lord*, written in 1937, Guardini laments that although human persons are made in the image of God, many people have a lack of desire to turn to God. Therefore, he asks how, "I who am nothing in myself, who exist only as he made me, an image or likeness of my Maker [can] be so ignorant of him?"[125] In the same book, Guardini wrote about Christian

---

120. Hitler, *Hitler's Table Talk*, 44.
121. Genoid, *The Testament of Adolf Hitler*, 101.
122. Guardini, *The Lord's Prayer*, 38.
123. Guardini, *The Lord's Prayer*, 37.
124. Guardini, *The Church and the Catholic*, 108.
125. Guardini, *The Lord*, 50. Here Guardini notes everything that is has its being through God alone. The words he uses for human person here, in keeping with the teaching of the Church Fathers is both image and likeness (*ebenbildung* and *gleichnis*)

Existence (*Christlichen Dasein*). And speaking about the Church referred to God's family where all are brothers and sisters. God's family is:

> The fullness of grace functioning in history. Mystery of that union into which God through Christ, draws all creation. Family of the children of God assembled about Christ, the first born. Beginning of the new, holy people. (heiligen Volkes) Foundation of the Holy City (Heilige Stadt) to be revealed."[126]

In Guardini's thought and notion of Providence, God, through Christ, calls all of creation and everyone into the union with God that can bring a transformed people and a transformed world into existence. One may ask if a person is predestined to such a world.

Predestination

Guardini refers to predestination in a chapter of *The Lord's Prayer*. This is important to his overall concept of Providence and may be fruitfully juxtaposed with writings of other theologians on Providence. Furthermore, in this aspect of Providence, Guardini shows how his readers can understand the importance of each person to God. The concept also serves as an interesting contrast to the concept of the racially predestined person held in such high esteem by the Nazis. Guardini believes that a person can reduce the idea of predestination to a dark and sinister prospect. Yet, to him, that would not reflect the loving Father of the Scriptures. Guardini doesn't want the idea of grace as a right or necessity to come in here. "One cannot reduce it to a system. It is not a doctrinal structure of 'ifs' and 'therefores' but a dialogue between the child of God and his Father—a prayer of love."[127] The grace given by God's benevolence enables existence to be changed but only when it is not "hedged in by rights or securities"[128] and trying to bargain with God. Guardini doesn't want a deterministic foregone conclusion similar to the one offered by Hitler from the perspective of nature and race. Thus there should not be any likelihood of considering God's grace and forgiveness a forgone

---

although it is not clear why he has used the term *ebenbildung* rather than the more common *ebenbild* for image. *Bildung* means formation or education. Perhaps Guardini is implying the necessity for development in order for the 'image' to exist.

126. Guardini, *The Lord*, 323.
127. Guardini, *The Lord's Prayer*, 103.
128. Guardini, *The Lord's Prayer*, 102.

conclusion. Rather, the sinner deserves eternal damnation but God has the capacity to give his love. Here he writes:

> God wills not the death of the sinner, but that he "be converted and live"; that all evil comes from man, not from the most holy God; that the eternal damnation of man is therefore his own fault and that God is only just when he pronounces that verdict.[129]

Eternal damnation, or salvation for that matter, is not pre-determined, or pre-destined, but rather indicates that one has a choice and must choose God and God's path. The God who is love pronounces the decrees which come from love. One must leave God free to choose to give God's grace. The person must relinquish all belief in the surety of eternal salvation but must risk the chance of failure, by loving God while allowing God the freedom of God's own response.[130] Guardini asserts therefore that the true meaning of the idea of predestination lies here and must come from God's freedom. That is to say, predestination must arise out of grace because only so can it remain love.[131] The freedom of love, with all its consequences is that which will lead us to the "bliss of heaven."[132]

> Thus does the Christian heart admit that God makes man, decides what he is to be, and directs his destiny as He will; and he renounces all opposition and right of appeal. . . . With it the Christian says to God: Thou art the Lord. Thou art free, also in regard to me . . . I long for heavenly bliss. . . . But I can possess Thee only if Thou givest Thyself; and that is love. . . . But how is one to love except in freedom?[133]

Thus Guardini's understanding is intersubjective and relational. It is this relationship which results in the harmony and union with the love of God with all of the risks that real love has. There is no predestination as such. Only the opportunity to love and be loved by God. Guardini considers, any other approach to the subject of predestination to be inappropriate. In particular, he is against the practice of reducing the idea of predestination to a system. Such a system could be associated with a type of security

---

129. Guardini, *The Lord's Prayer*, 100.
130. Guardini, *The Lord's Prayer*, 103.
131. Guardini, *The Lord's Prayer*, 102.
132. Guardini, *The Lord's Prayer*, 102.
133. Guardini, *The Lord's Prayer*, 102.

but is anathema to God's nature:[134] "One cannot reduce it to a system. It is not a doctrinal structure of "if's" and "therefore's" but a dialogue between the child of God and his Father - a prayer of love."[135]

Thus, God's incomprehensible love, known by the human person in a type of detachment,[136] is the only way to think of predestination:

> That is why the Christian lets go of everything which spells security, rights, demonstrable common sense. . . . In the measure that he renounces security and surrenders himself freely to the love of God, in that same measure does he experience a confidence beyond all reason, and a hope beyond all security.[137]

We note here that Guardini avoids expressing a more exclusivist view of predestination such as the view that some people are pre-ordained to be saved from birth. Rather, he associates predestination with the call for all to repent, and be changed by God, but leaves God and human persons free to decide how they will respond. That is to say, Guardini does not take the position which states that some people are predestined to be "saved" while others are not. God as God's-self pre-exists as love and, Guardini believes, has that care for the individual which Guardini has written of elsewhere.[138] The focus can therefore only be on God and abandonment to God's love, "Thou alone sufficest, O God!"[139] We turn

---

134. Guardini, *The Lord's Prayer*, 103.

135. Guardini, *The Lord's Prayer*, 103.

136. I use this term, detachment, to mean the type of indifference St. Ignatius of Loyola talked about. It indicates an attitude of relativity to all that is not God. See Rahner, "Ignatian Spirituality and Devotion," 54.

137. Guardini, *The Lord's Prayer*, 103.

138. This point about God's care for the sinner could also be associated with Guardini's writings about the afterlife and, in particular, purgatory. In relation to Providence, Guardini writes, "In its full meaning, being good is an endless process. We believe we are under God's providence. Each day brings us the tasks that God has assigned to us. Toil, work, effort, self-conquest, sacrifice, heavy unceasing demands are made upon us, and we know how rarely we fulfil them adequately. To be really good would mean perfectly to achieve what every hour demands, so that life might rise to its full accomplishment of what God has asked of us. What has been undone can never be recalled, for each hour comes but once, and the next brings in its own demands. What is to be done about these gaps and omissions in a life that is so fleeting?" Guardini, *The Last Things*, 43. Guardini's position, on this and other aspects relevant to Providence and predestination are commensurate with Roman Catholic Doctrine of that time and will be discussed later in the thesis.

139. Guardini, *The Lord's Prayer*, 104.

now to the importance of the world to an individual human person living with Providence.

Theme 4: New Creation and New Existence

To live with Providence is to live towards a new creation of the person and the world. I argued in chapter 3 that a person living with Providence lives in a different relationship to God and the world, which results in transformation of meaning for the human person and transformation of the world as the person lives in openness to the grace which transforms him or her. The world is a necessary part of a person's relationship to God in living with Providence. The new creation of Providence, I argued, begins as the Good touches a person from within and the person who responds with conscience, is able to help "complete" the world from within with moral deeds. The person lives a new existence. Here in this chapter Guardini's argument for creation rather than nature, as such, forms an important distinction in the development of Guardini's argument for Providence and the new creation. Before considering the details of nature and creation we turn to Guardini's conception of "world."

World

In Guardini's understanding the world refers to more than just the inanimate world. The created "experienced world" is an "all inclusive totality."[140] The world of creation is a world of being with a concrete exterior and, as the entirety of *all* being, it represents, for Guardini, a whole and structure in a meaningful form.[141] Guardini places the human person into this dynamic structure by asserting that the person exists in tension with one pole in the human person and the other pole lying objectively everywhere. It is the:

> whole which is constructed between two poles, one of which
> lies always in the individual person and the other in the

---

140. Guardini, *The World and the Person*, 64. As we will see below, Guardini makes a distinction between redeemed world and unredeemed world. Redeemed world is a world transformed in Christ assisted by the decisions of human persons while unredeemed world is one which is subject to destiny or trapped in that which just happens as in a determinist pattern.

141. Guardini, *The World and the Person*, 64.

multifariousness of things and events.... [I]t is realised as the believer encounters things, experiences and recognises them, evaluates them and assumes an attitude toward them, overcomes their power, masters, orders and forms them.[142]

World, for Guardini, is, primarily "experienced world" and is a living, active reality.[143]

Guardini's notion of world is integral to development of his notion of Providence in this period and strengthens his stand against the National Socialists. We recall that the National Socialists had elevated the concept of nature to a superior status commensurate with their philosophy of human election of the German people and the deterministic ideas of race. The concept of nature was extremely important in this period. Guardini demonstrates his opposing view with his words:

[I]n a world that was purely nature, there would be no choice, no history, no possibility of creation and with it no holy creation.[144]

In the dynamic, created and divine world of human persons and other things Guardini wanted to show a disjunction between what occurs out of necessity and that which is the result of an act or decision. God chose to create and, in this context, "holy creation" is the result of active choice. For the human person Providence cannot be a matter of passively allowing things to happen to him or her. Providence is not the acceptance of "fate." Providence occurs in the context of act and decision. Guardini held that nature, of itself, didn't exist. So-called nature was actually creation; God's handiwork (*Gottes Werk*). As will be seen below, Guardini argues that nature is a part but only a part of the world. The world is not "natural" but the work of God and under God's guidance. His assertion that God made an "act" of creation, supports his view that

---

142. Guardini, *The World and the Person*, 173.

143. In an earlier work Guardini asserted that there is a special relationship between things and human beings. He wrote, "The world consists not of things in themselves alone, but of that which comes about as we encounter these things." When we see things and experience them, when we approach things and come in contact with them, we become involved with them.... It is the world that God intends since God creates both things and human beings.... When human beings truly encounter things, the world emerges as God intends it. This world is always new." Guardini, "Tagebuch Aus Oberitalien," 18–19. See also Krieg, *Spiritual Writings*, 55.

144. "Aus der Biblischen Gotteslehre," 1–15. The publication of the journal *Die Schildgenossen* was suppressed by the National Socialists in that same year and unable to be published again until after the war.

human persons are called to volitionally participate in God's action; their decision for God is volitional rather than something proceeding from natural sources or forced upon them. Guardini's notion of nature and creation deserve more elaboration and we now turn to this distinction in his work.

Nature and Creation

Guardini's 1939 book, *The World and the Person*, begins with a consideration of nature (*Natur*). Guardini subordinates nature to creation (*Schöpfung*). Before considering creation we advert to Guardini's notion of nature, which considering the social background in 1939, is important.[145] Guardini notes that the term "natural" often denotes that which is "proper and healthy, wise and perfect—the "natural."[146] At the same time, the opposite, the unnatural, gives the impression of that which is "artificial, abnormal, unhealthy, spoiled."[147] For that reason, nature has been used in art, especially in the enlightenment, to express that which is classically beautiful. Guardini notes that, for these people:

> the concept of nature expresses something final. One cannot go beyond it. As soon as something is derived from it, it is definitely understood. As soon as something can be shown to have a natural cause, it is justified. As soon as something is recognised as being according to nature the problem disappears.[148]

Therefore, Guardini argues that, for antiquity, nature seems to have represented that which should be. Things have the character of a norm. In this sense, a quality of "absoluteness" was given to nature.

In opposition to these ideas of pure nature, Guardini argues that the Christian must distinguish between nature and creation because creation, unlike pure nature, didn't proceed from necessity. Rather, it was willed by God and is a result of grace. In the Middle Ages and time of the Renaissance nature had often been portrayed as the totality of existence. Some people considered the concept to have validity when it conformed to the

---

145. The National Socialists had elevated the "Natural" to an absolute, and it underpinned their determinist ideology.
146. Guardini, *The World and the Person*, 5.
147. Guardini, *The World and the Person*, 6.
148. Guardini, *The World and the Person*, 6.

ideas of the Graeco-Roman world.[149] Goethe, Spinoza, and Schelling see a numinous depth of God in the concept of nature, yet their ideas speak of a determinism Guardini can't accept. He writes:

> Here the consciousness of the believer must make a fundamental distinction: the world is not Nature but Creation, creation in the plain sense of a work brought about by a free act. It is not something "natural," self-evident, self-justified, but it requires a reason, and it is given this reason by the power which created it in its being and reality. And the fact that it was created does not depend upon the coming into operation of a cause constructed after the model of natural energy, but upon an act which . . . has the character of "grace."[150]

The world is not pure nature, which could herald the idea of a world of determinist necessity, but creation which is a gift of grace. As such, it is the act of the most Holy Living God. Guardini writes, "In creating, God is Lord, in the face of not only finite reality but his own absolute reality."[151] He adds, "God's Lordship is the Biblical expression of his freedom."[152] In linking God's freedom to the Biblical understanding, namely, God's Omnipotence and Lordship and ability to create, Guardini is able to argue that in the act of creation, "God is really God."[153]

Guardini is critical of modern philosophy, exemplified by Kant, where nature is shown to be essentially finite. Guardini says it stops at itself and is absolutized, or conversely is absorbed into the idea of the Absolute. In that sense, he believes that modern consciousness more appropriately recognized the meaning of finite reality which demands human action. God created the world out of love. It was a *free act* from the freedom of God's omnipotence and not out of the overflow of God's love as the Neoplatonists believed, since that would have made the world a natural phenomenon which evolved out of necessity. The initiative and action of God was involved. Having made those distinctions, Guardini writes that creation involves another aspect, namely, history, which is accomplished by God. In that sense, "Nature" (*Natur*), "Subject" (*Subjekt*)

---

149. Guardini, *The World and the Person*, 6.
150. Guardini, *The World and the Person*, 18.
151. Guardini, *The World and the Person*, 20.
152. Guardini, *The World and the Person*, 203n1. Guardini distinguishes God's freedom from human freedom by saying that human freedom implies obedience (to God) at its deepest level. God's freedom is truly free.
153. Guardini, *The World and the Person*, 19.

and "Culture" (*Kulture*) are abolished as entities in themselves because they form part of a whole.[154] Existence, therefore, is able to become a whole; it is given.[155] He writes:

> The world is created; it is entirely the work of God. But as such it has a reality, has a fullness of being and of meaning in its created finiteness. It has been put into the hand of man, who is also finite but real and powerful. Man's responsibility for the world is much greater than the middle ages could perceive, greater because he can know and handle it in far greater measure than that age could possibly foresee. . . . This also imposes an obligation on the Christian: namely, the responsibility for the world before God.[156]

Since God is the author of creation, it means that the human person, as created, is related to God. As we noted in chapter 1, Guardini considers Christian responsibility for the world to be a necessary part of living with Providence. Yet Providence - living involves the New Creation.

God in Creation

Guardini also believes that as creator of the world God lives within its being.[157] Since God is the author of creation, it means that the human person is already related to God. For Guardini, that means that one should not have their center outside of themselves even if that is God, because it would denote a "heteronomy"; the center in another. In other words, as argued above, one's self cannot exist under the power of another.[158] Guardini's dialogue partner, here, whom he opposes, is Nietzsche. He believes that Nietzsche reacted to this very aspect; the awareness that people felt controlled by God. His solution was to "kill" God. Conversely, Guardini wants to affirm that God is not the "other" but he is God.[159] Developing this point further, Guardini says:

154. Guardini, *The World and the Person*, 20.
155. Guardini, *The World and the Person*, 23.
156. Guardini, *The World and the Person*, 25.
157. Guardini, *The World and the Person*, 26.
158. Guardini, *The World and the Person*, 27.
159. Guardini, *The World and the Person*, 29 Nevertheless, Rudolf Otto whose work influenced Guardini's idea of the holy argued that God was "wholly other." His intention was different to many others who sought to show a dichotomy between God and human persons. Otto's aim was to show the enormity of God and the respect with which a person should regard God who deserves awe.

> Creating means that God places man in relation to Himself in which reason first says, "God is not I," and then adds "but he is not 'another'" either by this seeming contradiction pointing to something inexpressible which is beyond conceptual thought. But this inexpressible something can be immediately apprehended by the religious consciousness. Indeed it is likely that religious consciousness consists in this very apprehension. This relation then attains its ultimate clarity and fulfillment in the concept of actual grace.[160]

Because God is both intrinsic and non-intrinsic to the identity of the human person, the person is able to apprehend the incomprehensibility of God by non-conceptual thought. Fulfillment and clarity of the apprehension occurs through grace. It is this simultaneous awareness of one's finitude along with the infinity and incomprehensibility of God which constitute the religious consciousness. Guardini is able to assert that the special character one has as a person occurs because the rootedness is in God not in one's self.[161] The awareness of the place of one's rootedness gives one the possibility of relating to God and adopting an attitude towards God based on God's value of man himself. That value, as argued above, is the attitude of esteem.[162]

Christian World—New Heaven and New Earth

Here in this period of National Socialism Guardini develops his earlier argument further. While God is still central he shows how the human person has an indispensable role in the development of the new creation. The relationship of the human person to God enables a "new creation" to occur and reality in the world emerges in a different way for that person. Guardini attributes this capacity to the scope which arises out of a person's use of free will to trust God and to allow God's love to have sway. When living with Providence Guardini believes a person will receive what he needs for his life, even if it comes about through darkness and sorrow.[163] "His standards are divine; that means that the course of our destiny takes ways which are incomprehensible to us."[164] In the same way, Providence

---

160. Guardini, *The World and the Person*, 31.
161. The National Socialists believed one's rootedness lay in race.
162. Guardini, *The World and the Person*, 32.
163. Guardini, *The Lord's Prayer*, 76.
164. Guardini, *The World and the Person*, 198.

may also mean that the immediate necessities are denied at that time because, Guardini argues, the person needs trial.[165] Yet, if the person has faith he or she will be one with God in love and there will be a new unity. Nothing is imposed upon the human person. Rather, a new structure of existence, which Guardini calls the "new heaven and new earth" comes in to play around the person. Further nuancing of Guardini's notion of Divine Providence is made possible as Guardini considers destiny which he polarizes with Providence. This aspect will be developed even further in the post war period. We turn now to Guardini's concept of destiny.

Destiny

Destiny, writes Guardini in this period, is nothing more that the environment in the form of events and "that which happens."[166] In other words it is something over which the human person has no control. Yet to him the external factors are only a part of all that occurs. Providence has an active personal component. Guardini believes the human person can act to direct his or her future. We argued in chapter 2 that Guardini conceives of two poles in the human person. One pole is within the person and denotes that person as an individual, the other pole is outside the person and refers to the environment at large. The internal factors, within a person, play an important part, and a person can influence their environment to a very large degree. Here, Guardini argues that a person is artisan of their own fortune:[167]

> The world which concerns me is not the general physical or "objective" totality of things, but my environment, and that comes into being only in part from without. Half of it comes from within, from my own attitude at any time and receives its character from me. I am really "the artisan of my own fortune" taking this phrase in a much deeper and more effective sense than rational ethics usually gives to it.[168]

For instance, Guardini argues that when an accident happens the person could have had interior urges which "constitute that state of mind which

---

165. Guardini, *The World and the Person*, 198.
166. Guardini, *The World and the Person*, 191.
167. Guardini, *The World and the Person*, 192.
168. Guardini, *The World and the Person*, 192.

determines the environment of events."[169] That is to say a person's being can affect the environment in which they dwell. Likewise, the world around a person is not just an objective "world" but the environment, partly self-selected, of a certain person. Destiny, as such, can be influenced by a person's attitude. Yet Guardini knows that this may not be conscious. Furthermore, it is not just a matter of will or "basis of willing":[170]

> "Attitude" is rather the condition of the depths of the personality which precedes all conscious willing, the interior receptiveness or unreceptiveness, narrowness or magnanimity, fear or readiness, weakness or strength which determine the first willing and direction of life and so represent its basic disposition. To the extent to which this attitude changes—and it *can* change; here the real *metanoia* (repentence)[sic] takes place—the destiny also changes.[171]

In this important quotation, Guardini's position regarding Providence is clear. A person's attitude, deep within themselves can influence their destiny and conversion is needed.[172] When conversion takes place, that person's destiny changes. Attitude refers to an orientation and the capacity to focus on a goal which renders the present able to be fashioned by the future. Repentance and *Metanoia*, leading to conversion of the heart to God, can make a person's destiny different. Guardini holds that a person's destiny can change if a person becomes more truthful, more magnanimous, more unselfish, more free and loving.[173] Nevertheless, we can be critical of Guardini's position here, in the period of National Socialism,

---

169. Guardini, *The World and the Person*, 192. Guardini's overall argument is tempered with the assertion that a person is to be selflessly detached and magnanimous in living and when converted to a God-loving life can bring good into the world.

170. Guardini, *The World and the Person*, 193.

171. Guardini, *The World and the Person*, 193.

172. One could also argue for the influence of Heidegger here. Heiddeger had been a colleague of Guardini, and Heidegger writes, "Dasein has always understood itself and will always understand itself in terms of possibilities. Furthermore the character of understanding as projection is such that the understanding does not grasp thematically that upon which it projects-that is to say possibilities. . . . [P]rojection, in throwing, throws before itself the possibility as possibility, and lets it *be* as such. As projecting, understanding is the kind of Being of Dasein in which it is its possibilities." Heidegger, *Being and Time*, 185. Elsewhere Heidegger says, "The world is something the world projects outward, as it were, from within itself. . . . [S]o far as Dasein exists a world is cast forth with the Dasein's being." Heidegger, *The Basic Problem of Phenomenology*, 168. Guardini would have other things to add to this view as will be seen below.

173. Guardini, *The World and the Person*, 221.

which could be said to be too focused on the human person and that person's capacity for control.[174] While we could argue that, in the manner of Aquinas, Guardini believes in a God who allows secondary causes, his extreme position on this aspect raises the question of overall capacity or power of God, or God's inaction, and could even suggest a Deist tendency. Questions we might ask Guardini are: Did every person who was hit by a bomb bring it upon themselves? Did every survivor have a better internal attitude? What does this assertion by Guardini mean for God's will? How free is God in such a situation? These are questions about a position Guardini will not hold as strongly in his later work. We have said that if a person's attitude changes their destiny can change. We could also add that their being changes and underpins the attitude change. Faith has been shown to be important for Guardini. We must ask how destiny is different in the life of faith. We now turn to that argument.

Destiny in the Life of Faith

Destiny can change in the life of a person of faith. Three things important for the development of Providence here are: 1) The importance of focusing on the Kingdom of God and God's concerns; 2) Living with Christ within and allowing Christ to lead; 3) Living in a way which means the environment around a person will change.

For Guardini the crucial words are that a person should seek the Kingdom of God and God's justice first. This shows that God's idea of Providence does not operate as a law of nature, with the same for everybody, but rather it depends on the attitude of the person who fulfils that condition first. Such a person will learn to look beyond the non-essentials in this life, to the essential and eternal. Furthermore, the persons doing this will find themselves in accord with God, because God's object will become their object. Providence, which is not something already finished, becomes actual only when a person is in accord (*einvernehmen*) with God, because then his or her existence undergoes a profound change. In relationship with God the person doesn't need to focus on the needs of this world to the exclusion of everything else. The being of that person changes and a holy care surrounds him or her bringing things which the

---

174. We acknowledge that Guardini may be trying to counter a fatalist tendency or extreme passivity in this terror-stricken time of National Socialism.

person needs with it.[175] The focus is on God. Providence as Christ understood it is focused on transformation of the human person in God. The person of God the Father is central. Guardini argues that Providence is a work of grace and its existence is known only from revelation but we can see how it operates from the pattern of a person's life. There is more than an orderly system. As we have noted, Providence occurs in relationship with God.

Christ within the Believer: Christian Being

I argued, above, that the period of National Socialism was a period of extreme Christocentricism for Guardini. The relationship with Christ, who dwells within the person, forms the believer and the new creation which is essential for Providence living. Accordingly, Freedom *(Die Freiheit)* as understood in *The World and the Person*, comes from Christ. Christian discipleship or the following of Christ is not just a pedagogical relation.[176] Rather, the believer is given a new kind of being. Guardini's theology of Christian existence, may be understood from the Pauline doctrine of the inner-relation of Christ and human persons and in particular the notion of the "indwelling Christ." Working from St. Paul[177] Guardini notes that the person who is in Christ is a new creation. Guardini argues that according to this view, "the human whole, soul and body, spirit and matter, becomes the material in which a new kind of being, not given by nature, expresses itself."[178] Guardini holds that the "fleshly man" which, for him, is the natural whole, body, soul, environment and actions is in contrast to that which comes from grace. This "fleshly man" is juxtaposed, by Guardini, with a new possibility. Concurrent with his concentration on Christian existence, Guardini says that Christ within a human person, gives one, in the Holy Spirit, a new kind of being, which will prepare that person "for a holy existence, the 'Christ in us.'"[179] Guardini believes that because Christ lived his human existence he was able, when he became

---

175. Guardini, "Was JESUS," 9. The German reads, "ein heiliges Walten um gibt ihn, und die Dinge tragen sich ihm gleichsam zu."

176. Guardini, *The World and the Person*, 166.

177. 2 Cor 5:17.

178. Guardini, *The World and the Person*, 144.

179. Guardini, *The World and the Person*, 144.

spirit, to bring that earthly life into the eternal form. Clarifying this assertion, Guardini writes:

> This pneumatic (spiritual) Christ, who bears within him the whole fullness of reality and destiny of the historical Christ, forms the theme that is repeated in every believer, and not only the theme, but also the power which carries it out, for its accomplishment is grace. So the believer undergoes beside, or rather in, his natural development a second one, that from spiritual childhood to full maturity.[180]

In this way, then, the Christian undergoes transformation and becomes like Christ through the spiritual Christ. Nevertheless, the view that the historical Christ forms the believer anew from within might be challenged by one who could argue that despite individual integrity and development, the human person does not have complete freedom if the Spirit of Christ is replicated in every believer. The new kind of being the Christian can have is extremely important for Guardini and very appropriate for Guardini's argument here. It is completely contrary to the National Socialist argument that to have a truly holy being one must be Aryan. Furthermore, in a very positive way, Guardini is showing the way ahead for an alternative opportunity. A holy existence, a Christian existence, comes to all in Christ's humanity. "Those whom God foreknew he also predestined to be made conformable to the image of his Son (Rom. 8:29)."[181] In every believer, throughout all his actions, his experiences and developments, something deeper is to take place, the "mystical" life of Christ which forms the Christian.

In this section, in quoting Romans 8:29–30, Guardini brings the notion of predestination to refer to the preparation which occurs in this new kind of being and will gradually conform to the image of Christ.[182] Yet, despite Guardini's assertion, in *The Lord*, that Jesus Christ was Jewish, his Christo-centric turn during this precarious period of National Socialism and intended to help people live more Christian lives, may not have helped the Jews very much and could even have engendered further anti-Semitism from those so inclined. We have argued that living from the being of Christ is important for Christian existence and eventual personal transformation.

---

180. Guardini, *The World and the Person*, 144.
181. Guardini, *The Art of Praying*, 130.
182. Guardini, *The World and the Person*, 144.

A Door for God in the World

Guardini wants to image what it would mean to a person's destiny if that person was orientated to God in the way in which Christ speaks, and if the concern for the kingdom of God was central for him or her.[183] Such a person would be magnanimous, have an internal security and be tranquil in regard to all lesser values because of their focus on the ultimate.[184] Furthermore he or she would have a type of detachment. Guardini argues that the environment around such a person will be different because that person will not have the same degree of attachment and desire to fearfully hang on to things in this world and be a slave to its ways. He writes:

> Wisdom says that existence serves the man who does not need it; that the world bestows itself upon the man who is independent of it, and happiness is found by him who does not seek it.[185]

From this passage Guardini's point is clearer still. The attitude which can positively affect a person's destiny is that which has a focus on the things of God while maintaining an attitude of detachment for other values. In this way the environmental "pole" is drawn into a different and new relationship with the person thereby creating a new destiny since all things are transformed. For this is the beginning of the essential thing (*eigentlich*),[186] or rather the path to it. What is essential in living with Providence? It is, according to him, that which is to be found in Revelation. Furthermore, we are able to know from Revelation that possibilities for the world transcend the world itself. The individual human person has privilege with regard to the world. One can be a door for God to flow into the world.[187] He says:

> A man with the faith of which we have spoken forms as it were a portal of entrance for the creative power of God which is directed toward the world. . . . The world is not something ultimate but lies in the hand of God which shapes it. . . . The world constantly exists as a work of God's creative will; it is in a state of potentiality in relation to this will and obeys it. . . . Things

---

183. Guardini, *The World and the Person*, 193.
184. Guardini, *The World and the Person*, 193.
185. Guardini, *The World and the Person*, 194.
186. In the English translation of *The World and the Person*, the word *eigentlich* has been translated, "essential."
187. Guardini, *The World and the Person*, 195.

have, as scholastic philosophy says, a *potentia obedientialis* a potentiality of obedience in relation to every power which is really able to command whose possibilities cannot be measured beforehand.[188]

The person of faith lives in a world already full of possibilities, of potentiality known to God but not always to the human observer. God enables development of this potential, when the required conditions are present, through the believer. The believer's existence is central here because when a person loves God and focuses on the Kingdom of God, the potential (*potentia obedientialis*) of the world can be activated because circumstances around this person take on a new character.[189] According to Guardini, such a person helps the world to take a step towards developing the potential which lies within it so that it is moving towards being that world which is created for the child of God—the new creation.

Environment and Faith

The environment around a person of faith is different. The person of faith must make decisions which are important. Guardini has said that when a believer focuses on the Kingdom of God the reality around the believer will be transformed. Providence enables a person to experience Providence in the world. The "pole" of the "whole" is as important to that life as the subjective "pole" within the believer. Living in the world, the person is able to select which part he or she will interact with. In other words it is a chosen environment. The reality around the believer, the environment, is that which is: "selected from the world and given a form. It is part of that whole world which influences this particular person and also that which results from his activity. He is influenced by it and influences it in turn."[190] In other words, the believer is able to select with whom or what he or she will interact with and while the person's destiny is contained in this environment and the series of events, this too becomes a selection.[191] The selection is made by a person from the senses and the will, and the qualities

---

188. Guardini, *The World and the Person*, 195. In *The Lord's Prayer*, Guardini posits the possibility of bringing evil into the world, and not just good, but this time with an impure heart (i.e., a person could be a door for evil in the world).

189. Guardini, *The World and the Person*, 195.

190. Guardini, *The World and the Person*, 189.

191. Guardini, *The World and the Person*, 189.

of one's character. As one thing is accepted and another rejected, one is able to construct one's own environment. According to Guardini there is a type of play with the world in which the human person has a "centre of concern" with things further away at the borders which straddle the periphery, itself bordering the strange and unknown area. Guardini sees this area as that in which the individual is able to ward off the encroachment of the world or those elements which he or she does not choose to have. This aspect means that the environment will also have a varied effect on the person. Therefore Guardini holds that a person who is self assertive will be much more able to construct the environment according to their own choices and values than one who is less self-assertive[192] which means that a measure of self acceptance is important as well.[193] The type of environment one lives in is created externally and internally. To live completely from a heart filled with God is to live in an environment which helps to produce a positive effect in the "whole."

Conversely Guardini cites selfishness as the opponent of living with Providence:

> If a man is greedy and insecure in the depths of his nature, things about him behave differently than they do with a strong and unselfish person. If a man is always driven by personal motives, always intent on doing and attaining something, existence takes on a different character . . . than around a person who is disinterested yet living intensely. The person who loves has a different environment than the hard-hearted or envious one; the sincere and honest person a different environment than the liar and the cunning man; the magnanimous and candid person . . . (than) the narrow-minded or tyrannical one.[194]

Guardini illustrates his point by using an example of the ability to play an instrument and asserts that just as one man can take up an instrument to play and the instrument adapts well, another man may not establish that same rapport and the instrument may even break.[195] Since everything has a meaning of its own and in that sense a power, that same power can work positively or negatively according to the user.

---

192. Guardini, *The World and the Person*, 190.

193. Guardini developed this point well in a later work, *Die Annahme Seiner Selbst*. In that work he links self acceptance with the presence of Christ.

194. Guardini, *The World and the Person*, 191.

195. Guardini, *The World and the Person*, 191.

Human persons are children of God. Human decision and the guidance of God are important. Providence is not a passive acceptance of events, naturalism or something deterministic which is imposed on someone. That would be destiny or fate. The relationship with God has already been understood in the earlier chapter to be a type of loving covenant-style relationship. This relationship with God is lived out in a mutuality in which the human person is in God and God is in the human person. We have already argued in an earlier chapter that in Guardini's notion of Providence this way of living also constitutes a theosis; deifying participation in God's loving being. The relationship of the person to God enables a "new person" to develop. The new person is able to contribute to a "new creation" and the reality in the world emerges differently. We have argued that Guardini was concerned with Christian existence in the world and here we touch on Guardini's concept of living in a way in which the person's openness to God enables a new being to surround that person. A new structure of existence, the "New Heaven and the New Earth" comes into play around the person. The human minds, hearts and dignity must thrive, as the new existence comes into being. The order of Divine Providence comes from the heart of God and shines forth through human hearts.[196] In other words, the person lives from a new being; a new pattern that exists within, and because the person lives in openness to God, he or she is able to guide the Spirit from the heart of God into the world. *The relationship with God*, not adherence to order as such, enables the person to respond to God and where God is leading. As the person is one with God in love, grace surrounds the person and the order of Divine Providence shines forth from the human heart. This will be how Guardini is able to write that when person lives with Providence their destiny can change.[197]

Providence, Guardini has reminded us, is the totality of world events, having the governance of God its creator and director. Earlier, we referred to the interactive aspect of Providence as that which occurs in a world in which the human person has one pole within and the other pole externally in the world at large. Guardini brings these two realities together. The result comes as part of a faith response by the human person to place themselves, in responsibility, in harmony with the demands of the Sermon on the Mount and then the new existence will be formed as

---

196. Guardini, *The Lord's Prayer*, 77.
197. Guardini, *The World and the Person*, 193.

things around that person "behave differently." Consonantly, the meaning of the world around the person will be different because the motive for events is carried out in the context the love of the father for his child. The person, being transformed by the love of God the Father, is able to relate to things with the experience and the trust of a "child of God." The "new creation" is that which issues forth from this relationship. We said, above, that the relationship with God and the new creation arise in the context of the profound repentance felt by the creature. It is in this context, that Guardini can argue for the "new creation" as a consequence of purer faith and bolder love.[198] Faith and love are essential for living with Providence. Yet the Christian may have boundary experiences to which we now turn.

Religious Experience

Guardini puts boundary experiences with the experience of Christ within a person. Religious experience is integral to the movement towards the new creation. When one is reduced to an awareness of their own limits and the possibility of the "other," the most Holy God, one is able to experience the limit or boundary inherent in one's finite self. Guardini expresses it this way:

> I reach the true boundary only when I become interiorly conscious of the totality of my self standing in the totality of existence as such, and this is possible only religiously; that is, in such a way that I am reduced to my own limits, and defined as a finite being by the adjoining completely "other," the holy God.[199]

Guardini believes the same concept can be expressed psychologically as the depth or spark of the soul.[200] Yet, Guardini is explicit in his statement that only when the "Christ within us" is grasped by faith can the limits of our existence really be experienced. Therefore, for him the formation of the believer by Christ is a dynamic movement in which the believer is formed by "the constantly renewed self expression of Christ."[201] The movement from the immanence of God in Christ is also, for Guardini, an upward movement into transcendence, and is, furthermore, eschatological. In the consummation of the "new man" and the "new creation,"

---

198. Guardini, *The World and the Person*, 188.
199. Guardini, *The World and the Person*, 56.
200. Guardini, *The World and the Person*, 56.
201. Guardini, *The World and the Person*, 57.

polarities and time will no longer exist. Rather the wholeness will exist in immediacy. Guardini refers to this aspect which occurs, primarily in the Holy Spirit, as transfiguration.[202] Love abolishes the boundaries, making all things in God.[203]

Christian Responsibility

In Guardini's thought there is no dichotomy between God, the world and the human person. In other words there is a unity between all of these things and God who is also transcendent holds all things in God's being. The person who lives Providentially in relationship with God is open to the same Spirit of God which permeates creation. The Christian responsibility of the world is the proper province of the lay person, because a person's daily task is to be found in the being of the world as it is.[204] A person's daily task will be the will of God for that person and reveal to him or her, the future direction of that will. Guardini believes that the will of God does not hang above the world, but lies within its being as it is.[205] Furthermore:

> Responsibility for the world has been given to him as a Christian task. As a Christian, he must not only guard against the dangers of the world and "save his soul," but he saves his soul in providing that the world becomes right before God. In order to do that, he must see it as it is, and maintain himself in accordance with its possibilities. The will of God does not hang above the world but lies within it.[206]

Guardini's argument is existential and refers to living one's life as it comes. In the living of one's life, one may become aware of what is important and what must be done. Therefore Guardini argues that every

---

202. Guardini, *The World and the Person*, 60.
203. Guardini, *The World and the Person*, 60.
204. Guardini, *The World and the Person*, 26. The importance of human responsibility which emerges in a theology of covenant such as Guardini has, must be associated with Providence because God would act responsibly in the world. The notion of responsibility is even more important in the third period of Guardini's writing and we note here that the contemporary Jewish writer, Irving Greenberg, argues that in the Holocaust, God provided an opportunity for humans to uphold the human side of the covenantal relationship. See Greenberg, *For the Sake of Heaven and Earth*.
205. Guardini, *The World and the Person*, 26.
206. Guardini, *The World and the Person*, 25.

aspect of living life is important and writes that reflection on each day, and its tasks holds special significance. Guardini holds that the layman "represents the first and basic form of believer."[207] Furthermore, "the layman is in a particular manner related to the world, and the world is God's creation."[208] Therefore the vocation of the laity in their relationship with God lies in attending to the being of the world and taking responsibility for it. Here, then we see a re-emergence of an earlier priority, namely, the focus on the Kingdom of God.

The Kingdom of God

In *The Church and the Catholic*, which Guardini wrote in 1923, he wrote of the Kingdom of God. The text is quite foundational for his thinking on the subject, and Providence itself, and is therefore relevant in this chapter. We have seen that in that early article Guardini links Providence with the Kingdom of God, and identifies the experience of the Holy Spirit as axiomatic in forming this Kingdom. His vision in the early period is somewhat mystical. I argued that in Guardini's notion of the Kingdom of God there is a profound pneumatological element which points to the new creation and eschatological nature of Providence.

In the period of National Socialism Guardini develops his notion of Providence and the Kingdom of God further. In *The Lord's Prayer*, written in 1932, Guardini refers to this reality in another way. He writes that the kingdom of God is in the world and interwoven in human history.[209]

Guardini works from his belief that God is our fulfillment, yet in this passage he doesn't say that the Spirit of God is imposed on a person. Rather the person surrenders to God and God reigns in the person's heart and will with that person's consent. The person is sanctified by the holiness of Christ, not by their own efforts as such. The truth of God which illumines the mind and brings with it a meaning of the holy truth sustains a person and is so clear and fulfilling that the human person feels at

---

207. Guardini, *The World and the Person*, 25.

208. Guardini, *The World and the Person*, 25. We cannot say that Guardini advocates that only the priest follows Christ while the layperson has the world. In other writings, already mentioned, he makes clear the importance of following Christ for all believers and indeed his very Christological, even Christocentric theology is intended for all of his readers and hearers. This was in significant contrast to some Roman Catholic theology of the laity and "Catholic Action" at the time.

209. Guardini, *The Lord's Prayer*, 52.

one with it. As such, existence is transfigured by this immanent and most Holy God. Another concept is brought in here, namely, the assertion that God, in God's love and freedom, has forgiven sin and that the person is sanctified by the holiness of Christ. In short, the human person is fallible and in need but God in Christ can sanctify the person and God's truth illumines the mind[210] bringing with it an "open shining holy plenitude."[211] The human responsibility in this is that the human person surrenders his or her freedom to God.

Guardini chose not be too abstract in his writings and further on in the same chapter of *The Lord's Prayer*, in fidelity to his method of attending to the phenomenology of human lives, Guardini refers to this experience in a specifically concrete way. There he uses the example of the saints and, once again, St. Francis, to explain how the Kingdom of God might be lived in a human life. He says:

> The Kingdom of God surrounds Francis with openness, a holy nearness, a rich active fullness. . . . He is utterly human; he is human in a particularly beautiful and profound sense in that God works in him unhindered. But around him the world is different from what it is around others. The legends which are told of him—but is it so important whether the birds came to him or not; or whether the fishes listened to him; or the wolf of Gubbio laid its paw in his hand . . . ? But the fact that such things could be told of him is proof that around him everything was different from its ordinary self. For the kingdom of God had been able to reach him. . . . With him the kingdom of God was not something finished and arrested. With him too it was in a state of continuous coming; and if Francis had regarded himself as perfect, and had settled down to a state of fixed possession, he would have lost the most precious thing he had. The mysterious fullness which Christ calls the Kingdom of God streamed into him continually. And continually he opened himself to it and received it anew.[212]

---

210. Guardini is considered to be in a trajectory which includes St. Augustine and St. Bonaventure. Guardini wrote on both of their works. Here, then, we see the influence of St. Augustine and St. Bonaventure who both believed that spiritual knowledge occurs when the truth of God illumines the mind. See St. Bonaventure, *Journey of the Mind into God*.

211. Guardini, *The Lord's Prayer*, 41.

212. Guardini, *The Lord's Prayer*, 58.

In using this example, Guardini wants to encourage his readers to surrender to God and allow God's Spirit to flow through them into the world in the same way as St. Francis did. This passage, testifies to the way in which Guardini will not allow the theology to remain at a theoretical level and shows how he brings in the practical, educational aspect to balance it.

The Kingdom of God and the Environment

Speaking from Christ's words on the Sermon on the Mount, Guardini notes that Providence is the involvement of the Living God in each individual life. God wants to look after that person. Here Guardini is able to clarify further his understanding of what it means to "seek the Kingdom of God." A person must care for the Kingdom of God and God will care for that person. In order to do that one must think judge and act in accordance with Christ. They must make God's concerns their concerns. Although Providence may seem elusive if a person focuses on the Kingdom of God and not God's Providence there is a good reason for that. When a person lets go of everything permanent and fixed they can enter into a new understanding with God to care for God's kingdom and God will care for them in a special way. We saw that from his earliest writings on the subject, Guardini presents the view that a person's being may change when, in the surrender to God who acts, the love of God floods the being of that person and changes him or her. It is important to note that Guardini is not advocating a natural process here or an imposition on a person by an acting God. Rather there is a co-operative process in which the human person in surrender and relationship to God shares in God's life. In the example from St. Francis' life, it is possible to envisage a further assertion that Guardini is making, namely that when a person's life changes a new being surrounds that person. This new holy being not only brings God's Spirit to the things of the world but God gives the gift of a new special protection, namely, holy care which surrounds that person. The early work on St. Francis was foundational for the work written in this period of National Socialism in which Guardini continues this assertion. At that time Guardini recommended thinking only of good outcomes as the answer to fears that one might have in a city besieged with bombs and other acts of aggression. In the 1939 book *The World and the Person*, we are able to see an example of this in Guardini's notion of Providence when he writes:

> [T]he message of providence seems to be as follows: "believe in the God who discloses himself to you in the revelation and is quite different from the <u>nous</u> of the Stoics or the world-spirit of some religious experience, the God who is the Father in heaven, hidden in his own nature and only revealed by Christ. Take into your thought and mind, as the thing of supreme importance, the new possibility of existence which he offers, His "kingdom"; and place yourself in harmony with Him in concern for this kingdom, as it is expressed in the petitions of the Lord's Prayer, "Thy kingdom come," "Thy will be done." Then this kingdom will take shape around you and you yourself will receive what you need for your life. Notice that it does not say depend on the course of events.[213]

Thus, the new existence offered by God is God's kingdom. Guardini is opposed to any notion of Providence that envisages a passive response of resignation to the course of events.[214] Such an attitude, as shown above, would be more akin to Guardini's idea of destiny. On the other hand, to be pre-occupied with personal security is to be distracted and serving "two masters" (the world and God).[215] Rather, a person's focus is to be God's concerns and interests so that the world around that person will be transformed. Zachary Hayes notes that Guardini's focus on the kingdom of God enables human transcendence while the person remains in this world. Such a person doesn't become "other worldly" as such but experiences the conversion from a self-centered world to a God centered one.[216] Guardini argues, "The laws of existence will put themselves at your service; events will happen and things will turn out as is good for you."[217] Living with Providence, as we saw above, is concerned with having a transformed existence and assisting with the formation of the new creation. Guardini envisages that the believer will have a new hierarchy of values; a new set of priorities and concerns. The focus of that person's

---

213. Guardini, *The World and the Person*, 187.

214. Such as the words, "One can't do anything about it" in the face of social difficulties. Krieg notes that in the National Socialist period in Germany, many people felt a sense of social impotence.

215. Guardini, *The World and the Person*, 187.

216. Hayes, *Visions of a Future*, 50.

217. Guardini, *The World and the Person*, 187. Guardini's "good for you," is not necessarily that which is better in terms of "this world" benefits. There were, arguably, good people who acted in accordance with God's will at that time and were still executed or imprisoned.

life will be different because he or she will have a different relationships to people and things. The person is able to begin to live from a new paradigm. The new paradigm refers to the order of being yet Providence in this sense is not ready made or a hidden order to be discovered, but something "in the process of becoming."[218] In other words it will be formed at that time, in relationship with God, with the cooperation of the human person and according to the choices which that person makes. On the other hand, the presence of grace involves an inwardness. Thus the new creation is a world which is permeated with the grace of God. The human person living with Providence and God's guidance can live in conformity with God's guidance of the world.

In *The World and the Person*, published in the year the second World War commenced (1939), he writes that Providence may "consist in denying us immediate necessities. . . . Providence means the Providence of that God who knows not only what we think we need but what we really need."[219] Guardini considers our existence to be safer in the hands of God, in God's wisdom, than in our own. "His standards are divine; that means that the course of our destiny takes ways which are incomprehensible to us."[220] Guardini believes that this statement does not refer to fatalism but to the mystery of God's Providential action. Faith and confidence are the way to live with this action. Nevertheless, Guardini asserts, "the true purpose of Providence is not that man may prosper in time but that "the Kingdom of God" may come and his justice may be fulfilled: that the new creation and the man of eternity may be perfected."[221] This aspect of the Kingdom of God includes individual Providence and Providence of the whole and refers to the eschatological nature of providence in his writings, which will be developed further in the next period.

Conclusion

In chapter 4, *theme one* focused on the way Jesus Christ understood Providence which is a work of the Holy Spirit. The care of God is paramount and the God-loving person results from this. In *theme two*, Providence in relationship with God, Guardini developed his notion of the

---

218. Guardini, *The World and the Person*, 188.
219. Guardini, *The World and the Person*, 198.
220. Guardini, *The World and the Person*, 198.
221. Guardini, *The World and the Person*, 199.

I-Thou relation and development of the person. Sharing in the life of God is through Christ who dwells in the Christian person. In *theme three* the notion of person was developed to show how a person can live with integrity and the notion of human will is explored. Predestination was considered in this section with Guardini asserting that God would want the human will to be brought into the decision for salvation (or lack of it). In *theme four* Guardini showed how nature, of itself determinist, must be distinguished from creation.

5

Guardini's Writing on Providence after 1945 and Analysis

Introduction

THE FINAL PERIOD OF this study begins after the War and takes us to the end of Guardini's life. His major writings of interest to his study of Providence in this period[1] will be considered according to the same themes we have drawn out in the other chapters. In his book, *The End of the Modern World*, written in 1950, Guardini presents a picture of the world as it had become. His vision could be seen as pessimistic. Yet Guardini wants to look to a world of hope. He shows how earlier ages were a continuation of the time of Christ as the society adapted to changes in the world in certain ways. However in the time Guardini was writing everything was changing and those links of continuity of the past were going. He writes that the new world will be one which has few continuities with the past. Rather, everything will be completely different and a person needs to trust in God's Providence because there will be nothing else.

Guardini notes:

> Perhaps love will obtain an intimacy and harmony never known until this day. Perhaps it will gain what lies hidden in the key words of the providential message of Jesus that things are

---

1. *Freedom, Grace, and Destiny*; *The End of the Modern World*; "Living Freedom"; *Power and Responsibility*; *Gebet und Wahrheit* (first preached as a university sermon); *The Wisdom of the Psalms*.

transformed for the man who makes God's will for His Kingdom his first concern (Matthew vi,33).²

In an Introduction to *The End of the Modern World*, the distinguished American philosopher, Frederick D. Wilhelmsen, writes, "Guardini has dispelled the fog of secularization; he has cleared the air; he has shown us rising within our very midst the world which is to come. He offers us faith, neither in man nor in history, but in God alone and in His Providence."³ Guardini writes:

> Here too we dare to hope. This trust is not based at all upon an optimism or confidence either in a universal order of reason or in a benevolent principle inherent to nature. It is based in God Who really is Who alone is efficacious in His Action. It is based in this simple trust: that God is a God who acts and who everywhere prevails.⁴

God acts and is Omnipresent. With his prophetic ability to envisage the future Guardini has not lost hope in God's Providence. It is a timely message and one which led him into further reflection on the uses of power in the aftermath of the war.

A year after he published *The End of the Modern World*, Guardini published a sequel to the book called, *Power and Responsibility*. It was a timely reflection on the ills of the National Socialist period. He saw that power could have a constructive side to it. Yet he didn't leave his readers smarting with pain. He suggested a way forward. He knew that there are many deceptive things in the Modern World. He writes that a real piety is possible: "The mind which considers reality not from any subjective *a priori*, but purely objectively, ... to discover that finiteness is also createdness. It has been prepared to grasp the revealed nature of everything that is, and from there to reach a decisive affirmation of Biblical Revelation."⁵ The piety which Guardini believes is necessary would arise in that situation and would no longer be: "operating in a separate realm of psychological interiority or religious idealism, but within reality, a reality which because complete, is also the reality created, sustained, and willed by God."⁶

2. Guardini, *The End of the Modern World*, 109.
3. Wilhelmsen, "Introduction," in Guardini, *The End of the Modern World*, XIII.
4. Guardini, *The End of the Modern World*, 107.
5. Guardini, *Power and Responsibility*, 89.
6. Guardini, *Power and Responsibility*, 90.

Guardini believes that type of clarity of vision would enable a person to see through the illusions which the scientific or technological world might produce including the "'liberal's', the idolatry of culture, totalitarian's utopia, the tragicists's pessimism"[7] and other ways of looking at things. Guardini argues against a "new Sparta"[8] saying that the new person may come from many walks of life but should not be praised for toughness alone:

> All too many in Germany fell victim not so long ago to the "heroic" ideals of "fanatical will" "dogged determination," "ruthless sacrifice"! Those who tossed these slogans about were not strong but weak.... And if they actually were fearless in the face of danger, it was because for them the spirit counted as nothing. The strength we mean comes from the spirit, from heart's voluntary surrender; that is why it nurtures all that is known as reverence, magnanimity, goodness, considerateness, interiority.[9]

The way forward according to Guardini entails allegiance to the sovereign Lord, creator of all being, who called man into existence and sustains him in that vocation, who gave the world into his keeping and who will demand an account of what he has done with it.[10] He reminds his readers that "Freedom does not consist in following our own personal or political predilections, but in doing what is required by the essence of things."[11]

At the end of *Power and Responsibility*, he suggested to his readers that it would be good to recapture a contemplative attitude in order to reawaken the depths of a person. In accordance with his earlier work, linked to Providence, he wants them to contemplate, to pray to be still. He wants people to feel conscious of their responsibility for the world. Above all he wants them to know: "what the sick world needs is *a metanoia*, a conversion, a reappraisal of our whole attitude towards life, accompanied by a fundamental change in the "climate" in which people and things are appraised."[12] We turn now to a more detailed treatment of the themes in which Guardini draws on the experience of the war years for a new time.

---

7. Guardini, *Power and Responsibility*, 90.
8. Guardini, *Power and Responsibility*, 88.
9. Guardini, *Power and Responsibility*, 88.
10. Guardini, *Power and Responsibility*, 93.
11. Guardini, *Power and Responsibility*, 94.
12. Guardini, *Power and Responsibility*, 96.

With regard to the theme of Providence, there is development in the treatment of these themes that is consonant with the fact that Guardini is reflecting on the whole experience of the Nazi period from the fresh, post war perspective.[13] There is development in this period as he reflects on power and relates Providence to the judgement and justice. Actual Providence ends at the end of a person's life but it doesn't end for the God of Providence who will then answer the questions a person may have had in his or her life. The period effectively ends in 1963 with his last major writing on Providence, although in 1965 Guardini wrote *The Church of the Lord* where he reflected on the Church in the period between that time and his early book, *The Church and the Catholic*, showing the insights of the mature Guardini who had lived as a priest through one of the most difficult periods of German history. Because of illness, Guardini wrote very little from this point until his death in 1968, although previously unpublished writings continued to be published. At the end of this chapter a very short section will consider two of his last texts, which are relevant to our study. These texts effectively bookend the work which began with the 1916 text. Both texts stand alone yet are significant in the overall corpus studied in this thesis and affirm Guardini's ability to work independently yet in dialogue with the social context.

In relation to the first theme, Jesus Christ and Providence, we see in this period how Guardini sets Providence at the opposite pole from destiny. In Providence in relationship with God in the world, we see Guardini considering human freedom at length. In the third theme, the importance of the individual to God, Guardini writes of justice and judgement in the fulfillment of all things. Finally, Guardini writes of the place of God's grace under the fourth theme, New Existence and New Creation as he writes of the world as God's creation and focuses on the Kingdom of God. From this vantage point he reflects on the Holocaust and other atrocities of the Second World War. We turn, now, to our first theme.

Theme 1: Jesus Christ and Providence

We have argued that in the period of National Socialism Guardini's work was very Christocentric as he wrote about the way JESUS understood Providence. Now in this period we see the way Guardini not only explores

---

13. The social situation in Germany at this time has been written about in chapter 2.

how Jesus understood Providence, but how he lived a life completely guided by God the Father. Guardini shows how destiny was transformed in the life of Christ who thus provides an example to believers whose destiny can likewise be transformed in the life of faith. Before turning to the experience of destiny in the life of Christ, we will take a closer look at Guardini's view of destiny in the life of human persons.

Providence and Destiny in Human Existence

In a very extensive footnote in *Freedom, Grace, and Destiny*, Guardini draws attention to the use of the notion of destiny by the National Socialist regime. According to him it was linked to the Germanic notion of destiny and the this-worldly concept of Nietzsche. Bravery in the face of destiny was presented by them as a counterbalance to what they saw as Jewish calculation and Christian tender-heartedness. The National Socialists thought that the new man should be ready to encounter danger and thus rise to new planes of being in accepting destiny. The notion was used as a tool to manipulate the people who, according to Guardini, eventually had a collective psychosis. "When the leaders eventually had to face destiny themselves . . . they displayed a shamelessness without parallel. . . . [T]he whole belief in 'destiny' had been nothing but a cynical will to power."[14]

As human persons, we experience Providence while in this world, not only in the afterlife. We have argued that "world" in Guardini's understanding is always experienced world. That is to say, Providence in existence is experienced in an interactive world. In order to look at the way Jesus Christ dealt with Providence Guardini draws attention to the normal human condition and, in particular, the struggle of existence. His argument is important because Jesus was also human. Guardini's description of destiny is important to an understanding of his nuanced overall position. It will be seen that destiny (as unredeemed existence) and fate are synonymous for Guardini.[15] Redeemed existence, is destiny that is transformed, or is being transformed, in the life of faith and becomes Providence.

Guardini notes that many people consider destiny as a kind of force. In *Freedom, Grace, and Destiny*, Guardini polarizes Providence

---

14. Guardini, *Freedom, Grace, and Destiny*, 186.
15. Although Guardini continues to use the word destiny even for the life of Christ.

with destiny. What is destiny for Guardini? Destiny is "the impersonal *par excellence*. . . . [Destiny] knows neither justice nor wisdom, neither reverence nor goodness, but seems to provide a ground for that which is cold, indifferent and meaningless, and even for evil."[16]

Furthermore, asserts Guardini, destiny presents itself to the human person as a power and mystery. It is something that the person feels cannot be completely controlled. Yet, he notes, some people do try to control destiny. Indeed, some people consider destiny itself as task.[17] One may try to control destiny with fatalism,[18] stoicism[19] or humour.[20] Since many people experience destiny as a kind of force, the experience is considered to have a lack of human choice.

Guardini notes that "Destiny is the impact of reality upon myself."[21] He sees the possibility of destiny occurring in one of three different ways, conscious, unconscious and subconscious. It is not only that which confronts a person destiny "proceeds also from man himself."[22] Therefore it doesn't only have an outer aspect but also has an inner aspect which we will consider in some detail. While Guardini considers that destiny could be overwhelmingly influential and have a religious character about it, for him, destiny *per se* is negative. It is not the plan of God for a person's life. Yet a person can act to direct his or her own life. He writes, "I am actively engaged in creating my destiny in so far as I select and direct the events

---

16. Guardini, *Freedom, Grace, and Destiny*, 188.

17. Guardini, *Freedom, Grace, and Destiny*, 185. He argues that such people search for the intention of destiny and the existence of human persons in the concrete situation. Those who take this approach attempt to master destiny by recognizing a structure and responsibility in it. This means that when things go well, destiny as task can imbue its proponents with a sense of confidence but when not, all that is left is resignation which gives neither a way forward nor sense of meaning.

18. *Fatalism* here refers to an active tragic situation which purports to offer self-fulfillment because the goal was adhered to. Guardini notes that Nietzche's "amor fati" adopts such a pattern. Guardini, *Freedom, Grace, and Destiny*, 182.

19. By *Stoicism*, Guardini means that a person may reserve his or her own self as the last stronghold that will not submit. Such a person renounces all possibility of blessing from outside his or herself. He or she is able to stand strong in the face of enormous suffering. Guardini, *Freedom, Grace, and Destiny*, 183.

20. For another type of person, *Humour* provides the way of coping with the realities of destiny. Guardini's definition of such a person is one who may suffer, but has the capacity to use humour to transcend the world process with liberty and love and "hidden capacity for enjoyment." Guardini, *Freedom, Grace, and Destiny*, 184.

21. Guardini, *Freedom, Grace, and Destiny*, 163.

22. Guardini, *Freedom, Grace, and Destiny*, 163.

which come my way."[23] From this departure point, Guardini is able to show the way that Christian existence can transform a person so that he or she, with the guidance of God, gradually lives with Providence rather than destiny and can be open to God's plan for his or her life. The transformation is not immediate and therefore the person lives with some of the dispositions of the "old" person while the transformation is occurring.[24] Guardini believes choice and decision, in faith (and Grace), can transform destiny to become Providence. It is important for Guardini's overall view of destiny and Providence that he shows how some things are inevitable and must be accepted and other things are able to occur through choice so that destiny may be overcome. This process involves concepts that Guardini calls "fact" and the "spiritual element." Guardini uses the concept of "fact" to show how choice is important to Providence living and the possibility of not just accepting destiny or fate. What does Guardini mean by "fact"?

Human Decision

Guardini uses the term "fact" to distinguish events from destiny or fate from events that are chosen by the person. The term "fact" is a much-debated term in philosophy referring to something which is actual or true as distinct from a theory or value. It can mean the ontological difference between what is and what ought to be. Guardini defines "fact," as those things which are not necessary or pre-determining but are the result of human conditions and decisions of either the person themselves or of someone else which then impinge on that person's overall destiny.

Fact is: "everything which cannot be seen to exist necessarily but does exist de facto; in other words, fact is everything that proceeds from freedom. It is done because the agent wills it. . . . Facts continually emerge from my individual life. The words I utter, the gestures I bring about—these are facts."[25] Fact, unlike necessity, involves human choice. According to Guardini, human persons create their own patterns, which emerge as "fact"; and the way in which such patterns develop can say something about that person. In this way, Guardini is able to develop his assertion mentioned in the previous chapter of this thesis, that human persons are

---

23. Guardini, *Freedom, Grace, and Destiny*, 163.
24. Guardini, *Freedom, Grace, and Destiny*, 207.
25. Guardini, *Freedom, Grace, and Destiny*, 157.

artisans of their own fortunes. Here Guardini has linked human choice with freedom. The human person is able to will something and do it. "Fact" is able to help construct the experiential world the person lives in. The attitudes and activities of each person are closely related. He considers them to be determined by an inner form which he calls an "entelechy"[26] and is based upon the individual personality with further development by education and experience. Thus "Fact" is integral to Guardini's argument for allowing destiny to turn into redeemed destiny or Providence although "Fact," the internal 'entelechy' and the ability to choose are not the only aspects of human direction. Ultimately the spiritual element, to which we now turn, is decisive.

The Spiritual Element

Guardini considers that the spiritual element is able to:

> precede the individual's self-expression and self-development. Continuously and effectively it fashions interior and exterior attitudes and fashions both the individual and his *Umwelt*.[27] The process is not purely natural as with a plant or animal. Man has a spiritual element so that this form is not only the principle form from which he operates but also a task to be fulfilled.[28]

The Spiritual element is not finished until the human person takes action but it is integral to Providence as it is lived individually and communally. Although notoriously imprecise in defining this "element" Guardini argues that the spiritual element enables destiny to be overcome. He

---

26. *Entelechy* is a philosophical term from the Greek, *entelecheia*—the realization of potential into actual. In other philosophies, the term, entelechy, refers to the process by which things become their own highest expression—it can refer to the condition of a thing whose essence is fully realized or a vital force which directs a thing towards its own self fulfillment. *Encylcopedia Brittanica Online*, s.v. "Entelechy," accessed October, 24, 2014, http://www.britannica.com/EBchecked/topic/188810/entelechy; The Free Dictionary, s.v. "Entelechy," accessed October, 24, 2014, http://www.thefreedictionary.com/entelechy.

27. Environment. The translator has left the German word in place in the English translation. *Umwelt* means environment and according to the translator includes things or objects which exist to serve his or her purposes. *Mitwelt*, she says is the world in which the person exists with other human beings. See Guardini, *Freedom, Grace, and Destiny*, 165.

28. Guardini, *Freedom, Grace, and Destiny*, 166.

links this with freedom, conscience and morality.[29] Freedom is necessary for self realization to occur. He sees the spiritual element as presenting the individual with a kind of struggle yet this element is important for one's overall destiny:

> In man . . . self realisation belongs to freedom. His essential form is therefore the basis of his reality and his purpose. It must be fulfilled through conquest, superficial elements must be sacrificed to deeper factors crises have to be sustained and tensions resolved. Freedom can face these demands or run away from them; it can correspond with this essential form of life or do violence to it. . . . it becomes a living conscience which lays down the right rule of behaviour, attaches a moral value to it and recognises guilt when it is unfaithful to it, and attempts to punish or compensate for it.[30]

The spiritual dimension of a person, also responsible for the formation of conscience, is only fulfilled by overcoming superficial things which would draw a person away from that which is deeper. Conscience is an important part of choice. Guardini believes formation of conscience reveals a condition of things which, revelation shows, can only be explained through the doctrine of original sin and its consequences.[31] The spiritual element is a task to be fulfilled and is not finished. The task is "in process" or in the process of "becoming." In other words, development of the spiritual aspect of a person will continue. The inner form of a person must be informed by the spiritual. Yet, the self is also significant because human choice enables human persons to fashion their own "world." Freedom allows a person to transcend the mere notion of necessity and enter the world of free thought and imagination where depth is also possible. In freedom the person as "person" is able to live from the "blue-print" of a social existence while retaining the capacity to exist-within-oneself and to belong to oneself.[32] Spiritual development occurs in this context.[33] Decision making and integrity, while human and individual, is nevertheless informed by the spiritual being of a person. Thus, the spiritual

---

29. Freedom is an important concept for Guardini in this period and will be developed below.

30. Guardini, *Freedom, Grace, and Destiny*, 167.

31. Guardini, *Freedom, Grace, and Destiny*, 167.

32. Guardini, *Freedom, Grace, and Destiny*, 175.

33. This task, it will be argued later, is most effectively done in relationship with Christ.

element is crucial in the overcoming of destiny and openness to Providence. Choices involve a socio-psychological attitude and a spiritual one. We are now in a position to evaluate the life of Christ. Turning to the life of Christ we ask if he overcame destiny.

Destiny and Providence in the Life of Christ

Considering the life of Christ Guardini noted that Jesus is bound by all of the necessities of existence that we as human persons experience. Yet, he possessed an intense awareness of himself as Redeemer and sense of responsibility as Messiah; his consciousness was that of fulfilling and transforming history. Furthermore, whilst he wielded considerable power, shown in his mastery over nature and insight into the hearts of human persons, he existed in restricted circumstances.[34] In Gethsemane, Guardini notes, we are able to witness the severity of his experience. His victory over Satan in the accounts of his temptation shows that he never employs his powers to break through the barriers which have been imposed on him. Guardini also considers the various people who dealt with Jesus. He finds many of them defective. For example, both Pilate, and Jesus' own disciples, were weak in some way. Pilate washed his hands of the situation, and the disciples were unable to find a way to persuade the people to support Jesus.[35] Guardini writes of these things and adds, "throughout it all, humanly speaking, runs a disturbing strain, that is haphazard and meaningless."[36] Guardini attributes this aspect to evil. He says, "And Jesus evidently recognizes, amid these human and historical factors another lurking factor, the 'power of darkness', operating its own hidden evil."[37] If Jesus' life is transformational for us we may ask how Jesus handled such evil. How can we understand destiny in Christ's life?

Christ's Way of Addressing Evil

Guardini believes that in normal human existence one encounters evil. Christ's human existence was no exception. Guardini records that Jesus'

---

34. Guardini, *Freedom, Grace, and Destiny*, 189.

35. Guardini, *Freedom, Grace, and Destiny*, 190. None of these people used their own power of choice in a way that benefitted Jesus.

36. Guardini, *Freedom, Grace, and Destiny*, 190.

37. Guardini, *Freedom, Grace, and Destiny*, 190.

awareness of Satan goes hand in hand with his mission.[38] At one point, Jesus speaks of Satan as "prince of this world"[39] and recognizes that there is an evil order of things and relationships. "Satan possesses a real power in the world, a dominion over men and things. He is not as Dualists urge, an evil principle who constructed the world together with the good principle[40] but a creature of God, originally good but who in sinning became evil."[41] In fidelity to the Scriptural account in Genesis, Guardini believes that the power, concealed behind many things in this world, has been given to Satan because of humanity's disobedience to God at the first fall:

> Thus Satan is a ruler of a "kingdom" that permeates the whole of existence and influences all behaviour. This means . . . that he is active at the very source of destiny. The element of malice, evil and coldness we have mentioned is his will. Its intention is to dethrone God, to construct a world that no longer belongs to God. . . . [H]e tempts man to concentrate on himself, to transfer his allegiance to himself.[42]

In this present world, as in the beginning, the devil wants to dethrone God and make it his world and he does this by encouraging a person to focus on him or herself before transferring all allegiance to that self. Guardini links evil with the notions of autonomy and heteronomy referred to earlier. He believes that allegiance to self becomes sheer autonomy and selfishness. Conversely, as argued in chapter 2, if one transfers personal allegiance to something or someone outside of one's self, it is called heteronomy and doesn't allow the person to be guided by the deepest center of his or her being. With either of these alternatives, one cannot be true to one's own being.[43] Christ did not fall into this trap and was *not* untrue to his own being. His pattern of life has shown the way

38. Guardini, *Freedom, Grace, and Destiny*, 201.

39. Guardini, *Freedom, Grace, and Destiny*, 202.

40. Guardini, *Freedom, Grace, and Destiny*, 202. We have referred elsewhere to Guardini's assertion that evil is not the opposite of Good. The polarities of this world should not refer to an equal balance between Good and evil. Evil has no rightful place in this world.

41. Guardini, *Freedom, Grace, and Destiny*, 202.

42. Guardini, *Freedom, Grace, and Destiny*, 202. This point will be taken up more fully below.

43. For more about autonomy and heteronomy see the section in *The Person and the World*. To be true to one's own being, a person, ideally, is a *Theonom* (not an *autonom* or *heteronom*), giving allegiance to God through one's own being. This act is effected through Jesus Christ.

human persons can be true to their (God given) being. Yet, we may ask if Christ had a sense of his own destiny?

Guardini holds that there was no sense of destiny in the consciousness of Jesus. He writes:

> What happened to Jesus is unnatural, painful, destructive, yet it is not alien to but in a curious way familiar to Him. Right to the end He does all He can, in the spirit of His mission, to bring things to a right conclusion, but we have no impression of a special conflict with its flow, its possible victory or defeat. Nor can one say that He passively allows events to overwhelm Him; He lets them approach and takes them to His own heart, but it is not as if He—in the sense of *amor fati*[44]—decided to assent even to the most terrifying fate. It is rather as though everything is gathered into a personal relationship, and here we approach what in Him is unique. . . . The force that is operating is no "power," no metaphysical or mythical "something," but always and entirely a person. . . . "His Father" so entirely and exclusively His that He associates no man, however dear to Him, with this relationship . . . the Absolute that for its own part embraces the world.[45]

Christ's very personal relationship with God enabled him to live from the strength of the Spirit of God which pervades the world. There is harmony in his relationship with God as all events including the horrifying, destructive and painful ones, are taken into the heart of Jesus and become part of his personal relationship with God the Father. Experiences, in this world, are not lived apart from the love of God. Guardini writes:

> Whatever exists lies within His Divine-human consciousness and his relation to the Father that fulfils it. With His Father, Jesus' relation is that of one who is sent and is obedient: not like a creature whose insight and judgement lie outside God's designing mind, but on a plane of equality which is sharply emphasised (John 8:25–30, 42–47, 54–59 etc.,) . . . A fundamental harmony exists between Jesus and the Father.[46]

Thus, while Christ's life could have been subject to the cold pattern of destiny, it is lived in relationship with his Father and therefore

---

44. Guardini's dialogue partner, Nietzsche, used the term *amor fati*, love of fate, to argue for acceptance of destiny (see n18 above).

45. Guardini, *Freedom, Grace, and Destiny*, 193.

46. Guardini, *Freedom, Grace, and Destiny*, 193.

actualized in harmony as love.⁴⁷ "The mysterious element in destiny which may at times seem an absence or even denial of meaning vanishes in this harmony."⁴⁸ We, human persons, are imperfect and fail to live in accordance with God's intention. Conversely, when we live in relationship to God and in harmony with God's will, expressed as love, we know Providence. Guardini writes: "The manner in which events enter into the life of Jesus and are experienced by Him is not 'destiny' in any normal meanings. It seems impossible to find a positive name for it, since this would suppose a full understanding of His mind. It acquires a proper name only when the believer participates in it; then it is known as providence."⁴⁹

Christ's uniqueness consisted in His ability to remain in the will of God and stand strong. He was faithful to the filial love which occurs in harmony with his Father. In this way the filial harmony is borne out as the love of the "redeemer for the world." Jesus was able to make atonement for people's sins because he remained in His Father's will. Furthermore, this action was able to alter Satan's relation to the world:⁵⁰

> Despite the ferocity of the "power of darkness" unleashed against Him, Jesus remained in the Father's will and thus made atonement for men's sins. From that point onwards, Satan has no further direct power over things; and only so much over men as they give him because of their disposition or, correspondingly, what God permits for the working out of sacred history.⁵¹ . . . Christ's word, however stands guarantor that the believer, who entrusts himself to faith, is held firm and secure in Redemption.⁵²

47. Guardini, *Freedom, Grace, and Destiny*, 194.
48. Guardini, *Freedom, Grace, and Destiny*, 199.
49. Guardini, *Freedom, Grace, and Destiny*, 204.
50. The important thing for Guardini is that Jesus' loving relationship with God enabled him to remain in the Father's will, not that he accepted the cross in a fatalistic (Nietzchean) sense as such. In other words, if Jesus had not been rejected by those he came for, he could have continued his mission on earth, and his filial love would have been borne out in that way. Guardini holds that in such a situation, humanity would have come to its fullness at that time and would not be, in contemporary language, in an "already but not yet" situation.
51. Guardini holds that God allows some sinful action for the working out of sacred history. Guardini, *Freedom, Grace, and Destiny*, 204. This is evil in the service of God although, presumably, the perpetrators don't know that it is and perform it for their own needs.
52. Guardini, *Freedom, Grace, and Destiny*, 204.

By remaining in harmony with the Father's love, Christ overcame the direct power of Satan. In this sense Guardini refuses to say that Christ experienced destiny in the afore mentioned sense of uncontrollable fate. That is to say, Christ did not succumb to a controlling pattern of existence, he did not experience his existence as being dominated by mystery, and he therefore did not need to adopt popular ways of overcoming destiny. Rather, by his faithful action, Christ established a redeemed existence.[53] Christ's action is not only an example to human persons. Christ actually redeems. How does that occur?

Redemption by God in Christ

Guardini believes redemption occurs though the action of God taking our destiny upon Godself. This is done through the action of Christ. Thus he is able to argue that human destiny, is finally taken up by God in Christ. Redemption by Christ enables the human person to be transformed by and in God. Christ enables the believer to live according to God's will and when the believer participates in Christ's action, it is called Providence.[54] Thus Guardini's assertion indicates behavior that is far from a purely autonomous action. Relationship with Christ, and God, are central. Guardini's highly Christological position on destiny may be summarized thus, that Christ was not just an ordinary man who happened to partake of the Spirit of God to an extraordinary degree.[55] On the other hand God was not just an uninvolved God who rested after the act of creation (as some Deists believe), nor is God just the impersonal original ground of all being with everything in the world as the material expression of God's essence. Rather, God freely *chose* to enter into history in the form of Jesus Christ, in order to take human destiny upon God'sself. In *The Lord*, Guardini had written:

> Revelation's account of the incarnation and the relation of God to the world is something fundamentally different. According to the Bible, God entered into time in a specific manner, acting

---

53. Guardini, *Freedom, Grace, and Destiny*, 205. While obedience is clearly important in Christ's action, this obedience is to God. Guardini, it will be shown below, takes a cautious view in relation to secular or social obedience, asserting that too much adherence to rules or authority can work against Providence because God's ways are not always known.

54. Guardini, *Freedom, Grace, and Destiny*, 204.

55. This assertion also addresses potential Adoptionist notions of Christ.

on an autocratic decision made in complete freedom. The free, eternal God has no destiny which is a matter for mortals living in history. What is meant is that God entered into history, thus taking destiny upon himself.[56]

(The destiny which Guardini refers to here is the destiny of humanity which was addressed by Christ in his cross and resurrection.) God in Christ took destiny upon God's-self at that time.[57] That is to say that, the responsibility of history was taken up by God. In that sense we could say that to look at history is to look at God. God has assumed history's guilt. This assertion will enable Guardini to argue that conversion of the whole person to God, through Christ, is necessary if the person is to live a life of Providence and change his or her destiny. A person does not do this in his or her own strength.[58] Redemption is completely effected by Christ who lived his earthly life so completely in the power of the Holy Spirit of God that his own being became Spirit. Guardini holds that the Pneuma abolishes earthly-historical existence as an entity in itself. Christ's existence is completely directed to God. God the Father directs the being of the believer to Christ, and out from him in a gradually, redeemed existence. For Guardini this is Providence in the proper sense.[59] We turn, now, to the details of a person's relationship with God in Providence living.

Theme 2: Providence Occurs in Relationship with God— in the World

As noted in the introduction to this chapter, an important aspect of this theme in the post war period is Guardini's extensive treatment of persons within the context of our relationship with God. Integral to his

---

56. Guardini, *The Lord*, 15.

57. G. C. Berkouwer would argue that "Providence does not remove the seriousness of history, it charges history with responsibility." Berkouwer, *The Providence of God*, 198. Guardini's position would be concurrent with this view. We recall that for him, the laity are responsible for the world.

58. We argued in the previous chapter that Providence exists when a person participates in the existence of Jesus and lives from the existentiality of Christ. In *The World and the Person*, Guardini showed how Christ was able to transform the human person's being and change them from within.

59. Guardini, *Freedom, Grace, and Destiny*, 206. Here we understand Guardini's intention as referring to God in Christ and God the Holy Spirit but we recall the criticism referred to earlier that his pneumatology is too Christocentric.

understanding of the relationship with God, is the relationship with Christ in the Holy Spirit. Thus we will note a clear Trinitarian dimension to Guardini's account of our relationship with God in this period. Yet freedom is integral to this relationship and is so important to Guardini's developed notion of Providence that consideration of the way Guardini nuanced his exploration of freedom is now in order.

Free Activity and Human Choice

Guardini juxtaposes freedom with human action to consider freedom in a number of different ways including freedom in act and content, freedom in the realization of values, freedom and power, freedom in personal relationship, freedom in solitude, moral freedom, and sacred initiative. The aforementioned notion of choice comes in here and will be considered below. The philosophy of Immanuel Kant is no longer the main issue for Guardini in this period as it was earlier. His dialogue partners and those he wants to argue against are Nietzsche, Schliermacher, and other philosophers such as the Actualists and Pragmatists, all of whom, have defective ways of thinking in his view. Working from the idea that God made a conscious decision to create human persons, Guardini sees human action as very important. He sees intentional action as the way that human existence is distinguished from pure nature which just exists. He will eventually argue that intentional action in Providence–living reveals a conscious and transforming relationship with God, in Christ, which is sustained through Christian spiritual practice. Guardini believes that human persons discover themselves in free activity in which they are the agents.

His argument is as follows. Just as God created the world out of choice and not necessity, human persons are able to use their own volition in constructing their lives. They must also take responsibility for their actions. Their acts proceed from an interior and original ground of existence in the person. One brings one's own self into realization. Guardini writes: "It happens because I want it to happen, because I bring it *originally* out of myself; I am the *original* power that lifts it above the threshold of existence."[60] The translator notes that the word Guardini uses here is *Ur-heber*, (author or original lifter) the one who lifts the act into existence and not the *Ur-sache*, (original thing or cause) the original

---

60. Guardini, *Freedom, Grace, and Destiny*, 16; see also p. 28.

ground of the action because the action is not done to us, rather, we do it ourselves.[61] Guardini believes that in this action, one is oneself in a special way because, "I was not only the *original ground* but also the *original active force* in its production."[62] To really be oneself, one must act, and act from one's own interior existence. Guardini wants to affirm that human persons are not part of Nature in the evolutionary or necessary sense.[63] Choice is involved. He believes that an omnipotent Nature would absorb both the freedom and responsibility that is only appropriate in relationship with a sovereign and personal God.[64] This view needs further illumination and is an important aspect of living with Providence. It may be recalled that Providence is lived out in relationship with God. We are arguing further that, for Guardini, Providence is not just natural, it is lived out in freedom and responsibility with God.

What then is the attitude to living with Providence? We see immediately, that Guardini wants to bring the reader beyond a passive reception of Providence. This basic attitude of being able to stand on one's own feet, and take responsibility is developed here as Providence that is not only a "gift and help but a task and demand"[65] as well. He writes: "What is essential to belief in Providence is not that we should throw ourselves into the arms of a friendly Father who puts all things into order but that we should participate in God's care for his kingdom, and share the responsibility for this absolutely decisive concern."[66] Again, Guardini draws attention to action. In initiating an action one possesses the action and ultimately oneself.[67] As one acts in freedom, one is able to own one's action and take responsibility for it.[68] The person is a type of "co-creator" with God as they share responsibility for God's kingdom.[69] Participation in God's Spirit means that participation in responsibility is part of that privilege. Expressed differently one could say that becoming like God,

---

61. See translator's notes, Guardini, *Freedom, Grace, and Destiny*, 16.
62. Guardini, *Freedom, Grace, and Destiny*, 16.
63. We recall that the National Socialists absolutized nature.
64. Guardini, *Power and Responsibility*, 76.
65. Guardini, *Freedom, Grace, and Destiny*, 230.
66. Guardini, *Freedom, Grace, and Destiny*, 230.
67. Guardini, *Freedom, Grace, and Destiny*, 59.
68. Guardini, *Freedom, Grace, and Destiny*, 60.
69. We use the term "co-creator" carefully because Guardini is adamant that human persons can only create from created things and are not the initial causal agent as God is.

means becoming caring and responsible as God is for this world. Freedom, for the other, must be in that context.

Guardini has dialogue partners in the prevailing thought of the time and given the prominence of the thought of these philosophers, even today, his view here is important. He would like to distinguish his position from two other philosophical positions which he believes to be in error. The first, prevalent in critical philosophy, polarizes "real being" with freedom putting real being with nature and therefore, biological determinism. Freedom, in this view, is placed with (intellectual) ethical principles that he believes are not essentially "real." The other area of philosophical error according to Guardini is that of the "Actualists" who put forward the idea that the person only exists at the moment of free activity but they don't take the existent "self as ground" into account. Drawing on his work in *The World and the Person*, Guardini notes that this explanation is flawed because Guardini believes that freedom is located in personal behavior and the person must actualize their being with orientation towards freedom. Free behavior is axiomatic for the actualization of the human person from the original ground of their existence, that is, to absolute being, although there are different ways of realizing this activity.[70] Furthermore, freedom in Guardini's view is a quality of the responsible person rather than just being an intellectual quality or abstraction. Responsible freedom is exercised by a person of integrity. Personal freedom is also the locus for Guardini's consideration of power.

Freedom and Power

Guardini considers power in relation to freedom by saying that one may search for an even fuller freedom by dominating in a certain situation to become an "overlord." Every action can be taken too far and become a situation of power.[71] Guardini asserts that: "True dominion is rooted in obedience to the higher nature of things. The true master is the man who guided by higher purposes, is able to fulfil this service in sovereign form."[72] Guardini believes that relation to one's own body preserves this freedom if the relation is a balanced one. Yet, Guardini cautions against

---

70. Guardini, *Freedom, Grace, and Destiny*, 19.

71. Guardini, *Freedom, Grace, and Destiny*, 35. The notion of power will be further explored below.

72. Guardini, *Freedom, Grace, and Destiny*, 36.

the mentality which views the physical body as absolute, and actually enslaves, because physical vigor and beauty is sought and the spirit is forgotten.[73] Other values are relevant to the Spirit of God. For instance, truth is important.

Freedom and Truth

In the freedom relevant to values, truth is important. Guardini agrees with Socrates who argued that in contemplating truth a person becomes assimilated to truth and thus develops a capacity for eternity. On the other hand Guardini doesn't agree with Nietzsche and the proponents of Pragmatism. Their idea was that the value of truth consisted in its positive effect on life (they said it gave assurance energy and intensity).[74] Guardini argues that truth is not utility, it is truth, has its own intrinsic validity and dignity, and is not subordinate to life. Truth is important to life as a measure of excellence to which a person may aspire to in their life.[75] In that sense life is, rightly, subordinated to truth. Thus in the realization of Spiritual values, relevant to the freedom of being and Providence, truth is paramount. Yet living with Providence means that relations with others are also important.

Freedom and Personal Relations

In personal relations, one experiences freedom of relations when encountering another. Since human persons are made for encounter one may realize oneself in communion. In encountering something one may be "touched by the light of its being."[76] Guardini holds that encounter may occur with human persons but it may also occur with something inanimate or a natural object such as a tree although presumably not to the same degree. With human persons, if the encounter is mutual both may be influenced by the other. Developing his argument from the "I-Thou" concept outlined in the previous chapter, Guardini writes that the

---

73. Guardini, *Freedom, Grace, and Destiny*, 36. In the period of National Socialism, a lot of emphasis was placed on development of the physical body and youth groups concentrated on such aspects as health and beauty.
74. Guardini, *Freedom, Grace, and Destiny*, 37.
75. Guardini, *Freedom, Grace, and Destiny*, 37.
76. Guardini, *Freedom, Grace, and Destiny*, 40.

most intense form of this freedom is love because the person is aware of moving from self-centeredness to the concerns of the other while paradoxically being more "oneself."

On the other hand, solitude is as important as personal liberation if properly viewed. In solitude one is able to challenge one's ego and develop body and spirit. When one lives without this solitude and is always with others, this center is lost and one becomes part of the pattern of others. This aspect was referred to previously in reference to heteronomy which Guardini sees as negative. The ideal is Theonomy and conversely, true freedom in Theonomy is only achieved in the presence of God which also guards against the possibility of excessive autonomy because in Guardini's framework (excessive) autonomy can herald decline. Here, then, Guardini is restating his assertions about heteronomy and autonomy that were discussed in Guardini's early thought in chapter 3 and picked up again in chapter 4. Living with Providence involves balanced relationships with others and is sustained by Theonomy which is best lived in moral freedom.

Moral Freedom

Guardini considers moral freedom to be the content of freedom which embraces all other types of freedom. Morality, for Guardini, is "the sum of what ought to be done, the good."[77] Furthermore, the reason it should (not must) be done is its intrinsic worth. There is an inherent link with Providence here because in living Providentially a person is, ideally, concerned with God's concerns and not their own self interest. The intrinsic worth of the situation is relevant. Guardini writes, "It is not subordinated to a biological or psychological instinct or to a cultural activity but to a particular responsibility of the person, his conscience."[78]

Here Guardini unites the idea of the Good with conscience and human action. He writes further:

> Ultimately the Good is founded upon God. It is a Divine attribute; more accurately, an original aspect of His living being, as also a direction of His living mind. God is the Good, in person ... [it] is His very self, of which we have knowledge only though his revelation.... What confronts the individual conscience as

77. Guardini, *Freedom, Grace, and Destiny*, 44.
78. Guardini, *Freedom, Grace, and Destiny*, 44.

ethically good is God's holiness in so far as it penetrates into conscience and makes itself an objective for man's action.[79]

In this reconsideration of the Good, written many years after his work in *Conscience*, Guardini says that the Good is related both to Being and its content, and the sense that, in the human person, the Good needs Being for its development.[80] Without Being, the Good remains limited and inarticulate. In the case of God, unity between Being and the Good is realized. That is to say, the Good is realized perfectly in God's Being but in human persons that is not always so. Guardini believes that God's reality, will and the value of the good are identical."[81] In the existential situation Being enables the Good to become action. That is to say, Being is not only potential but also act. Guardini wants to affirm that the Good is practical and can be lived as specific in a particular situation and with the obligations of a person in that situation.

The Good "is not good in general but ... what is right here and now ... immediate practical needs ... the whole interior truth of things ... man with his complete nature, and all of it envisaged against the supreme holiness of God."[82] The important thing here is harmony with God's love and intention made possible in relationship with God. Nevertheless, Guardini acknowledges that in some people the obligation and drive toward good may be perverted and be used in the service of evil.[83] Thus the Good is clearly linked to moral actions here and the negation of evil.

Guardini believes that Good preserves life and saves it when good is done for its own sake. That is to say, the chief motive must derive from the intrinsic goodness of a thing. In this action a person is really free. Guardini writes, "It is characteristic of moral freedom that it expresses

---

79. Guardini, *Freedom, Grace, and Destiny*, 46. Guardini holds that a person's action with the Good is not determined by education or capacity. Rather, the action is that which establishes one's meaning, worth and "fundamental character as man." We recall that in the preceding period of National Socialism moral worth was placed with the "natural" acquisition of the Aryan race.

80. Guardini, *Freedom, Grace, and Destiny*, 47.

81. Guardini, *Freedom, Grace, and Destiny*, 47n19. Here we may observe a subtle difference from Guardini's earlier work where Guardini referred to the Good as a characteristic of God, God's holiness. In this passage, it may be seen that, while not retreating from that position he includes a position much more akin to the Western "identity principle" referred to earlier in the thesis.

82. Guardini, *Freedom, Grace, and Destiny*, 47.

83. Guardini, *Freedom, Grace, and Destiny*, 51.

itself in detachment from the immediate self with its desires."[84] The end point of a morally free decision, is that the person experiences the breadth of the moral value and assents to it. The ideal which Guardini believes is never reached on earth is where a person is completely morally free and is unable to do a wrong action. Conversely, enslavement as we see in injustice, occurs when there is untruth or real evil. Likewise, various personal dispositions may enslave. For instance, anxiety, impatience or domination can enslave a person. In this type of situation, good is used as a means to an end.

While not explicitly blaming Nietzsche for the rise of Hitler, Guardini is critical of Nietzsche on this point. He believes that Nietzsche's criticism of moral doctrines were influential and then put to the test by the Nazi leadership. According to Guardini, Nietzsche painted: "a picture of man, rooted in Nature and sensitive experience, acting not from a conscience determined by good and evil but from the direct instincts of overbrimming life and natural creative energy."[85] Guardini believes such a position is in error because a person's being and worth should be founded on an orientation to the Good to which conscience bears witness. Nietzsche's position is akin to the absolutist ideas of the National Socialists who subordinated God the Creator to "pure nature." He doesn't believe anyone is devoid of conscience and morality. For Guardini, Nietzsche's picture of human persons is not only primitive but possibly even mentally ill.[86] Yet conscience and morality also speak of holiness. We turn then to Guardini's understanding of holiness and religious freedom.

Religious Freedom and the Holy

In chapter 3, I argued that in living with Providence, a new holy world and holy creation could replace the present one when the Kingdom of God was attended to. In this period, in his search for the definition of real freedom, Guardini considers aspects of the "holy" especially through Rudolph Otto's work.[87] Guardini holds that the enlightenment, wrongly, produced the idea that the essence of religion lies in "rationalist

---

84. Guardini, *Freedom, Grace, and Destiny*, 49.
85. Guardini, *Freedom, Grace, and Destiny*, 51.
86. Guardini, *Freedom, Grace, and Destiny*, 51.
87. Otto, *The Idea of the Holy*.

knowledge and ethical conduct" but Otto's work addresses this error in thinking.[88]

In religious experience, Guardini believes that a person has a type of freedom during the experience of the Divine or the "numinous" although he will ultimately argue that can also be ambiguous. Such an experience which is clearly beyond anything which is "earthly and world—bound,"[89] is able to have an enormous effect on a person. The experience might occur:

> in Nature, under the sky at night time or in the still mountains; it may be prompted by works of art, as when you walk through a cathedral or listen to music; it may be inspired through men of very impressive character; it can be caused by elevating or shattering historic events or amid day to day affairs; in fine, it can arise without any special environment, at any time and from any direction, it can just happen.[90]

Guardini notes that this experience can be actual and powerful. Guardini would like to distinguish this type of experience from Schliermacher's theology and writing on the "religious factor." Only after the work of Phenomenology could the "religious factor" be studied. Guardini writes:

> Religious experience is no mere state of excitation; it is not a feeling without an object, nor is it a subjective function. It is a true state of apprehension, awareness, and certitude; in it something is "given" and the person who has the experience knows a definite object just as a man who sees, knows an object under the light. This object is real. It is related to the reality of this world, though it is not itself this-worldly.[91]

Guardini believes that God is beyond any possible conception or real ability to "grasp" God and yet in this God empowers and leaves one free. Guardini notes here that even contact with objects and events can reveal what something is or an ultimate meaning.[92] Rudolf Otto used the words "the Holy." Guardini finds the concept restrictive. "The Holy," as a concept

---

88. Guardini, *Freedom, Grace, and Destiny*, 52.
89. Guardini, *Freedom, Grace, and Destiny*, 52.
90. Guardini, *Freedom, Grace, and Destiny*, 52.
91. Guardini, *Freedom, Grace, and Destiny*, 53.
92. Guardini, *Freedom, Grace, and Destiny*, 56.

must be tempered with a more powerful idea of the freedom which God provides.

Yet in *Living Freedom*,[93] first written in the 1927 but re-presented again in 1950, Guardini suggests caution with the notion of religious freedom. He had written, "Religious sentiment has a tendency to go immediately to the last step in all things, to take cognizance of the ultimate as the solution of the problem and to want to see in the will to attain that ultimate the fulfilment of the task."[94] Furthermore, the religious attitude could actually destroy culture or "rob natural activity of its responsibility and joyousness."[95] In other words, God-given natural activity or culture itself could be destroyed by a narrow religious attitude.

Rather, the person changed by faith is able to live with Providence with the clear notion that he or she lives by grace.[96] The twin aspects of human action and grace prevail. The "whole," history, sacred history and human actions, are "borne along by God's Providence and man's decision."[97] In *Living Freedom*, Guardini links freedom with the notion of person, with Christ and the Holy Spirit. Relationship with God is through Christ. A person must believe in Christ and go with him *in the Holy Spirit* to live in the Spirit of God in union with Christ. A new existence occurs in this way. Guardini writes that, "Once a man believes in Christ, Providence takes the place of destiny in directing his existence."[98] The person lives according to a new *Gestalt* or paradigm and set of values. That person's choices are different. Christ remained in the Father's love and in harmony with God was held secure and firm by God. Christ, whose existence was not controlled by unknown forces or mystery had no need for popular conceptions of destiny and was therefore able to redeem existence by his faithful action to God. Thus, when a person believes in Christ, God in God's love is able to direct one's existence and in this sense one's destiny can be changed because the person lives according to a new *Gestalt* or paradigm and set of values.

---

93. Guardini, *Living Freedom*. 184–99.
94. Guardini, *Living Freedom*, 150.
95. Guardini, *Living Freedom*, 150.
96. Guardini, *Living Freedom*, 147.
97. Guardini, *Living Freedom*, 148.
98. Guardini, *Freedom, Grace, and Destiny*, 207.

The Challenge of Evil

Redeemed existence is existence where the person is able to exercise choice and, self-determination and where the choice and decision can be made with openness to God's grace and guidance. Conversely, Guardini considers destiny as part of "unredeemed existence." By this he means, an existence which is open to forces around it over which the person has or may have no control. In Guardini's view destiny is open to events which occur where the person has not exercised choice. Guardini considers fate to be a product of the pattern of things which exist in a world which has "revolted against God."[99] Guardini notes that such an existence "was the consequence of sin, that is, punishment inflicted as such by the justice of the Lord of the world."[100] In other words, human volition was involved and found wanting. Human existence in this scheme of things means that the person has a "narrowed vision" which makes it impossible for a person to view things as they really are. Furthermore, the human person may encounter evil in this world. We have considered Christ's response to evil and said that Christ was able to remain loyal to God. What is Guardini's understanding of the challenges an encounter with evil would bring?

Guardini believes the meeting of faith with Satan and evil is akin to the meeting of faith and extreme autonomy with evil. In other words he links extreme autonomy with evil. He argues that such autonomy is contrary to true being and living with Providence. Guardini believes that human persons have an essential orientation to unique and absolute Being and as such their truth is found in "service."[101] That is to say, when they live authentically from the ground of their being, they are not likely to be ego-driven and are in a position to bring the love of God to others. Openness to the "other" will also open them to themselves while paradoxically turning from self. This outpouring of love for others finds expression in the service of God to those same people. Therefore according to Guardini, autonomy can only be a transitional moment because, "[if] man deserts his true Lord, 'whom to serve is to reign,' then he falls a victim to the arch-rebel, whose service is slavery and shame."[102] That is to say, to serve God is also to share in the life of God, and have real

---

99. Guardini, *Freedom, Grace, and Destiny*, 205.
100. Guardini, *Freedom, Grace, and Destiny*, 205.
101. Guardini, *Freedom, Grace, and Destiny*, 203.
102. Guardini, *Freedom, Grace, and Destiny*, 203.

freedom and mastery, but to serve the devil brings intractable slavery. Guardini believes that Christ was able to break the evil pattern of Satan with His own Divine purity: "on which temptations can lay no hold, in the sacred truth of His message, in his unerring faithfulness to the prescription of His Father's will even though it led him through straights and self-abnegation, through humiliation and suffering, to a terrible death."[103]

Guardini believes that Satan is real—not some evil principle floating around, but a real and wilful person who has set himself up in opposition to God and aims to draw people to himself in place of God. Satan is the epitome of extreme autonomy. Christ overcame Satan and has made another way possible. This new way is the way of Providence not fate.

Yet, the consequences of sin prepare human persons for redemption and it was Christ who revealed that reality is not existence as destiny but existence in a world which has fallen away from God.[104] The person living in the world without the redeeming power of Christ lives in a more diminished way and is thus subject to a disposition which may be more closed and therefore more subject to undesirable influences (to which the person may succumb), but the believer is invited to participate in the grace of God with the indwelling Christ who can bring complete freedom. The Son elevates nature itself into the divine life where true freedom is found. True freedom is not to be found in the world of destiny nor is it "unredeemed existence." True freedom and redeemed existence is the result of grace. We turn then to the notion of grace and Christian freedom.

Grace and Christian Freedom

Grace is central to Guardini's notion of freedom. The Christian message does not raise a person to a completely spiritual dimension but liberates that person to live a full holy existence in the world.[105] Living with full freedom in this world is important for Guardini. For him, grace is the order of our freedom. Without grace a person is not really free. Guardini's insistence on grace as the term of our freedom is important because this same grace enables Christians to stand within themselves with integrity, to have participation in God, the ground of their being. We argued above

---

103. Guardini, *Freedom, Grace, and Destiny*, 203.
104. Guardini, *Freedom, Grace, and Destiny*, 206.
105. Guardini, *The Church of the Lord*, 75.

that in Guardini's notion there is interpenetration of the human and Divine. As one is held in the grace of God made possible in Christ, or as one allows God to guide one's life, one is open to the enormous range of possibilities of God in Godself and in this way one is both rooted in God, and completely free for the whole of reality. Christian freedom relates directly to Providence as we have understood it.

Guardini holds that only one who is truly free is able to attain self-realization and exist in one's self. Providence is experienced in that context. In that context he also believes that freedom stands out from all other human behavior and is fundamental to it. We have considered his writing on types of freedom. He writes that although there are a number of ways human freedom may be exercised, true freedom is a work of the Spirit and in that sense will ensure that only Christian freedom is real freedom. We have argued, above, that for Jesus Christ, Providence is a work of the Holy Spirit. Relating freedom to being, Guardini argues that: "freedom that derives from the content of the act, consists of a man's right relationship to being; he senses the truth in its essential nature, notes the worth it incarnates and makes a place for it in his life. Revelation now sets man before the richness of being and the supreme dignity of God, His truth and holiness."[106] Later, Guardini asserts that "self-conquest and detachment for growth in freedom of the spirit and heart"[107] are a task for the Christian. He believes that this growth of spirit and heart in the process of freedom will assist the believer to become "independent of created things through the grace of God but also on account of his own courage, discipline and sacrifice, in which he is wholly open to the truth and richness of God and is master of his own power of action."[108]

Christian freedom is, for Guardini, a process rather than being static. Christian Baptism awakens the freedom which already exists and which grows in everyday Christian life.[109] Nevertheless, Guardini employs an already but not yet caveat. The freedom now possible in Christ, is still not complete but will become so when Christ returns. The relationship to God in this world is centered on Christ who is able to bring true freedom and the transformed life necessary in Providence living,

---

106. Guardini, *Freedom, Grace, and Destiny*, 70.
107. Guardini, *Freedom, Grace, and Destiny*, 76.
108. Guardini, *Freedom, Grace, and Destiny*, 76.
109. Guardini, *Freedom, Grace, and Destiny*, 78.

The Christian message, affirmed by Guardini is not world-denying but life affirming and lived out, as discussed in chapters 2 and 3 as the "new man or woman" in the "new creation." Each individual person is important to God in living with Providence and it is to this aspect that we now turn.

Theme 3: The Individual Person Is Important to God

We argued in chapters 3 and 4 that Guardini believes the individual human person is of infinite value to God. In this postwar period, the notion of transformation in the pneumatic, cosmic Christ is strong and integral to God's love. Providence is developed further and is shown to end in the judgement and justice. Guardini argues here that God loves God's people so much that God was prepared to take human destiny upon God's self to enable them to participate in God's own life. Not just mind but the mind of Christ, can create a positive meaning for the human person and becoming a "child of God" is the work of the Holy Spirit which occurs simultaneously with the natural human development of "person." Guardini affirms the importance of love in living with Providence and shows how living with Providence ends in God's justice and judgement which is integral to God's love. We turn now to Guardini's notion of judgement.

Judgement

The notion of the Judgement of God in the fulfillment of God's Providence, is very strong in this period just after World War II and Guardini refers to it at length in his book, *Freedom, Grace, and Destiny*. Here in post-war *and* post-Holocaust Germany, Guardini asserts that Providence ends in justice and Judgement. It was vital that Guardini dealt with this aspect adequately in the post war period. His words on justice and judgement are a clear development of his earlier work on Providence. He argues that the doctrines of the Apocalypse and Providence are "inextricably connected."[110] Providence shows the workings of God in this world.[111] "If the significance of the pattern of Providence is to be known, it must be revealed ultimately in some special event, and this is the final Judgement"

---

110. Guardini, *Freedom, Grace, and Destiny*, 215.
111. Guardini, *Freedom, Grace, and Destiny*, 132.

he writes.¹¹² Judgement is the way God shows that each human person is important to God and is that aspect of Providence that addresses the issue of both earthly life and what lies beyond it. Judgement, a positive act, in Guardini's view, is the process which comes from God in which the full significance of Providence is made clear.¹¹³ It is linked to history because during a person's historical existence the way he or she lives either helps God's presence in this world or hinders it. Guardini states that Providence is the way that God develops his kingdom to be "the absolute significance of history."¹¹⁴ In other words, history does not stand alone because God gives the opportunity for God's significance to emerge from historical decisions of individuals. The full significance of Providence can only be made clear by God, and this occurs in Judgement.¹¹⁵ One cannot effect Judgement on oneself nor another.¹¹⁶ Judgement belongs to God. Guardini's concern is how God effects this Judgement. The details of this action, by God, are important to Guardini's notion of Providence and it is to this aspect that we now turn.

The First Act of Judgement

Guardini argues that Judgement is completed in two acts. There are those who will be eternally saved and those who are eternally lost. Others must have purification.¹¹⁷ Guardini's idea of purification means guidance in the full love of God.¹¹⁸ The first act of Judgement follows after the death of each person and refers to the life he or she has just lived. There is salvation if a person has believed in and obeyed God or eternal loss if the person has repudiated God in some way. Purification must follow for those who are attached to evil even if their intention was good.¹¹⁹ The other type of Judgement occurs at the end of time or when Christ returns.

---

112. Guardini, *Freedom, Grace, and Destiny*, 215. Here Guardini quotes Matt 25:31–46; Rom 15:10–12; Rev 20:11–13.
113. Guardini, *Freedom, Grace, and Destiny*, 215.
114. Guardini, *Freedom, Grace, and Destiny*, 215.
115. Guardini, *Freedom, Grace, and Destiny*, 215.
116. Guardini, *Freedom, Grace, and Destiny*, 215.
117. Guardini, *Freedom, Grace, and Destiny*, 216.
118. Guardini, *The Last Things*, 33.
119. Guardini, *Freedom, Grace, and Destiny*, 216.

The Second Judgement

At the second Judgement at the end of time (universal Judgement), the history of the individual will be judged. By comparison with the privacy of the individual existential Judgement, the universal one is public. Guardini asserts that at the universal Judgement, God will be known as all in all and the larger mystery of God, which is hidden in temporal existence, will be revealed. The history of humanity with each individual history contributing to it while receiving from this larger historical whole, will be judged and seen in the light of the greater wisdom of God. God's Providence is revealed here in this second judgement because the existential questions are able to be addressed.[120] In Judgement God reveals the intention and reasons for God's actions in the person's life.[121] Guardini holds that unlike destiny, which is silent, the God of Providence answers these questions. For Guardini, it is God's holiness and justice that demand the clarification of history. According to Guardini, at this time the individual is able to see, in the complexity of his or her life's pattern the meaning of their own life, the pattern of the whole and the way their life fits into it.[122]

Judgement in the Overall Sense

In the light of seeing one's life in the larger context of the whole, Guardini argues: "[the final act of] Judgement is the final expression of the historical character of experience. Existence had a general beginning in creation, which is a free act of God's majesty; it will have a genuine end given by the same God. After this end there follows the assessment of existence for eternity."[123] The overall act of Judgement whether individual or universal is the final act in which the person is able to see all of the result of choices in totality. Wrong choices may have been made. The historical setting also enabled a type of "concealment," as the person's interior and that of others has been unknown. In a person's life, the past and future may not have been immediately obvious or were unknown, thus making disguise, or deception possible. Sometimes God himself appears to have absconded from temporal existence. Therefore the person finds

---

120. Guardini, *Freedom, Grace, and Destiny*, 222.

121. Guardini, *Freedom, Grace, and Destiny*, 222.

122. The being of human persons, in their wholeness, is for Guardini, clarity and courage, insight and obedience, truth and love, 224.

123. Guardini, *Freedom, Grace, and Destiny*, 216.

legitimacy in complete autonomy and a life lived away from thoughts of God.[124] In relation to this last point, Guardini writes that the: "cunning human will, in its resistance to God, makes use of this last concealment in the temporal order to fabricate the lie of autonomy, to act as though God did not exist and as if history were the only reality and the fullness of reality, self-contained and self-sufficient."[125] Guardini continues with insights about God himself: "If God openly exercised His sovereignty, then His truth would illuminate everything, His holiness would dominate everything, and the finite spirit could neither err nor choose evil. Consequently God must in some way restrain Himself, limit Himself so as to allow the creature room for choice—an attitude that can only be understood as kenosis."[126]

At Judgement, God, formerly hidden and kenotic in Christ, assumes God's full sovereignty and power. Guardini writes that the rejection of Christ by God's chosen people, the Jews, found expression in the destruction of Jerusalem in AD 70 (i.e., not, as some have claimed, in Auschwitz). God in Omnipotence, limits Godself in order to allow human freedom. Guardini understands this aspect as co-existing with God's continual and personal presence. God enables human choice by giving freedom for it. Guardini believes that Judgement takes away the concealment of God, and God's truth illuminates Spirit enabling God's holiness to permeate conscience so that God's sovereignty is known. The person feels the gravity of his or her life's acts.[127] Guardini holds that loyalty to truth and goodness are tested in history.[128] Therefore reality can be correctly seen as identified with truth and goodness rather than the way it *appears* to be in destiny. The characteristics of power and "life" which evil appeared to have, are now seen to have been deceit, and evil's "creative power" is known to be a destructive force. Guardini's description of events is compelling. He believes that the individual who is undergoing Judgement experiences an exclusive encounter with God which is based on the I-Thou relationship that was possible in his or her life.[129] In the open honesty of the encounter in God's immediacy, one receives

---

124. Guardini, *Freedom, Grace, and Destiny*, 217.
125. Guardini, *Freedom, Grace, and Destiny*, 219.
126. Guardini, *Freedom, Grace, and Destiny*, 218.
127. Guardini, *Freedom, Grace, and Destiny*, 219.
128. Guardini, *Freedom, Grace, and Destiny*, 218.
129. The I-Thou relationship was considered in chapter 4.

God's final "definition" on oneself. The new eternal being is based on the decisions of that person's finite existence.

Guardini sees Judgement as revealing a two-fold significance. On the one hand God is assuming God's rights and is given significance. On the other hand, human persons are given significance and respect. In this sense Providence differs from destiny which is impersonal.[130] Judgement is really encounter with God and is individual and intensely personal.

Both the personal encounter with God and the way Guardini links Providence to human responsibility, including accountability to God with it, show a development of Guardini's assertion in the earlier periods we have been considering. The human person is precious in God's eyes but is also called to be responsible for such a gift. A person's being is determined by personal freedom and ultimately freedom of being which is possible in relation to God as a person lives the will of God. The Judgement is able to show the way humanity has mis-portrayed God, as unwise, unjust or powerless as justice comes to the fore[131] and injustice is able to be addressed. We have referred to Guardini's argument for an image of the human person in the heart of God and the word from God which may be given to each human person at their birth. Now in this period Guardini argues that the moment of Judgement can yield a new name, a new identity, bestowed by God on the heart of the person. Guardini quotes the Apocalypse here, saying the identity is that "which no man knoweth, but he that receiveth it (Ap. 2:17)."[132] The new name may be given by God and as God's final judgement on his or her temporal life will reflect the sum total of his or her life's decisions. Guardini re-asserts, "Eternal life comes from temporal life . . . as the final existential form of the particular man out of his personal decisions."[133]

We are reminded of the importance of human initiative and action. Guardini is opposed to the notion that Providence be understood from one side only, as care from a loving Father (God) while the person, totally passive, accepts what comes without taking action. Rather, Providence refers to action and boldness. The human person must act and take responsibility for his or her own life because Providence is profoundly linked to responsibility in and for the world. As a person grows in harmony with

---

130. Guardini, *Freedom, Grace, and Destiny*, 221.
131. Guardini, *Freedom, Grace, and Destiny*, 222.
132. Guardini, *Freedom, Grace, and Destiny*, 220.
133. Guardini, *Freedom, Grace, and Destiny*, 221.

God, they grow in harmony with God's mind.[134] In the final Judgement at the end of all time the remaining mysteries will be revealed and the person will really understand why certain things happened. Guardini believes that at the Judgement, God's design will be open and every action clear because everything was created from God's love.[135] In a "this world" sense we may understand that love as grace.

Providence in Judgement

The judgement holds very positive significance for Guardini. It is not only intensely personal, it is also the time of justice: "Judgement gives man also his rights against existence in that it determines the "injustice" suffered by the individual on account of his body-soul heritage, corrupted through sin, the distribution of property and power, the mutual dependence of men upon one another, and the course of history. It gives him, finally, his right against other men in making clear, condemning, and punishing the injustice they have committed against him."[136] Thus, in the judgement, the individual human person can look forward to the justice denied to him or her in earthly life. Furthermore, the awareness of God's Providence will prevail:

> God unveils his Providence in judgement. He takes up the basic question about the meaning of existence which men have been continually asking throughout history. "Why did this happen to me?" "Why am I what I am?" "Why do I exist at all" Destiny is eternally silent. The God of Providence answers all in judgement. His holiness and justice both accept and demand the complete clarification of history; this will constitute the final revelation of God's mind. It is His "Justification."[137]

Guardini holds that the final Judgement will also reveal the ways of God's grace:

> His redemption and forgiveness, His operations and His paths, His enlightenment and assistance, vocation and guidance, foundations and constructions. The mystery will be revealed that man is responsible for all operations – beginning, continuance,

---

134. Guardini, *Freedom, Grace, and Destiny*, 224.
135. Guardini, *Freedom, Grace, and Destiny*, 224.
136. Guardini, *Freedom, Grace, and Destiny*, 222.
137. Guardini, *Freedom, Grace, and Destiny*, 222.

and fulfilment – and yet that man is responsible for all his action: a mystery expressed earlier in the sentence that the more forcibly God's grace is operating, so much more personally free is man. Judgement in point of fact is the completion of the realm of grace.[138]

In this sense then, the Judgement at the end of time is both the final revelation and the fulfillment of God's dispensation of grace that has been operating through time and history. Guardini doesn't believe that fulfillment without Judgement is possible. Judgement, for him, continues the "process of salvation" as the above quotation reveals, and is historical because it "proceeds by decisions taken and actions performed."[139] Guardini argues that Judgement manifests and completes Providence through the verdict of salvation and the acceptance or rejection of Christ.[140] God's integrity is preserved. One part of God's wisdom remains a mystery, and is held within God's innermost self. This center of God is, according to Guardini, the center where the entire pattern of things is held.

Guardini believes that while the minds of human persons reach towards the absolute, they are only able to proximate to it and not actually attain it. He takes the position of St. Thomas Aquinas here.[141] Guardini holds that the relation of a person's whole existence to the significance of that same existence, is the relation of the knowing act to truth. This leads Guardini to assert that an extra-noetic act is necessary in the relation between subject and object of knowledge to "decide" the knowledge as such. He argues that a person's full knowledge takes place in the meeting with God after death when the person is able to understand their experience in the light of the vastness of God's knowledge. We have argued that this takes place in Judgement.[142] In order to understand Christ's role in Providence and Judgement we have already considered the concept of Providence and destiny, juxtaposed, and polarized by Guardini. Living without the guidance of God could result in destiny or fate becoming dominant in a person's life. Rather the guidance of God can lead to a redeemed existence.

138. Guardini, *Freedom, Grace, and Destiny*, 225.
139. Guardini, *Freedom, Grace, and Destiny*, 226.
140. Guardini, *Freedom, Grace, and Destiny*, 228.
141. Aquinas asserted that God is so incomprehensible that perfect knowledge of God could never be attained because as the knowledge increases, the incomprehensibility increases to the same degree.
142. Guardini, *Freedom, Grace, and Destiny*, 227.

Theodicy and Guardini's Theology of Providence

Guardini's theodicy may be understood in this section. A theodicy is an attempt to show that God is just and good despite possible evidence to the contrary.[143] Yet, in recent post-holocaust literature, some writers refute the validity of a theodicy because they do not want to justify the unjustifiable. Guardini's position may be summarized thus. God created the world and wanted it to reach its culmination in humanity's freedom. That freedom, given by God, was misused because human persons did not use the freedom for God, but used it against God. Guardini believes that God knew from eternity that the result would be the rejection of God. He believes that God had foreknowledge, but not foreordination, because that would have implied human persons were not completely free. Guardini's position, therefore, is that God, as a loving God, gave human persons freedom but knew, because of his foreknowledge, what they would do. Nevertheless, because human persons must be left free, God did not intervene to force humanity to accept God or God's intentions. At the same time, God has involved God's-self in the world to a large degree, giving the world the gift of God's own being and embracing it with "an earnestness peculiar to himself."[144] Non-intervention has not meant non-involvement. We have argued that God also works through secondary causes. The touch of God will be known through people and things and people will know they are cared for. God made human persons in God's own likeness and each person is significant in God's eyes. God's grace is given to each person and as a person grows in God's grace, becomes more like God. "Participation" in God occurs in this way. Guardini describes this aspect of humanity thus, "The Creator impressed on it the significant forms that are founded in His own Being (cf. John 1:1–3) and has thus, as it were, staked His own honour upon it."[145]

The imprint, of God, is upon each person but human persons misused this privilege and rebelled against God. Therefore, because God is a loving God, redemption was brought into play. Guardini writes:

---

143. The term was introduced by the philosopher Gottfried Wilhelm Leibniz (1641–1716) in response to someone who had raised the question: If God is all good and all powerful, where does evil come from and what does it mean? See "Theodicy" in *A Concise Dictionary of Theology*, 239.

144. Guardini, *Freedom, Grace, and Destiny*, 242.

145. Guardini, *Freedom, Grace, and Destiny*, 242.

> When the Son assumes human nature into the unity of His Being, He elevates created Nature into the Divine life. To be sure, this human nature is absolute in its purity. The eternal Son comes, however, as Redeemer, with the consequence that the whole being of Christ belongs to the category of "for us." Thus he makes sin his own, not as an act He has committed but as guilt He has representatively assumed.[146]

Revelation, Guardini asserts, is to be assessed from "inside."[147] In other words a person must have an interiority which, by the experience of Christ, within, is able to assess revelation effectively. This action by the human person will eventually involve conversion of that person's whole being; whole existence, to God. Guardini states, "I have to say that according to revelation God does this and reveals Himself in it to me. This is a Copernican inversion of thought, part of that "conversion" demanded by Christ, on which Christian experience is based. It includes religious conversion of the heart to God, the ethical conversion from evil to good, and in addition the conversion from natural to Christian thinking."[148]

We should note here that Guardini draws attention to the absence of a pattern for "right thinking" as such; Christian thinking is not just "right thinking." Rather, one must believe that, "the beginning lies with revelation and what it declares to be the truth is the truth."[149] Furthermore the person must acknowledge God in God's Being as absolute Lord who has already revealed himself in His sovereign glory. The God who reveals himself is the "I Am" God of Mount Horeb. The believer is the one who stands before the Lord of all creation and makes God the Lord of his or her life. Thus, the relationship with God, *in humility*, is paramount. For Guardini, the cross is the absolute symbol of God's love. The world is open to the person who is orientated to the cross, and the really Christian heart will be "warmed by its radiance."[150] In other words, when one feels and understands the love of God and God's kenosis which Christ's cross reveals, one is experiencing a truly Christian heart.

---

146. Guardini, *Freedom, Grace, and Destiny*, 243.
147. Guardini, *Freedom, Grace, and Destiny*, 243.
148. Guardini, *Freedom, Grace, and Destiny*, 244.
149. Guardini, *Freedom, Grace, and Destiny*, 244.
150. Guardini, *Freedom, Grace, and Destiny*, 249.

"Co-creator"[151]

The Christian lives in and for God, in a position which is sustained by the human quality of hope.[152] Guardini declares that the believer must participate in "God's destiny."[153] Participation in God's destiny occurs completely through Christ. Thus the task of being "co-creator" is really orientation to God through Christ. While the believer must assume responsibility for the world, the person becomes a "co-creator" with God by going with Christ to God, in harmony with God. Two dangers, according to Guardini are: 1) Toning down Christ's will and secularizing one's life according to social norms; 2) Adopting a ghetto mentality and taking refuge in the paranoia of "them" and "us" by completely renouncing all possible control of the world.[154] Guardini's vision is eschatological. A person can respond to Christ's call with their whole person. Such a person must direct the world with the seriousness appropriate to carrying out Christ's will which is the will of the Father.[155] He writes: "In this process, consists man's essential development—the figure of the new man in the new creation, what one day, when it has passed through the fire of judgement, will abide eternally."[156] For Guardini, such a position epitomizes Christian hope. We turn now to a greater elucidation of Guardini's notion of the new existence and new creation.

Theme Four: New Existence and New Creation

Guardini believes an ontological transformation of the world and everything in it can occur through the grace of God that permeates this world. Participation in God and the community of the Holy Trinity is integral to the new existence and new creation and a new deified world. This process would be a radical transformation of God's creature, and all of creation in God, as human persons live with Providence. Christ gives a person a redeemed consciousness and conversion in every aspect of his

---

151. We have noted, earlier, that Guardini has expressed reservations about the term "co-creator." Only God can be a prime creator but human persons can create from that which is already created by God.

152. Guardini, *Freedom, Grace, and Destiny*, 251.

153. Guardini, *Freedom, Grace, and Destiny*, 249.

154. Guardini, *Freedom, Grace, and Destiny*, 250.

155. Guardini, *Freedom, Grace, and Destiny*, 250.

156. Guardini, *Freedom, Grace, and Destiny*, 250.

or her life. As part of this transformation Guardini shows how power and responsibility are borne out in service. While Guardini holds that nature began as an act of God and is to be seen in that context, he aims to bring his assertions into line with the extant thought in the scientific world. In his later work, he writes that since God created both natural law and the revelation of God in Jesus Christ, both are expressions of God's wisdom. Thus he is able to restate that the environment is God's world. Christians should be responsible for the environment especially as it is the locus for God's Providence. To understand Guardini's intention further we turn to his writing on conversion in this post war period.

Conversion—The "New Person"

The being of human persons can change; be transformed and gradually, in God's time, the person becomes a new person.[157] The "new person" comes into being after acceptance of Christ. Conversion to God and God's way of thinking occurs through Christ. According to Guardini, conversion, on which Christian existence is based, includes;

> religious conversion of the heart to God, the ethical conversion from evil to good, and in addition the conversion from natural thinking to Christian thinking. . . . [I]n spiritual conversion I have to acknowledge God as being, first and foremost in His Being, the absolute Lord, who reveals Himself in his sovereign glory and declares: this is Myself. He has willed a finite world at His side and before Himself . . . and has willed this "from now and forever."[158]

In order to have the "inner secret" of God's mind, Guardini does not advocate absolute values and motives. Rather, one must have the mind of Christ. Then one will have the inner secret of God's mind which is love. A person's vision of Christ's life and the development of his life come into play here.[159]

Here in this period, we are able to appreciate Guardini's development of the concept of Providence. We may say that for Guardini, this means conversion in the fullest sense possible. He writes: "To the degree

---

157. We recall Guardini's words that wisdom is knowledge of the time that belongs to things.

158. Guardini, *Freedom, Grace, and Destiny*, 244.

159. Guardini, *Freedom, Grace, and Destiny*, 247.

to which the 'old person is put off' and 'the new person put on' - and this happens in every genuine act of the Christian life - the notion of destiny is changed into that of Providence."[160] In Providence-living the transformed and converted consciousness enables the person to be continuously moving towards an ever fuller likeness of Christ and away from sheer destiny. The "person of the Father" takes the place of the mysterious impersonal force of destiny at the same time as Christ empowers the person themselves, because this conversion involves the person's will. The responsible person has made a decision to ask Christ to direct their lives and will have a mind of love.

The Place of Love in Providence

Love is a central way of living with Providence. We have said that when a person's attitude changes, their destiny changes too. Yet God and God's grace are preeminent. Guardini argues that a God who foresaw all of human failure and self-destructiveness could have kept his own slate clean, by refusing to go ahead with flawed creation. Instead, he foresaw, then continued to will, the ultimate in human freedom, and planned redemption for those who would accept Christ. For Guardini, every aspect of this action can be summed up in the words "this mind is love."[161] This mind, God's mind, can be manifest to the believer when, supported by grace, the believer acts in faith and accepts this mind of love given in revelation, and fulfils it.[162] In the process of conversion to God, therefore, destiny refers to the destiny of love, as the person's life is transformed into the destiny of the lover.

For Guardini, the redeemed person has a special relationship with God which entails mutual respect because the person is as God willed that person to be. Yet Guardini would say that the world and the human person are not linked to God in a natural sense because "between Him and the world there lies the abyss of absolute sovereignty [yet, the] love of the Father"[163] is able to fill the space where indifference and emptiness could have resulted. When one lives in harmony with the love of God, one also lives with truth justice and power. In that sense, God has

---

160. Guardini, *Freedom, Grace, and Destiny*, 207.
161. Guardini, *Freedom, Grace, and Destiny*, 246.
162. Guardini, *Freedom, Grace, and Destiny*, 246.
163. Guardini, *Freedom, Grace, and Destiny*, 209.

been able to establish genuine being and freedom in that person. As the human person focuses on seeking the Kingdom of God, love is the central behavioral and attitudinal concept in Guardini's notion of Providence. In the action of giving love, the process will order the person's being to the greater and all-encompassing love of God. More precisely, grace, effected through Christ, brings the love of God the Father to the human person. Providential Christian living involves the balance of grace and human action which will enable them to be open to the leading of Christ and God's wisdom.

Redeemed Existence

In the period of National Socialism a person was exhorted to live from the existentiality of Christ. Now in the post war period, Guardini has refined his position further. A new form of existence is the transformation which Jesus effects in the life of a person living with Providence and is commensurate with being a "child" of God. Guardini believes that Jesus was able to establish a new existence by discovering and living his existence according to a new way, thus becoming an encouragement, and example. More importantly, he is the one who acts and through whom the action is to be performed for others. Guardini writes: "His life and action form the beginning of a new existence. To be redeemed means to enter into [Christ] through the grace of this new beginning and to live from him."[164] Such a person lives, by grace, from the existence of Christ. For this to be possible, Guardini believes that the basic acts of such an existence are faith hope and love. Faith begins with Christ and develops in a "stable personal abiding in Christ."[165] Love is "personal union with Christ as absolute lover . . . [and hope is the] certainty that this new beginning . . . will be realised in complete richness and stability and will finally be consummated in eternity."[166] Yet, personal integrity continues for the human person because: "This does not mean that in Christian existence the human 'I' is blotted out, and that Christ enters in its place. It means precisely that because Christ lives in me, I am finally able to be *myself*—that *self* which God had in mind when he created me and there awoke in me

---

164. Guardini, *Freedom, Grace, and Destiny*, 205.
165. Guardini, *Freedom, Grace, and Destiny*, 205.
166. Guardini, *Freedom, Grace, and Destiny*, 205.

my power of initiative, decision, and self development."[167] The presence of Christ enables a person to live as God intended. Yet Christ's life entails a kenosis. As the incarnation of the Son of God, Jesus is the foundation of Being and, in his life, "he confined the divine sovereignty of His Person within the limits of human nature."[168]

Ultimately Guardini argues that in Providence-living the Christian lives with a new being where there is togetherness of the grace of God and human freedom. We have already noted that the spiritual aspect of a person is important in their ability to "stand in themselves" and have personal realization. Now we may also say that in living with Providence "the order of being" implies a freedom of being which is bonded to the will of God through Christ. The providential design, by which God guides the world, is fashioned in love. The human person lives with the guidance of God and their being and life's purpose is gradually brought to fruition and the purpose intended by God. Providence can be lived out in this development. Human action is important both for the bond with God and action in the world. Yet, conversely, human action is greatly influenced by freedom of being which is made possible in a life in God.

Holiness of Existence

Guardini considers that God directs the world and the love of God (shown as God assumed a human existence) is at the center of God's guidance (*Lenkung*) of the world.[169] Guardini quotes Romans 8:28 ("to those that love God, all things work together unto good") and says:

> Only God understands what is the right thing, and therefore belief in Providence takes us back to his judgement that surpasses all comment and to his impenetrable design. But these are wisdom and love. The step taken into the incomprehensible is a positive one: it consists of confident love as an answer to provident love. It is convinced that whatever happens, in its absolute

---

167. Guardini, *Freedom, Grace, and Destiny*, 73.
168. Guardini, *Freedom, Grace, and Destiny*, 191.
169. Guardini, *Freedom, Grace, and Destiny*, 211. *Lenkung* means to direct or steer. *Walten* means to govern or to rule. Thus, Guardini's more frequent use of *Lenkung* indicates his notion of God who gives the human person the capacity for freedom and that person is able to take some action for him or herself.

vigour and delicacy, is pure precision and its immense solemnity, corresponds with the exigencies of the sacred process.[170]

The wisdom and love of God can guide the world. Yet, the believer can co-operate with God, since God's knowledge is unsurpassable. This implies that one uses one's responsibility in this regard. Furthermore, Guardini is able to argue that the cold, empty mystery of destiny is replaced with the incomprehensible mystery of the God of love. For Guardini, the Providence of God is given to human persons as a task to be fulfilled and not only as a consolation. Guardini says:

> Providence, as heralded by Jesus, is to develop from this harmony of the believer with God's creative and active will. . . . [I]t involves the will towards a new community of care and concern with God, an activity and a suffering in union with His will that makes the deepest possible demands. It is, in a very true sense, the "achievement of faith and, because things continue seemingly to contradict it, "the victory which overcometh the world."[171]

For Guardini, the believer is able to share God's love and care for his kingdom as God guides the believer in a way that is formative for his existence. Human responsibility involves love, suffering and care which deserves further illumination.

Human Action—Responsibility

Earlier I argued that human responsibility was important in living with Providence. Human action involves responsibility towards all of God's creation and responsible use of power. In post-war, post-Holocaust Germany Guardini relates new creation to responsibility and notes that emphasis on authority and its obedience in the Nazi period has detracted from human responsibility. "It . . . has diverted man's attention from the responsibility of individual judgement, moral decision and personal participation."[172] Human persons therefore, in his mind, ought to be responsible, involved and capable of independent moral assessment and in that context participate in society in a personal way. These characteristics make the use of power possible. Guardini believes that "Power is

---

170. Guardini, *Freedom, Grace, and Destiny*, 211.
171. Guardini, *Freedom, Grace, and Destiny*, 213.
172. Guardini, *Freedom, Grace, and Destiny*, 232.

good to the extent to which it is wielded responsibly and morally, and secured by sound judgement and self control."[173] For Guardini, this assertion does not mean that a person gives way to self-seeking control of events. Rather, the person needs to have a "redeemed consciousness."[174] Guardini asserts that human persons often go to extreme action, either wanting to take all power and Providence under their own control, irrespective of the dominion of God, or throwing oneself into the Dionysiac "all or nothing" in order to organise their experience. Transformation is personal and ultimately social. Yet Christ himself, would have changed the "religious element" and "replaced it with firm faith and obedience to the living God."[175]

Responsibility—Guardini's Example

Responsibility is integral to Providence and Guardini's words were matched by his actions. This was shown in the actions which Guardini took on behalf of people, Jewish and non-Jewish, after the war. Immediately after the end of the war, a ceremony was held at the University of Munich (Ludwig Maximilian Universität). This was a memorial service for the five young students and professor; members of the White Rose resistance group who had been executed by the Nazi regime for their opposition to National Socialism. Guardini spoke at this ceremony.

The address was entitled "The Scales of Existence," and he spoke of the sacrifice of the members of this group and his own unworthiness to say something on behalf of these people. From 1943 onwards, Guardini had maintained contact with a friend of the leaders of, the resistance group, The White Rose. This public address after the war was to be the first of a number of public acts which Guardini would make on behalf of those who had sacrificed their lives. In this action, after the war. Guardini was one of the few who involved himself in the public arena while so many preferred to remain silent about what had happened. It was in keeping with Guardini's belief that a theologian must involve themselves in society and take responsibility for their own action and for the society they call their own.

---

173. Guardini, *Freedom, Grace, and Destiny*, 232.
174. Guardini, *Freedom, Grace, and Destiny*, 240.
175. Guardini, *Freedom, Grace, and Destiny*, 241. In other words, the interior aspect of belief is important. Belief cannot be only the external practices.

What would Guardini say about Providence in the lives of those young people who were executed for their opposition to Hitler? How could that be Providence? Providence in Guardini's thought refers to fulfillment of purpose and may appear to involve good or bad things for that person. While Guardini may not say that they were born for that purpose or that there was no choice involved Guardini would say that they had made the choice to look to God and there was harmony between their wills and that of God. Guardini writes that this does not mean that the person will be spared pain and sorrow but that the person will have what they need and then everything that happens will serve the true end of that person's life.[176] These young people were reading his work before they were arrested and probably *were* in harmony with God. Providence means that "the living God is personally concerned with every single human being and ready to look after him."[177] The young people, reading Guardini's work on Providence would have known he advocated seeking the Kingdom of God and God's justice, "that is before and more than anything else."[178] Guardini says that whoever thinks this way is in agreement with God because that person wishes that, "His kingdom and holy justice should come. Out of this understanding, Christ says, the course of events will fall into place around the faithful."[179] Providence is apprehended by the eyes of faith.[180] The young students in Munich would have known that they were in the care of God. The lawyers convicting them had choice and chose to murder them just as Pilate had a choice but offered to free Barabbas to the people instead of Jesus. After their deaths the pamphlets they had been distributing were taken to Britain where they were copied and the British wrote that they had been executed for their actions. These leaflets were then distributed by a bomber pilot all over Northern Germany as they flew over which would have shocked the people who found and read them. A belief in God's Providence would enable a person to understand the situation as one in which all things worked together for good to those who loved God who were called according to his purpose (Rom 8:28).

---

176. Guardini, *The Art of Praying*, 130.

177. Guardini, *The Art of Praying*, 128.

178. Guardini, *The Art of Praying*, 129. This was one of many books where Guardini advocated this attitude.

179. Guardini, *The Art of Praying*, 129.

180. Guardini, *The Art of Praying*, 130.

After the war, on May 23, 1952, Guardini gave an address at the University of Tubingen. In it he addressed the question of a national collective guilt of the German people. The address was titled, "Verantwortung: Gedanken zür Jüdischen Frage" (Responsibility: Thoughts on the Jewish Question). His argument addressed the need to take moral responsibility for what had happened to the Jews, the need to make amends and the need to overcome the evil that had taken over the lives of the German people.[181] Guardini is adamant that human responsibility is necessary in living with Providence.

Power and Responsibility

Related to responsibility is Guardini's afore mentioned writing on power and the use of power. Guardini believes Christ lived his power as obedience and humility. Providence involves living responsibly within the world with courage and the guidance of God. The use of power in Guardini's thought, and connection with Providence, can be nuanced further.

In 1951, when Guardini wrote *Power and Responsibility*, he analyzed the notion of power. Responsibility, part of Providence-living, was integral to this notion. In his post-war reflection Guardini addresses the notion of power which was linked to Providence in the thought of Hitler. Power is defined by Guardini as having two elements. Power is: "real energies capable of changing the reality of things, of determining their condition and interrelations; and awareness of those energies, the will to establish specific goals and to direct energies towards those goals. All this presupposes spirit, that reality in man which renders him capable of extricating himself from the immediate context of nature in order to direct it in freedom."[182] Such power is able to give purpose to things.[183] Furthermore, power, which is determined by the user, can be used for good and the positive as well as destruction and evil.[184] Power is demonic when it is unable to give, "respect for the human person, for his dignity and responsibility, for his personal values of freedom and honor, for his initiative and way of life."[185] Power such as this, Guardini believes, is no

---

181. Krieg, *Romano Guardini*, 130.
182. Guardini, *Power and Responsibility*, 2.
183. Guardini, *Power and Responsibility*, 3.
184. Guardini, *Power and Responsibility*, 6.
185. Guardini, *Power and Responsibility*, 7.

longer able to be morally answerable by the human person. "What does happen is that the void is succeeded by a faithlessness which hardens to an attitude, and into this no man's land stalks another initiative, the demonic."[186] In other words, a destructive vacuum may follow an abuse of power, leaving space for evil influences.

Yet, power is universal and can be related to every aspect of a person's being, activity, and competence.[187] Guardini clarifies this statement: "every act of doing and creating, of possessing and enjoying, produces an immediate sense of power. The same is true of acts of the vitality. Any activity in which a man exercises his vitality directly is a power-exercise, and he will experience it as such."[188] Thus, power as a behavioral characteristic is normally used and experienced in action which can be positive. Furthermore, Guardini understands power as having an ontological expression: "Consciousness of power has also a general, ontological aspect. It is a direct expression of existence, and expression which can turn to the positive or the negative, to truth or its semblance, to right or wrong. With this, the phenomenon of power crosses over to the metaphysical, or to be precise, the religious."[189] Thus, in this sense power can be used for good or evil and a person actively living with Providence exercises choice with this aspect in order to live with fidelity to God.

Guardini considers the theological concept of power from the perspective of Revelation. He notes that the foundation of power is revealed at the beginning of the Old Testament "in connection with man's essential destination."[190] After the creation of the world God created man and woman in God's own image. Guardini argues that God's own intention was to give human persons dominion over other beings.

According to this view, a person's natural God-likeness is shown in his or her capacity for power and ability to use it. In this sense, a person has "Lordship."[191] In this context, power may be understood as great, serious and grounded in responsibility. Arguing for responsibility in human use of such sovereignty, Guardini writes:

---

186. Guardini, *Power and Responsibility*, 8.
187. Guardini, *Power and Responsibility*, 9.
188. Guardini, *Power and Responsibility*, 9.
189. Guardini, *Power and Responsibility*, 11.
190. Guardini, *Power and Responsibility*, 12.
191. Guardini, *Power and Responsibility*, 14.

> If human power and the lordship which stems from it are rooted in man's likeness to God, then power is not man's in his own right.... [He or she] is lord by the grace of God and must exercise... dominion responsibly, for [he or she] is answerable for it to him who is Lord by essence. Thus sovereignty becomes obedience, service.... Sovereignty is service also in that it operates as part of God's creation, where its mission is to continue what God in his absolute freedom, created as nature, to develop it on the human level of finite freedom as history and culture. Man's sovereignty is not meant to establish an independent world of man, but to complete the world of God as a free human world in accordance with God's will.[192]

God's Providence would surely be seen in such a world. The exercise of power must respect the self-determination of each present thing according to God's plan for its existence. A link with Providence occurs as the "name" of a person or thing is respected. For human persons the true self is able to be expressed and fulfilled. Thus as human persons come to fulfillment in God's Providence they are being empowered to do so in accordance with their essential being; their "name," rather than being impeded in their life's task because someone had wanted to exercise unethical power.

Power and Humility

Salvation is not an improvement in the state of being according to Guardini. He believes it ranks with creation itself and originates in the pure freedom of God.[193] Christ's person and attitude are important because salvation is linked with humility which Guardini considers to be a virtue of strength. Christ's strength, dominion and supreme power is converted into humility:[194] "Jesus' whole existence is a translation of power into humility. Or to state it actively: into obedience to the will of the Father as it expresses itself in the situation of each moment.... For the Son, obedience is nothing secondary or additional; it springs from the core of his being."[195] Guardini argues that the obedient strength here is not

---

192. Guardini, *Power and Responsibility*, 15.
193. Guardini, *Power and Responsibility*, 22.
194. Guardini, *Power and Responsibility*, 26.
195. Guardini, *Power and Responsibility*, 27.

weakness. It is "*kyriotes*, lordship, giving itself into slavery."[196] Salvation is therefore able to mean that a new beginning of existence has been established by God and is God's answer to the question of power.

According to Guardini, trials and difficulties will still occur, and destiny can once again show its upper-hand, but the real achievement will be shown at the end of time. Thus, he is asserting that Providence in its fullest sense is eschatological. Furthermore a note of caution must be made since Guardini writes here that the concept of destiny may, in some believers or some theologians, take on a veiled form under the cloak of the sovereignty of grace or predestination.[197] For Guardini this belief goes against the very core of the idea of Providence because in Providence human decision and freedom should prevail. He writes, "The God who destines the individual man to salvation without bringing his human freedom into the decision is no longer the God of the revelation of Jesus Christ but a revival of the ancient power of destiny concealed in Christian terminology."[198]

Thus, in this way, Guardini makes his position on predestination very clear. He does not believe that God foreordains human persons to the quality of their existence and survival in their earthly lives. Rather each person is presented with the opportunity to make his or her own decision. The guidance of God can enable such a person to live a transformed transfigured life which as lived out in absolute love, in the manner of Christ and the Saints, enable the redeemed person to live in a redeemed world and contribute to that world as a type of "co-creators" of God. Loving and Christian living in Guardini's understanding may therefore be said to be grace, freedom and destiny transformed into Providence.

Later Texts of 1959–66

The Providence text, *Gebet und Wahrheit (Prayer and Truth)*, was written in 1960. In a similar manner to the 1916 text, it stands alone as the other "bookend." Although many aspects of it are similar to the previous Providence texts, there are several differences which show that Guardini is continuing to engage with the society of the time. In his writing about 'nature' he is no longer arguing that pure nature doesn't exist and the

---

196. Guardini, *Power and Responsibility*, 28.
197. Guardini, *Freedom, Grace, and Destiny*, 214.
198. Guardini, *Freedom, Grace, and Destiny*, 214.

natural world must be called creation or God's work as he did earlier. Rather, Guardini just refers to nature as if his meaning is understood and he shows ecological concern. The same God gave Revelation and the laws of nature which belong to God as well and are images of God's wisdom. These two things need to be at peace with each other.[199] Science is to be acknowledged and worked with and not distanced. God's world must be cared for and human persons must have responsibility for this. Christ is the center of creation. Yet, some people may have found discipleship of Christ difficult. Perhaps this is why the Saints are referred to in this text. This would seem to be an awareness, on Guardini's part, that The Saints had clearly lived life as human persons do and therefore the situation is manageable. Guardini urges his readers to follow the Saints in their lives and devotion to God. In these people there is only love which means the kingdom of God is being made.[200]

Order of Being—Kingdom of God

In *Wunder und Zeichen*, Guardini's image is of God, the Lord of the World, the builder of his Kingdom, who gives the person, a co-builder, what they need, so that his kingdom may come about. The concept of order, here, is far from a rigid set of rules. Guardini uses the passage in Matthew 6 to show that this process is not a law of nature which would be effected through necessity or a world order which could be determinist. Rather, Providence is not finished but "on the way" or in process. Human action is an integral part of this. Providence is experienced in the world not apart from it. He writes:

> We should not spiritualise this text at first sight before we have tried to sense its true meaning. For it does not say: 'focus your attention upon heavenly things and if earthly concerns turn out badly brush them aside saying, "Well it doesn't matter!" No, put the Kingdom and its Justice, its order and worth, in the first place, as well as its priorities of values and motives, and worldly activities will become the Kingdom of heaven in your concrete life.[201]

---

199. Guardini, *Gebet und Wahrheit*, 125.
200. Guardini, *Gebet und Wahrheit*, 129.
201. Guardini, *Wunder und Zeichen*, 69.

Furthermore, continues Guardini, the development of the Kingdom of God will be built with the earthly human life and thus also the foundations of Christian history. It is in that context that the hand of God might also be seen:[202] "for the Christian message is not concerned with raising the soul to complete spirituality but with liberating man for a new and holy existence. The message of Jesus does not concern the spirit alone but the whole man."[203] The human person lives in a concrete, created world. We turn now to Guardini's recapping of this world's importance in his theology of Providence. The praise is to God.

Doxology

The Wisdom of the Psalms (*Weisheit des Psalmen*)[204] was published in 1963. Just as the 1916 text drew heavily from the Breviary with its Psalms and prayers, this book returns to the importance of the Psalms enjoyed by Guardini in his youth.

While Providence is not explicitly mentioned, Guardini's theological understanding in this book show the same vision of God's World which has been paramount in this book. Importantly, given the acts of the Holocaust, the religion of the Psalmist, Judaism, is not belittled nor is his own religiosity seen as defective. Guardini recognizes the Psalmist's commitment to God. In this book the mature and elderly Guardini appreciates the love of God and devotion of the Psalmist who also had a love of God's creation. The pure "nature" of the National Socialists is no longer there. Yet, divine mystery underlies creation:

> What the Psalmist sees here is not "natural" nature, not something that can be grasped by the senses or reason alone. The man who wrote these words felt the spirit of God in the world. In these great phenomena—the sea, the sun, the stars, the living and growing things—he sensed the presence of God. Everything was permeated by divine mystery. This is what he realised. It filled him with wonder and gratitude, and he gathers it all up in this word: Praised be he who made it.[205]

---

202. Guardini, *Wunder und Zeichen*, 69.
203. Guardini, *The Church of the Lord*, 75.
204. Guardini, *The Wisdom of the Psalms*.
205. Guardini, *The Wisdom of the Psalms*, 72.

Noting that God is active in all events Guardini is keen to note the link with science when he says, "Science has determined events and made them transparent. This is right and proper."[206] Fittingly, Guardini's work, and this thesis, end with the praise of God—doxology. Guardini holds that praise to God is only possible if the world is the work of God:

> If it is "nature" in the modern sense then there is no praise. Then nothing ascends from the world to an eternal holy source. Then nature does not proclaim truth and breathe forth joyousness, does not in gratitude lift up its being to its creator. . . . [E]verything simply exists dull and mute. Praise proceeds only from the knowledge of the inexpressible fact that "in the beginning"—not of time, for time came into being when God created the world but in the beginning absolutely—when there was nothing . . . and now in the heart and mind of him who knows by faith gratitude springs up because the magnanimity of the creator permits him to exist.[207]

Guardini believes that the glory of God generates praise in human persons but while the natural world lives in praise to God, it has no voice to give verbal expression.[208] He reflects on Psalm 148 and says that it is the function of human persons "to translate into words of praise the essential praise that lies in all things":[209]

> The nations are called upon, and the rulers who represent them; princes and judges who rule them, young men and maidens, old men and children—all shall praise the name of the Lord. The name of the Lord is he himself, God in the form of the word. The majesty of God is what provokes praise, the fact that power and glory are in him personified and so can receive and can receive and appreciate the praise. This majesty . . . is revealed in creation, revealed as that which surpasses all that is created.[210]

Guardini believes that the form of divine praise that is exemplified in the Psalms and is the basis of the Liturgy and the Divine Office, the prayer of the Church, is also found in Christian poetry and most perfectly in St. Francis' *Canticle of the Sun*.

206. Guardini, *The Wisdom of the Psalms*, 50.
207. Guardini, *The Wisdom of the Psalms*, 64.
208. Guardini, *The Wisdom of the Psalms*, 67.
209. Guardini, *The Wisdom of the Psalms*, 72.
210. Guardini, *The Wisdom of the Psalms*, 75.

Praise can be integral to living with Providence as the Christian adverts to the God of creation, and Providence, who also evokes responsibility. "But we must re-acquire the ability to praise; not in an artificial way, certainly, but we can, for instance, when we are out of doors, accustom ourselves to think: 'God has created this.'"[211] Guardini notes that for some people religious acts must be entirely spontaneous but he considers this a misunderstanding of prayer. Rather, while there is a kind of prayer that is spontaneous, it must be granted, but "there is also the prayer of service, of practice and this is the rule. The thought: The world is created, the heavens the light of the sun, the mountains, the trees, all are created, and praise be He who has created them—all this is prayer and we must strive to acquire it again."[212] Thus Guardini speaks of human action that may dovetail with other more instrumental action in God's world. Living with the awareness of Providence involves living with full human capacity directed towards God's world. Guardini says: "faith still means remaining in knowledge and confidence within the providence of a personally acting God, His works and deeds are now carried on within the confines of humanity as a whole."[213]

He continues:

> To believe means . . . that God is acting, throughout all time, from the creation of the world until its end. It means doing at any time that which is demanded of us, and following God towards His actions toward their goal; that is the return of Christ and the victory of the Kingdom of God. So it is good if we break through the appearance of a mere doctrinal system and say, "God is acting here and now, doing something with me also. I place myself in his activity, go with him act and strive." In this connection the meaning of "hope" becomes clear: it is the confidence that in spite of all opposition of disbelief and disobedience, in spite of seeming impossibility, the promises of the Gospel are being fulfilled and the birth of a new life will be realised for us and for the whole creation.[214]

Guardini believes human decision and action are important. Many believers have a view which is "too placid"[215] and as such are unable to ap-

---

211. Guardini, *The Wisdom of the Psalms*, 76.
212. Guardini, *The Wisdom of the Psalms*, 77.
213. Guardini, *The Wisdom of the Psalms*, 126.
214. Guardini, *The Wisdom of the Psalms*, 127.
215. Guardini, *Freedom, Grace, and Destiny*, 235.

preciate the grandeur of the responsibility which God has given them.[216] For Guardini, Christian responsibility is active and instrumental. He writes:

> We must not regard God's control of the world as a system of protection in which men live piously and securely; if we do, we are leaving the grandeur of human existence to the unbeliever, and belief becomes identified with timidity. All grandeur belongs, of course to God.... God's Providence has made use of human foresight, direction, and formative skill.... Consequently, Christian belief must develop an ethic of self-dependence, an awareness of the rights and duties of man, entrusted with the world's development, and a corresponding power of action.[217]

A Christian believer understands the rights of human persons and is always responsible. Guardini charges the Christian with responsibility for every aspect of God's creation and says that "God will demand a reckoning of everyone who by sin or negligence spoils his work."[218] Care of God's creation is important. Here we are able to see a mature expression of the idea of Providence that moves from an individual's life to a social one; the redeemed (or becoming redeemed) individual person, who is living as God made them to be, helps to bring the light of God into the world which can become a redeemed world where justice, love and responsibility and praise coexist side by side. Thus the Kingdom of God exists as a world where the love of God permeates each aspect of a person's heart and the world in which a person lives with courage, bravery and trust in God. In the Kingdom of God there is responsibility and care for God's concerns, including every aspect of creation and human persons.

---

216. Guardini, *Freedom, Grace, and Destiny*, 235.

217. Guardini, *Freedom, Grace, and Destiny*, 236. In a footnote, Guardini notes that this is not a doctrine of Activism. Rather each person has duty and work to fulfill, and if they have lost means and resources in the "disasters of recent years" (the years of National Socialism) their actions in trusting Divine Providence and moving with the will of God is a way of making a positive contribution to world problems. Guardini believes the Judgement will reveal who have been the real workers in the Christian relations to the world.

218. Guardini, *The Wisdom of the Psalms*, 67.

Conclusion

In this chapter dealing with Guardini's postwar writings we have considered Guardini's writing on the four themes studied in the other chapters. Guardini studied the way Jesus Christ lived with Providence, yet because he lived in openness to the love of God and in perfect harmony with God, the Father, he could not be said to be living with Providence. Providence is for human persons who fail to always live in harmony with God and God's intentions yet are open to the grace of God. In Christ, God took our destiny upon Godself.

Providence has been compared with destiny in all it's forms and freedom considered in many different ways. Guardini has asserted that a person is more free when God is acting. In this chapter while asserting that one brings oneself to self realization, he argues that one must have the mind of Christ. This involves religious conversion of the heart to God and conversion to God in every possible way. To the extent that the "old person" is removed and the "new person" put on, destiny changes to Providence. The central way of living with Providence is to love which Guardini says orders a person's being to God. Providence is not just a consolation but a task to be fulfilled. In a similar mode to the first period, where Guardini argued that a person is most themselves when God is acting, in this period of time, he argues that because Christ lives within a person they are able to be themselves. Responsibility in every way is important in this period; responsibility for one's own destiny or Providence, responsibility for the their actions that will be known in the judgement and responsibility with regard to the use of power. In living with Providence the human person lives according to the order of Christian being—God's love. True fulfillment comes to that person when he or she lives in a way that is true to their own being. When that person is able to bring himself or herself into accord with God's plan, fulfillment of the individual occurs alongside fulfillment of the whole. The "name" uttered to each person by God at the beginning of his or her life can be evaluated in the light of the whole. Providence ends in the judgement which is the last stage in a person's life, considered in the light of the whole. God may "re-name' a person according to his or her life. Thus Providence ends in judgement and justice and is a time for the love and mercy of God.

Overall Conclusion

God's World. No String Puppets: Providence in the Writings of Romano Guardini

GUARDINI'S WORK ON PROVIDENCE has been covered over the course of his long life. A range of sources have been used and the notion of Providence considered chronologically in order to study development and to see the changes at different times and different social contexts. My central research question was: Did Guardini's writing on Providence change or develop in each period of Guardini's writing, and if so, how and why? We have shown that there was been development in Guardini's Providence writing although there is also a basic *Gestalt* or form which was there from the beginning. This *Gestalt* has enabled different aspects to of Providence to come to the fore at different times. Like much of Guardini's work, his notion of Providence comes primarily from Scripture and is nourished by theology from the Christian tradition. Guardini grounds his theology of Providence in the theology of God the Creator who also acts with human co-operation. Providence for the individual is not fixed or finished and proceeds with Providence of the whole. The context of Providence is God's love which is both the path and the goal. Providence is known in this world but is also eschatological and ends in judgement and justice after the person's earthly life. Justice which was denied a person in his or her life can occur at that time. Providence for the individual can proceed with the whole. Furthermore, Providence for the human person has been shown to be fulfillment for that person. Fulfillment for the person comes as the person matures according to his or her own nature and deep being, which is rooted in the being of God but particular for each person, and is that person's "call." There is a vocational aspect with it because that person is held in the being of God who has created each human person to be uniquely him or herself. When a person lives in authenticity according to that uniqueness they are more able to live providentially. The redeemed person has a redeemed existence through Jesus Christ and, can be "a door for God" in the world and able to contribute to a changed, redeemed world. God is a God of love, and Providence, primarily understood under four themes, develops in each period of Guardini's life although the overall *Gestalt* or form was there from the beginning. We turn now to specific differences in the themes.

The thesis considered Guardini's notion of Providence according to four themes which proved to be important for making distinctions according to each period of time. They are: 1) Jesus Christ and Providence; 2) Providence is understood in Relationship with God; 3) The Individual Person is Important to God; 4) New Creation and New Existence. **The first theme considers Jesus Christ in relation to Providence**, but although Guardini referred to the centrality of Christ in some of his early work, the first Providence text I have used grounds Providence in the context of the nature and characteristics of God. Guardini argues that God has infinite wisdom, power, patience, simplicity, fullness and absolute love. This enabled Guardini to argue that God can be trusted, and the person must have faith. The notion of trust was an important part of the first text. Guardini developed the notion of the wisdom of God and God as the Good which, he argued, is God's Holiness. Building on the attitude of faith, in the next period, *chapter 4*, Guardini considered the question of *how Jesus Christ understood Providence*. It was the period of National Socialism and Guardini noted that, unlike the National Socialists, Jesus did not speak about an order to things, but Providence was the work of the Holy Spirit and is understood from the heart. Although many in German society searched for order at this time, they needed to know that Providence may take an unpredictable path. In this chapter, the care of God is still there as in *chapter 1*, but Guardini notes that Jesus taught the person living with Providence to have an interior attitude of a quiet heart. The person must be God-loving and focus on the Kingdom of God. This notion of the Kingdom of God involves a new structure of existence around such a person and all that happens will be from God's love. *Chapter 5* showed development in this theme as Guardini looked at *the way Jesus lived with Providence*. This direct approach showed the place of Christ in the personal relationship with his heavenly Father and God was paramount. Destiny was transformed in the life of Christ and Guardini considered Christ's freedom. The atonement of Christ on the cross is well developed in this chapter where Guardini argued that God freely entered into history in the form of Jesus Christ and took the destiny of human persons upon God-self. Christ's life demonstrated many things including the way everything in Christ's life was brought into his love and harmony of the relationship with the Father. In this chapter, Guardini shows the action of Christ that is redemptive. Jesus was able to make atonement for people's sins, and alter Satan's relation to the world, because he remained in his Father's will where he was able to continue standing in integrity.

There was development in the second theme, **Providence is understood in relationship with God**, when Guardini moved from the more instrumental concept of conscience and the Good *in the first (early) period* to the very personal "I-Thou" relationship with God as the person's true "Thou" *in the second period*, although the importance of a mutual relationship with God had been asserted in the early period as well. In this period of National Socialism, Guardini argued that in living with Providence, Jesus Christ must live within a person. The reality and not an image is meant. Having the indwelling Christ is an important part of living with Providence. The context is the love of God. In *the third (Post war) period* we looked at the presence of evil and possible ways that relationship with God might be hindered. The experience of Christ in dealing with evil was instructive there. All forms of freedom, and finally, grace and Christian freedom showed that Providence is experienced when a person is free and able to attain self-realization. True freedom comes from the grace of God. Providence is known in relationship with God lived in the world and Guardini highlights the importance of love in living with Providence. The redeemed person has a special relationship with God because God willed that person to be and when a person believes in Christ, God in God's love is able to direct that person. Christ is important but here we can see the importance of the love of God that is paramount in Guardini's writing on Providence in this period.

Development of the third theme, **the individual human person is important to God**, was enabled after Guardini laid down the argument for later work, *in the first period*, and asserted that not only was God in the heart of the human person but the human person was in God's heart, valued and uniquely formed by God. The human person can share in the life of God. Guardini urges repentance and conversion to God ("being born again"). *In the second period, in the time of National Socialism*, that uniqueness, noted in the early period, was developed and was a mode of opposition to Hitler who announced that the individual human person was not important and could be replaced. Guardini considered the notion of person who is much more than *individuum* but someone able to be self-possessed and stand with integrity in their own right. Each human person is valuable. Human will was considered in this chapter. Each person has been called, he asserted, drawing on earlier work as well. *In the third and post war period* Guardini's notion of Providence was developed further when Guardini argued that Providence ends in the Judgement and justice. The National Socialist period had seen many atrocities and it is fitting that Providence should end in this way. Judgement is a positive concept for Guardini because it is there that the individual human person will find the mercy of God and justice for injustices suffered in this life. The total love of God is the context.

In theme four, **Providence is new existence and new creation** Guardini showed how the world is important. *In the early period, chapter 3*, he showed how creation can be renewed through God's love and human action, especially the moral actions of human persons. Moral deeds formed in every situation are important because with moral actions the world can be "finished from the inside" through that person. Providence can be experienced in this world, of God's creation. An ontological and ethical transformation is possible. Christ is the center of the world. The kingdom of God exists when a person is open to God and a person who is prayerful and trusts God can have a holy existence and care of God. This chapter laid down the foundation for the subsequent chapters where we are able to see development. *In the second period, chapter 4*, Guardini addressed the issue of nature and creation in an environment where the National Socialists had absolutized nature and used it to underpin their racial concepts. Guardini argued that the natural world was not just nature but God's creation. During this period, Guardini once again argued that the environment around a person was important and that the human person was artisan of his or her own fortune. Guardini's position here was strong, and it could be argued that it bordered on Pelagianism as he wrote that a person who lived in fear and thought about negative things such as a bomb dropping on his or her house might bring that actual situation upon him or herself. This was expressed too strongly, but the notion of the environment around the person was well developed in *The World and the Person*. Guardini's point was that when a person's attitude changes their destiny will change. He focused on the importance of conversion to God and God's way of thinking. In addressing the idea of the "superior person" of the National Socialists, Guardini wrote of the importance of being a God-loving person. The God-loving person, the person of faith, forms an entrance for the creative power of God which is directed towards the world. *In the third period, chapter 5,* Guardini still argues for a transformed world from human hearts yet there is soberness. In the wake of the events of the wartime period Guardini writes of responsibility. In particular this relates to power. Human persons can act with power in a positive sense and power can be good if used correctly. Guardini took action on behalf of the Jews in this period and spoke of responsibility towards others and all of creation. In this period Guardini shows a similar way of thinking to the first period—God is the God of nature and there should be no disjunction between the laws of nature, science and God. The world is important for living with God's Providence. There is still a double agency in Guardini's work, and the human person can become a "co-creator" with God. Looking again at the example of St. Francis, he argues that when a person is God-loving and focused on the Kingdom of God, and God's concerns, the person is surrounded by Holy care and the environment and everything else around that person will be different. That person can be a door for God in the world. In that sense the redeemed person will help to usher in a redeemed world. The world itself can be a holy and transformed world brimming with the grace of God.

We have argued that in Guardini's early life the Providence form was developed from Scripture and theology. The first Providence text clearly grounds Providence in the nature or characteristics of God the Creator. We said that the argument from God's characteristics is important for understanding that God can be trusted. Acts made in communion with God are more than just natural acts. Assent to God is volitional and mutual. In this way, Providence is lived in communion with God. Guardini shows that in order for a person's destiny to be fulfilled, God works though the community where a person lives and works and his notion of Providence is world affirming, not world denying. The human person lives as a *Theonom* and is therefore able to have God-guided integrity. The world has polarities and, at another level, the human person's relationship with the world occurs in the context of a "pole" in the person and a "pole" in the world. This enables learning and influence which bears on the awareness of Providence. Finally, in the living out of Providence, a person living in relationship with God is able to reflect on their life in association with God and see the movement of God's action in his or her life.

The importance of the individual person is understood in the context of God's love. The life-transforming Providential nature of God is given to the person, already linked by existence, when that person responds to God. In the early period Guardini shows that a person is not only cared for by God but is also in God's *heart* and named by God. The relationship with God, which already exists, can enable the person to be "born again." Guardini argued for a theosis at this time of writing although he doesn't use the term. He understands the person and the world to be in the same process of deification which enables a person to live a new and holy existence while in the world. Repentance is necessary for transcendence from the earthbound state.

Guardini believes that God is able to guide each individual life in a way in which it is in harmony with God's own plan for the world. It doesn't happen just naturally or automatically. God wants this guidance of the individual and the world to be loving, and understood in relationship with God's self. In this sense, Providence, for God, is intensely personal and involves human decision. Furthermore in living with Providence God can guide the individual and the world in a way in which they "dovetail" together.

Later sections also continued many of the themes which first appeared in Guardini's early writing on Providence. Many of these questions hinge on an understanding of God and God's nature and mode of operation as well as an anthropological and ontological understanding, yet in Guardini's thought these categories are only understood in the context of personal relationship to God which God has initiated. Guardini's understanding of transcendence is only understood in the context of God's immanence in the personal relationship which is offered and is not contextualized in a Deist or even semi-Deist position. Rather it indicates the absolute incomprehensibility of God even in God's immanence.

A Deist position would have spoken of a world in which God did not intervene in any way. The world would be controlled by a physical or moral order. In this sense, the individual would have to fit in with the rules of the overall order. Some Christian theologians who could be categorized as a semi-Deist for instance, believe that God does not intervene in this world.[1] For the Deist, God exists but is not directly involved with the day to day dealings. The world is left to its own resources so to speak. There are some strengths to such a model. For instance, were such a God

---

1. See Wiles, *God's Action in the World*, 96.

to exist, one would feel that one had full-self determination and was not fully and deterministically controlled. Likewise, one would not have a sense of being a puppet-on-a-string doing whatever God wanted while having no real self-expression of one's own. The person would have the sense that all of their personal integrity was intact. In that sense, we must also answer that while Guardini would not see God as uninvolved in the world, he does not understand God as absolute controller either. Guardini believes that God gives people freedom to act in the world without God's direct control. At the same time he accepts the notion of the indwelling Christ who, acting as grace of God in the Holy Spirit, is able to guide the believer to live as God wants and thus create harmony between the overall direction of world history and the personal history of the individual believer. It could be argued that Christ's guidance also gives way to a lack of self-determination for the believer. Guardini would answer that Christ within a person enables the believer to be brought to sharing in the life of God and to a greater fulfillment and therefore the person is more themselves. He has argued that a person is more themselves when God is acting and therefore, because of the grace, they have more freedom. Guardini holds that a person's actions are important. In the second period, Guardini makes that even clearer. To passively accept one's fate by letting external events, or internal passivity, determine one's life is destiny but not Providence for him. Providence involves active orientation to the world and events of people and things in an attitude in which human action and the human spirit are combined with the grace and action of God. In that sense, a person is also able to be a door for God in the world.

Guardini believes that Providence is not finished or fixed but "becoming" and the actions of each individual are important. We should be careful to distinguish the concept of Providence as "becoming" from that of God (himself) as "becoming," which could imply that God is unfinished. Some Process theologians would appear to hold this view. That is not Guardini's position although he believes that God in God's being is dynamic. There is some similarity and dissimilarity with the position of some Process theologians in Guardini's thought. One such area of similarity is the notion of God as an empowering God. Guardini believes that God is able to empower people in the sense that they can be all that they are meant to be through the power of God's grace. Unlike some Process theologians, Guardini does not hold that the being of God contains evil in an opposite pole to the Good. He has specifically refuted such a notion and, as argued above, considers such a position to be an error in the writings of some German authors.

Guardini has written that God takes Christ's suffering (and humanity's suffering) into himself and makes it his own. Yet when discussing the Good, Guardini refutes the notion that "the Good" and human persons form a unity in which each are mutually determined by the other since that would be to introduce a relativity.[2] God is God. In terms of God's love, Guardini states that God continuously works in every situation and attempts to move things in the direction of the greatest Good. We have noted that for Guardini, when human persons allow evil to enter their lives and do that which is contrary to God's will, God, who will consider creative life to be lost, can re-create, ordering things anew to God's purposes although someone must pay for the mistake.

There is a double agency in Guardini's work. It is interesting to note the arguments of critics of Process thought, who argue that Process theologians give too much credit to beings for action which can affect God's response to situations and therefore affect God negatively. Perhaps this is why when Guardini speaks of human action in Providence he not only holds that Christ must live within a person living a committed spiritual life, but he recommends Christian discipleship in the footsteps of Christ and the Saints who despite human difficulties were able to cooperate with God and work for God in the world with exemplary lives. The cooperation of human persons with God, is able to bring the greatest Good, which is God, into the world for the benefit of others also. While Guardini believes that God has given human freedom, he holds that God will ultimately determine the outcome of events by God's guidance and continued action for God's Kingdom.

Guardini does not share the view of the "Openness Theologians" who argue that God is not omniscient for the future. That is to say, their argument is that God doesn't know the future and "takes risks" by allowing his creatures full freedom to act although he does not know the outcome. Nevertheless, there are aspects of this thought that Guardini would agree with such as the approach to prayer, which was discussed in more detail in this thesis. Guardini would also have disjunction with any thought which gives evil a place in the being of God. Although Guardini believes that God permits some evil for the working out of sacred history, he has said that evil has no ontological status and comes from the freedom

---

2. Guardini, *Freedom, Grace, and Destiny*, 47.

which God allows. For that reason, he places evil in the category of contradiction rather than the category of contrary because unlike a contrary, evil cannot be the opposite of good. It is completely irreconcilable.

Guardini's theology is incarnational. Christ is the Redeemer and only through life in him, indeed as innermost principle, is a person able to share fully in the life of God. Guardini relates this life to a life from the divine ideas of God through Christ. In the post-war period, Guardini based his argument on the atonement of Christ. Human persons can participate in Christ's love for God, the Father, and relationship with him. In *The World and the Person*, Guardini asserted that God's standards are divine. Therefore it is fitting that Christ is divinely perfect: the exemplar who is able to fulfill the divine ideas of God. In the last chapter, Guardini showed how the relationship of Christ with God was lived out in perfect harmony and accord. Christ was faithful to his Father in the living of his life, and everything was brought into this relationship with God. With Guardini's Christocentric theology, reminiscent of St. Bonaventure, Christ has a central place—seen very clearly in his Providence writings, especially from the time of National Socialism. In that second period of his writing on Providence, Christ is brought out more strongly than in his early writings, and we have understood that this Christocentric position represents a way which is religiously opposed to that of Hitler and the National Socialists. The centrality of Christ in Guardini's concept of Providence places Guardini alongside Karl Barth in this aspect. Jesus Christ was central in Barth's conception of Providence as well. Arguably, for Barth (and we could affirm that for Guardini as well) Jesus Christ heralds the election of the whole human race. The centrality of Christ in Guardini's thought and the social environment in which he wrote in this period, enabled Guardini to contextualize his own view of God's Providence in Jesus Christ's understanding. Christ therefore is not just an instrument through whom God works, nor is he just an example, but he is God the Son and really understands God's purposes. He is able, within this understanding, to turn our hearts and minds to God the Father as he brings us into relationship with the inner self of God. The wisdom of God is brought by Christ himself. In this way, when human persons care for God's kingdom the focus is on God in God's self.

Guardini shows that the world is created and proceeds from God; it is God's world. Furthermore, Providence can usher in a transformed world. According to Guardini, when a person changes within and *metanoia* occurs, the person's destiny can change. Here we find the aspect which is unique to Guardini: the assertion that one's inner *Gestalt* can be changed according to one's choices in a way which enables Providence to enter a person's life. The person can be surrounded by "Holy care" and when a person focuses on the Kingdom of God, there is a new hierarchy of values, priorities, and concerns. This new hierarchy creates a different relationship to people and things. We have said that Guardini believes human persons can be a door for God in the world, and we can understand his understanding to be commensurate with the assertion that Providence can usher in a transformed world so that the world-in-transformation is not just a matter of changed perception on the part of the believer.

The world is essentially God's world and can be what God intended if God's wisdom is brought into it. A link between the first period of Guardini's writing and the fifth occurs in the assertion that every person must stand in the wisdom of God with all of their actions and, in the final judgement, be assessed in that light; the light of God's wisdom. God guides the world and human persons can cooperate by electing to put themselves with God's wisdom and thus guide their choices in a way which is commensurate with God's plan for the world. Guardini believes that God has the capacity to guide the individual and the world in such a way that fulfillment for each occurs simultaneously.

God's will is important in Providence. Expressed as wisdom, one can understand wisdom as having God's omniscience, intention, and will together. The world is essentially God's creation and can be the way God intended if God's wisdom is allowed full sway in the world. God guides the world but human persons can co-operate by electing to allow God's wisdom to light their paths and thus guide their choices in a way which is commensurate with God's plan for the world. This can occur in complete commitment to God and Christian living aided by Christ. Guardini uses the term "God's intention" but it is more than just intention. Rather, it is what God in God's wisdom actually wants, while allowing for human freedom and human cooperation. The person does not get "taken over" as such but is able, in grace, to move to a position where God's wisdom in the Holy Spirit is able to guide that person. This can occur as Christ within guides the person according to Christ's understanding of God's will which has been informed by Christ's innermost understanding. One day every person must stand in the wisdom of God with all of their actions and be assessed in that light; the light of God's wisdom. The wisdom meant here is therefore the wisdom which guides the world and which one accepts or rejects in choices throughout one's life.

While Guardini doesn't believe that God takes risks in the sense that Openness theologians refer to it, he argues that living with Providence may entail some risk for the person since the future is open, although known to God. Trust and faith find a place in that context. The new creation can be made through the hearts of human persons and since human persons have responsibility for the world, their hearts are the door for the love of God in the world. This occurs, Guardini believes, when the human spirit and the Spirit of God mix together in the human heart. The grace of God can grow in a heart in which the person is more open and lives as God wants.

The grace of putting something into action can strengthen the will and engender patience. Guardini doesn't believe that one can influence God's decision in prayer. He believes that prayer establishes the relationship in which a person may know what the will of God is because of guidance through the wisdom of God. Contemplation is important in living with Providence because the world and meaning of things may be clear. One may then pray for guidance. Guardini holds that prayer for others can only have legitimacy if one prays that God's will is done.

Providence is to be lived in the world not apart from it. Prayerful reflection on each day will reveal the intricate workings, the unseen hand contributing to the world and the lives of the people in it. A focus on God's concerns will help to usher in this transformed world. Holy care will surround those who love God and respond to God's grace. The environment around them *will* be different. Such people are a door for God in the world.

Romano Guardini's theology of Providence is unique in the areas he addresses. His notion of Providence is Trinitarian; it is grounded in the theology of God the Creator and is focused on Jesus Christ and the Holy Spirit. His theology of Providence is well developed, as this thesis makes clear, is personal and relational rather than abstract and rigid, human experience is integral to it, and he is able to show how freedom and grace lead to destiny which is transformed into Providence in the love of God. Guardini's theology is unique in the study of Providence through the experience of the human person and in his focus on the importance of human action and was especially so for his time. When a person's attitude and being changes, his or her destiny changes as well.

Everything in God's plan is directed to the New Heaven and New Earth in which all will find fulfillment. Guardini has consistently argued that in order for Providence to come into play a person must seek the Kingdom of God. In that sense, Providence can seem to be somewhat elusive. The human person is not asked to seek Providence but the Kingdom of God and God's righteousness. One is then able to move from a focus on self to a focus on God and God's concerns. When the focus is on God's concerns, the nature of God is also clearer. Focus on God and God's concerns, and Christian consciousness will allow an openness of being in which God's grace can be operative in the world, because instead of projecting anxiety or negativity, the Christian can project the Good and God's Grace. (To "be," when actualized in a person's life, can allow God's grace to be active and the direction clearer.) This occurs in relationship since openness to another also allows openness to the grace of God. Guardini holds that the real "Thou" of a person is God, and the relationship with God allows openness to God's grace which grows in a person's heart, and it is in this way that the individual becomes a "door" for God in the world. Human interaction is an important part of Providence.

Guardini holds that Providence must be lived in the world and not lived by moving in retreat from the world. The world is essentially God's world and not just natural. Creation is meant to be different from pure nature although the laws of nature are there. Creation doesn't just proceed from God but reveals God's continual decision and act. This could mean that God is always in control. Guardini speaks of God's governance (*Walten Gottes*) but more frequently speaks of God's guidance (*Lenkung*). Human decisions are important and can affect the future of a person. Guardini's idea about this is not so much that God's omniscience is limited but that God allows human freedom and human beings are essentially alienated from God. Often their decisions do not allow God's wisdom to prevail in this world and therefore God in God's wisdom does not finalize the Kingdom of God right now. That is to say, God does not bring a completely redeemed world, as God wants it, to completion at this time. We have said that, for Guardini, when the will of God is not done or evil is allowed to thwart the plan of God, God will re-create, but someone must pay for the mistake. Often in such a situation, suffering has been created by such a mistake. Guardini holds that the way God wants things to proceed in the world is for human persons to decide in favour of God's will and, by their actions, bring God's grace into the world, working therefore towards the new heaven and earth that God wants by becoming a door for God in the world. Conversion to God gives a person the new redeemed existence that is no longer mere destiny but a converted, renewed Christian existence whose being is the result of grace yet reflects that person's decisions. People are free, but God knows what they should do for their best interests and those of God's plan, for Providence is open and not fixed. Therefore a person can work with God as a type of "co-creator." The Christological focus of Guardini's notion of Providence means that when Christ dwells within the believer, one not only allows Christ to change and guide one's life but one can share in Christ's own communion with God the Father. Guardini believes that Christ's human life was so transformed by the Spirit of God that Christ is completely Spirit, *Holy Spirit*, and it is this Christ that lives within the believer transforming the person from glory to glory. That is not to say that Guardini has a two person Trinity. He doesn't, and he still continues to refer to the Holy Spirit who places Christ in a person's heart.

Guardini concentrates on God in God's unity in his last word on Providence. He shows how the concept of the Kingdom of God is understood in the Scriptures before showing how it develops in Providential living. According to the biblical pattern, Providence is again clearly linked to God the Creator. God the Creator is clearly working through God's creation which is God's expression, yet Guardini's theological anthropology allows for a resolution of the problem of Divine Causality and human responsibility and freedom. The centrality of God and human response, to the invitation to relationship with God, enables Providence to develop in a way in which the characteristics of God are not reduced. Rather, their effect on the being of the human person enables that person's being to be ordered and enhanced according to God's wisdom. Providence is known in relationship with God and lived in the world. It is this relationship which enables development of one's life's purpose in accordance with a person's name or image held in the heart of God. In living in accordance with that image the human person is able to contribute to the world and exercise care and responsibility for God's kingdom according to the gifts and disposition given by God.

Ultimately love, offered by God, and, from that standpoint, given by human persons to others, is the human action which determines the way the person is in the world and in which Providence will be lived out. Holy care will surround such persons. The person is loved by God. In this sense, Providence is intensely personal and, concomitantly, communal as a person acts with his or her whole being with a community of care for God's kingdom. The context is the love of God for it is God's world.

Providence—Guardini's Prayer

O Lord, you made all things "in their measure and number and weight," and all that happens takes place according to your wisdom. You gave freedom to man, that he might act on his own accord. But as soon as he has ended a deed, it stands within the structure of reality; he can no longer undo it, but must proceed onwards from it.

Thus you have fashioned his existence. In all things your justice and goodness should shine, but man has become lost to you, and the order of love has become changed into the dark image of fate.

But in Christ, your Son, you have revealed your countenance and begun a new work, O Father. He triumphed over fate and in so doing showed us your providence.

Now all things must be for us a disposition of your love. That is given us as a comfort, but also as a task. The message is not permission to let things take their course, nor to shut our eyes to your seriousness, but a call to holy action. Your kingdom must be the only necessity for us. Our first care and consideration must be directed to seeing that your kingdom come and that its justice be done. But then we may know that everything however obscure is for our good. Whatever we experience as fate, we should faithfully transmute to the picture of your providence, confidently overcome the strangeness and assist with love in your work.

Help me, O Lord, to lighten the confusion of things with the clarity of faith, and to lift off the weight of all that burdens me through the strength of trust.

And may your Holy Spirit bear witness in my heart that I am truly your child and am in the right when I accept all happenings from your hand. Let those questions which no human wisdom can answer be answered in the confirmation of your love. That I am loved by you is the answer to every question – grant that I feel it when the testing time comes.

Amen

Romano Guardini, *Prayers From Theology*

Bibliography

Allen, John, Jr. "How Romano Guardini Helps to Shape the 'Spirit of the Papacy.'" https://cruxnow.com/news-analysis/2018/02/romano-guardini-helps-shape-spirit-papacy/.
Allen, Paul L. *Theological Method: A Guide for the Perplexed*. New York: T. & T. Clark International, 2012.
Amico, Charles. *The Natural Knowability of God According to John Henry Newman with Special Reference to the Argument from Design in the Universe*. Rome: Urbania University Press, 1986.
Arendt, Hannah. *Eichmann in Jerusalem: A Report on the Banality of Evil*. New York: Viking, 1963.
———. *The Origins of Totalitarianism*. London: Allen and Unwin, 1951.
Babolin, Albino. "L'Esperienza Religiosa in Romano Guardini." *Studia Patavia* 15 (1968) 313–22.
———. *Romano Guardini: Filosofo dell'Alterita*. 2 vols. Bologna: Zanchelli. 1968–1969.
Balthasar, Hans Urs von. *Romano Guardini: Reform from the Source*. Translated by Albert K. Wimmer and D. C. Schindler. San Francisco: Ignatius, 2010; *Romano Guardini: Reform aus dem Ursprung*. Freiburg: Johannes, 1995.
Bärsch, Claus-Ekkehard. *Die politische Religion des Nationalsozialismus: Die religiösen Dimension der National Socialisten – Ideology in den Schriften von Dietrich Eckart, Joseph Goebbels, Alfred Rosenberg und Adolf Hitler*. Munich: Fink, 2002.
Berkouwer, G. C. *The Providence of God*. Translated by Lewis Smedes. Grand Rapids: Eerdmans, 1952.
Bernhardt, Reinhold. *Was Heißt Handeln Gottes? Eine Reconstruktion der Lehre von der Vorsehun*. Gütersloh: Gütersloher, 1999.
Bevans, Stephen B. *An Introduction to Theology in Global Perspective*. Maryknoll: Orbis, 2009.
———. *Models of Contextual Theology*. Maryknoll: Orbis, 2003.
Biser, Eugen. *Interpretation and Veränderung: Wirk und Wirkung Romano Guardinis*. Paderborn: Schöningh, 1979.
Blanning, T. C. W., and David Cannadine. *History and Biography: Essays in Honor of Derek Beales*. Cambridge: Cambridge University Press, 1996.
Bonaventure, Saint. *Journey of the Mind into God* (Itinerarium Mentis in Deum). https://www.crossroadsinitiative.com/media/articles/journey-of-the-mind-into-god/.
Borghesi, Massimo. *Romano Guardini dialettica e antropologia*. Rome: Studium, 1990.
Borsig, Lina. *Das Personale Antlitz des Menschen*. Mainz: Matthias–Grünwald, 1987.

Bougerol, Guy J. *Introduction to the Works of Bonaventure*. Translated by Jose de Vinck. Paterson: St. Anthony Guild, 1964.

Boyd, Gregory A. *Trinity and Process: A Critical Evaluation and Reconstruction of Hartshorne's Di-polar Theism Towards a Trinitarian Metaphysics*. New York: Lang, 1972.

Brockelman, Paul. *Cosmology and Creation: The Spiritual Significance of Contemporary Cosmology*. Oxford: Oxford University Press, 1999.

Brunner, August. "Foreword." In *On the Eternal in Man*, by Max Scheler, translated by Bernard Noble. London: SCM, 1960.

Brüske, Gunda. *Anruf der Freiheit: Anthropologie bei Romano Guardini*. Paderborn: Schöningh, 1998.

———. "Epilogo." In *Tra Coscienza e Storia: Il problema dell 'Etica in Romano Guardini*, edited by Michele Nicoletti and Silvan Zucal. Brescia: Morcelliana, 1999.

Buber, Martin. *I and Thou*. Translated by Ronald Gregor Smith. 2nd ed. Edinburgh: T. & T. Clark, 1958; *Ich und Du*. Berlin: Schocken, 1923.

Bucher, Rainer. *Hitler's Theology: A Study in Political Religion*. Translated by Rebecca Pohl, edited by Michael Helzel. London: Continuum, 2011.

Caine, Barbara. *Biography and History*. London: Palgrave Macmillan, 2010.

Caputo, John D. *Heidegger and Aquinas: An Essay on Overcoming Metaphysics*. New York: Fordham University Press, 1982.

Carbone, Vincenzo. *Una contemplativa nella vita attiva*. Venice: Instituto delle Suore Maestre di Santa Dorotea, 1993.

Certeau, Michel de. *The Writing of History*. Translated by Tom Conley. New York: Columbia University Press, 1988.

Cesarani, David. *Eichman: His Life and Crimes*. London: Heinemann, 2004.

A Concise Dictionary of Theology. Edited by Gerald O'Collins and Mario Farrugia. London: HarperCollins, 1991.

Cooper, Jordan. *Christification: A Lutheran Approach to Theosis*. Eugene: Wipf & Stock, 2014.

Cowburn, John. *Freewill, Predestination and Determinism*. Milwaukee: Marquette University Press, 2008.

Delio, Ilia. "Theology, Metaphysics, and the Centrality of Christ." *Theological Studies* 68 (2007) 254–73.

De Caussade, Jean Pierre. *Abandonment to Divine Providence*. Translated by John Beevers. New York: Image, 1975.

De Mesa, Jose M., and Westyn Lode. *Doing Theology: Basic Realities and Processes*. London: SCM, 1985.

Dessain, Charles C. *The Problem of Polarisation*. New York: Mellen, 1992.

Dietrich, Donald J., ed. *Christian Responses to the Holocaust: Moral and Ethical Issues*. New York: Syracuse University Press, 2003.

Ebeling, Gerhard. *Theology and Proclamation*. Translated by John Riches. London: Collins, 1966; *Theologie und Verkündigung*. Tübingen: Mohr, 1962.

Edwards, Denis. *How God Acts: Creation, Redemption, and Special Divine Action*. Hindmarsh: ATF, 2010.

———. *Jesus the Wisdom of God. An Ecological Theology*. Homebush: St. Paul's, 1995.

Evans, Richard J. *The Coming of the Third Reich*. London: Penguin, 2003.

———. *The Third Reich in Power: How the Nazis Won over the Hearts and Minds of a Nation*. London: Penguin, 2005.

Farrugia, Mario. "Romano Guardini 1885–1968." In *Dictionary of Fundamental Theology*, edited by Rene Latourelle and Rino Fisichella, 403–6. New York: Crossroad, 1994; *Dizionario di Teologia Fondamentale*. Edited by Rene Latourelle and Rino Fisichella. Assisii: Cittadella, 1990.

Fiddes, Paul S. *Participating in God: A Pastoral Doctrine of the Trinity*. London: Dartman, Longman and Todd, 2000.

Flynn, Gabriel, and Paul D. Murray, eds. *Ressourcement: A Movement for Renewal in Twentieth-Century Catholic Theology*. Oxford: Oxford University Press. 2012.

Genoid, Franscois. *The Testament of Adolf Hitler: The Hitler-Bormann Documents, February–April 1945*. Translated by R. H. Stevens. London: Cassel, 1961.

Gerl, Hanna-Barbara. *Romano Guardini: La Vita e l'Opera*. Translated by Benno Scharf. Brescia: Morcelliana, 1988.

Gerl-Falkovitz, Hanna-Barbara. *Romano Guardini 1885–1968: Leben und Werk*. Mainz: Matthias-Grünwald, 1985.

———. *Romano Guardini: Konturen des Lebens und Spuren des Denkens*. Kevelaer: Topos, 2010.

Göbbels, Joseph. *Final Entries 1945: The Diaries of Joseph Göbbels*. Translated by Richard Barry. Edited by Trevor Roper. New York: Putnam's Sons, 1978; *Tägebücher 1945: Die Letzen Aufzeichungenen*. Hamburg: Hoffmann and Campe, 1977.

Godman, Peter. *Hitler and the Vatican: Inside the Secret Archives That Reveal the New Story of the Nazis and the Church*. New York: Free, 2004.

Graham, Elaine, et al. *Theological Reflection: Methods*. London: SCM, 2005.

Greenberg, Irving. *For the Sake of Heaven and Earth: The New Encounter between Judaism and Christianity*. Philadelphia: JPS, 2004.

Gremillion, J. B. "Interview with Romano Guardini." *America* (1958) 193–95.

Griener, George E. "Herman Schell and the Reform of the Catholic Church in Germany." *Theological Studies* 54 (1993) 427–54.

Guardini, Romano. *The Art of Praying: The Principles and Methods of Christian Prayer*. Translated by Prince Leopold of Löwenstein-Wertheim. New Hampshire: Sophia Institute, 1985; *Vorschule des Betens*. Mainz: Matthias-Grünwald, 1943.

———. *Der Anfang aller Dinge: Meditationen über Genesis Kapitel i–iii*. Würzburg: Abteilung Die Bürg, 1940.

———. *Die Annahme Seiner Selbst: Christliche Besinnung*. Eine religiöse Hausebibliotek 6. Würzburg: Werkbund, 1953.

———. *Ansprachen, Vorträge und Artikel von und über Romano Guardini*. Edited by Ernst Tewes. Munich: Tewes, 1997.

———. "Aus der Biblischen Gotteslehrer." *Die Schildgennossen* 18 (1939) 1–15.

———. "Die Bedeutung der Psalmen feriae quintae für das geistlichen Leben." *Vortrag auf der Konferenz des Dekanantez Mainz-Stadt in Der Katholik* 197 (1913) 83–97.

———. *Berichte über mein Leben: Autobiographische Aufzeichnungen*. Schriften Der Katholische Academy in Bayern. Edited by Franz Heinrich. Dusseldorf: Patmos, 1984.

———. "Betrachtungen über Gestalten aus der Heiligen Schrift." *Burgbrief* 2 (1933) 17–19.

———. *The Conversion of Aurelius Augustine: The Inner Process in His Confessions*. Translated by Elinor Briefs. Westminster: Newman, 1960; *Die Bekehrung des Aurelius Augustinus: Der Innere Vorgangin seinen Bekenntnissen*. Die Schildgenossen 15, (1935): 2–17.

BIBLIOGRAPHY

———. *Christliche Besinnung*. Bd. 1. Würzburg: Werkbund, 1950.

———. "Die Christliche Innerlichkeit." *Die Schildgenossen* 13 (1934) 465–72.

———. *Die Christliche Liebe: Eine Auslegung von I Kor. 13*. Würzburg: Abteilung Die Burg, 1940.

———. *The Church and the Catholic and The Spirit of the Liturgy*. Translated by Ada Lane. New York: Sheed and Ward, 1935; *Vom Sinn der Kirche*. Mainz: Matthias-Grünwald, 1922; *Vom Geist der Liturgie*. Freiburg: Herder, 1918.

———. *The Church of the Lord: On the Nature and Mission of the Church*. Translated by Stella Lange. Chicago: Regnery, 1996; *Die Kirche Des Herrn*. Würzburg: Werkbund, 1965.

———. *Conscience*. Translated by Ada Lane. New York: Benzinger Brothers, 1932; *Das Güte, das Gewissen und die Sammlung*. Mainz: Matthias-Grünwald, 1929.

———. *Die Waage des Daseins: Rede zum Gedächtnis von Sophie und Hans Scholl, Christoph Probst, Alexander Schmorell, Willi Graf und Prof. Huber*. Translated by Michele Nicoletti and Paolo Ghezzi. Tübingen-Stuttgart: Wunderlich, 1946.

———. *Diario-Appunti e Testi del 1942 al 1964*. Translated by Nerea Ponzanelli. Brescia: Morcelliana, 1983; *Wahrheit des Denkens und Wahrheit des Tuns. Notizen und Text. 1942–1964*, Paderborn: Schöningh, 1980.

———. *The End of the Modern World: A Search for Orientation*. Translated by Joseph Theman and Herbert Burke. London: Sheed and Ward, 1956; *Das Ende der Neuzeit: Ein Versuche zur Orientierung*. Basel: Hess, 1950.

———. "Es Lebe die Freiheit: Festrede, gehalten bei der Enthüllung des Mahnmals für Professor Kurt Huber und sein studentischen Widerstandkreis am 12 July 1958." Translated by Michele Nicholetti. In *Jahrbuch der Ludwig-Maximillian-Universität München*. München: Universitätsgesellschaft, 1958.

———. *Ethik, Vorlesungen an der Universität München*. 2 vols. Edited by Hans Merker and Martin Marschall. Mainz: Matthias-Grünwald, 1993.

———. *The Faith and Modern Man*. Translated by Charlotte E. Forsythe. London: Burns and Oats, 1953; *Glaubenserkenntnis*. Basel: Hess, 1944.

———. *Freedom, Grace, and Destiny: Three Chapters in the Interpretation of Existence*. Translated by John Murray. Chicago: Regnery, 1961; *Freiheit, Gnade, Schicksal. Drei Kapitel zur Deutung des Daseins*. Munich: Kösel, 1948.

———. *Freiheit und Verantwortung: Die Weiße Rose–Zum Widerstand im "Dritten Reich."* Mainz: Matthias-Grünwald, 1997.

———. *"Von der Freudigkeit des Herzens." Brief über Selbsbildung, Zum Geleit [Preface]* Rothenfels: Deutsches Quickbornhaus, 1921.

———. *Gebet und Wahrheit: Meditation über das Vaterunser*. Würzburg: Werkbund, 1960.

———. "Gedanken über das Verhältnis von Christentum und Kultur." *Die Schildgenossen* 6 (1926) 385–91.

———. *Der Gegensatz: Versuche zur einer Philosophie des Lebendig-Konkreten*. Mainz: Grünwald, 1925.

———. "Die Geistlicher Lehrer Caussades." *Die Schildgennossen* 18 (1939) 282–88.

———. *Geistliche Schriftauslegung: Im Anfang War das Wort, die Christliche Liebe, das Harren der Schöpfung*. Würzburg: Werbund, 1949.

———. *Gläubiges Dasein: Drei Meditationen*. Würzburg: Werkbund, 1951.

———. "Der Glaube im Neuen Testament." *Die Schildgenossen* 10 (1930) 97–125.

———. "Der Heiland" [The Savior]. *Die Schildgennossen* 14 (1935) 96–116.

---. *Der Heilbringer in Mythos, Offenbarung und Politik*. Stuttgart: Deutsche Verlagsanstalt, 1946.

---. "Die Heilige Franziskus zum Gedachtnis." *Die Schildgennossen* 7 (1927) 2-18.

---. "Heilige Gestalt: Von Büchern und Mehr als Büchern." *Die Schildgennossen* 4 (1924) 257-68.

---. *The Humanity of Christ*. Translated by Ronald Walls. New York: Pantheon, 1964; *Die Menschliche Wirklichkeit des Herrn*. Mainz: Matthias-Grünwald, 1958.

---. *Im Anfang war das Worte: Eine Auslegung von John 1:1-18*. Würzburg: Werkbund, 1940.

---. *Jesus Christus: Meditations*. Translated by Peter White. Chicago: Regnery. 1959; *Jesus Christus: Geistliches Wort*. Würzburg: Werkbund, 1957.

---. *Jesus Christus: Sein bild in den Schriften des Neuen Testament*. 2 vols. Würzburg: Werkbund, 1940.

---. *Johanneische Botschaft: Meditationen über Worte aus den abschiedsreden und dem ersten Johannes-Brief*. Würzburg: Werkbund, 1962.

---. *The Last Things: Concerning Death, Purification after Death, Resurrection, Judgement, and Eternity*. Translated by Charlotte E. Forsyth and Grace B. Branham. Notre Dame: University of Notre Dame Press, 1954; *Die Letzten Dinge: Die christlichen Lehre vom Tode, der Läuterung nach dem Tode, Auferstehung*. Würzburg: Werkbund, 1940.

---. *Die Lebensalter: Ihre Ethische und Pädagogische Bedeutung*. Würzburg: Werkbund, 1959.

---. *Letters from Lake Como: Explorations in Technology and the Human Race*. Translated by Geoffrey W. Bromily. Edinburgh: T. & T. Clark, 1994; *Briefe vom Comersee*. Mainz: Matthias-Grünwald, 1930.

---. "Lex Orandi: Gedanken über die Liturgie." *Akademische Bonifatius-Korrespondenz* 34 (1919) 106-12.

---. "Die Liebe im Neuern Testament." *Die Schildgenossen* 10 (1930) 97-125.

---. *The Life of Faith*. Translated by John Chapin. Westminster: Newman, 1961; *Vom Leben des Glaubens*. Mainz: Matthias-Grünwald, 1935.

---. "Die Liturgie und die psychologischen Gesetz des gemeinsam Betens: Ein Beitrag zur religiösen Sozialpädagogik." *Pharus* 8 (1917) 241-55.

---. "Living Freedom: The Spirit of Man and the Spirit of God." In *The Focus of Freedom*, translated by Gregory Roettger. Baltimore: Helicon, 1966; "Lebendiger Geist." *Die Schildgenossen* 7 (1927): 349-68.

---. *The Living God*. Translated by Stanley Godman. New York: Pantheon, 1957; *Vom Lebendigen Gott*. Mainz: Grünwald, 1930.

---. *The Lord*. Translated by Elinor Castendyk Briefs. Chicago: Regnery, 1954; *Der Herr: Betrachtungen über die Person und das Leben. Die Macht: Versuch einer Wegweisung*. Würzburg: Werkbund, 1951.

---. *Prayers From Theology*. New York: Herder and Herder, 1959; *Theologishe Gebete*. Frankurt: Knecht, 1944.

---. "Die Psalmen vom Brevier des Donnerstags und das Geistlichen Leben." Reprinted in *Würzeln eines grossen Lebenswerks. Aufsätze und kleine Schriften I*. Mainz: Grünwald, 2000.

---. *The Lord's Prayer*. Translated by Isabel McHugh. New York: Pantheon, 1957; *Das Gebet des Herrn*. Mainz: Matthias-Grünwald, 1932.

———. "Das Objective im Gebetsleben: Zu P. M. Festugières 'Liturgie Catholique.'" *Jahrbuch der Liturgiewissenschaft* 1 (1921) 117–25.

———. *Pascal for Our Time*. Translated by Brian Thompson. New York: Herder and Herder, 1966; *Christliches Bewußtsein. Versuche über Pascal*. Leipzig: Hegner, 1935.

———. *Power and Responsibility: A Course of Action for the New Age*. Translated by Elinor C. Briefs. Chicago: Regnery, 1961; *Die Macht: Versuche einer Wegweisung*. Würzburg: Werkbund, 1951.

———. "Der religiöse Gehorsam." *Pharus, Katholische Monatsschrift für Orientierung in der gesampten Pädagogik* 7 (1916) 737–44.

———. *The Rosary of Our Lady*. Translated by H. von Schücking. Manchester: Sophia Institute, 1994; *Der Rosenkranz unserer leiben Frau*. Würzburg: Werkbund, 1940.

———. *La Rosa Bianca*. Translated by Michele Nicoletti and Paolo Ghezzi. Brescia: Morcelliana, 1994.

———. *The Saints in Daily Christian Life*. Philadelphia: Dimension, 1966; *Der Heilige in Unsere Welt*. Würzburg: Werkbund, 1956.

———."Siebter Sonntag nach Pfingsten: Die göttliche Vorsehung." *Chrysologus* 56 (1916) 540–46.

———. *The Spirit of the Liturgy*. Translated by Ada Lane. New York: Sheed and Ward, 1935; *Vom Geist der Liturgie*. Freiburg: Herder, 1918.

———. *Der Sonntag: Gestern, Heute und Immer*. Mainz: Matthias-Grünwald, 1958.

———. *Systembildende Element in der Theologie Bonaventuras: Die Lehren vom lumen mentis, von der gradatio entium und der influentia sensus et motus* (= studia et documenta franciscana 3). Edited by W. Dettloff. Leiden: Brill, 1964.

———."Tagebuch aus Oberitalien." In *In Spiegel und Gleichnis: Bilder und Gedanken*. Mainz: Grünwald, 1932.

———. *Unterscheidung des Christlichen*. Mainz: Grünwald, 1935.

———. *Verantwortung: Gedanken zur jüdischen Frage*. Munich: Kösel, 1952.

———. *The Virtues*. Translated by Stella Lange. Chicago: Regnery, 1967; *Tugend: Meditationen über Gestalten Sittlichen Lebens*. Würzburg: Werkbund, 1963.

———. "Was JESUS unter die Vorsehung Versteht." In *Christliche Besinnung*, Bd. 1, 1–16. Würzburg: Werkbund, 1950.

———. *The Way of the Cross of our Lord and Saviour Jesus Christ*. Translated by Ada Lane. London: Sheed and Ward, 1932; *Der Kreuzweg unseres Herrn und Heilandes*. Mainz: Matthias-Grünwald, 1919.

———. "Der Weg zu Gott im Neuen Testament." Reprinted in *Würzeln eines großen Lebenswerkes: Aufsätze und kleine Schriften* 2. Mainz: Matthias-Grünwald, 2001.

———. "Das Wesen des Christentums." *Die Schildgennossen* 9 (1929) 129–52.

———. *Wille und Wahrheit: Geistliche Übungen 1–5*. Mainz: Matthias-Grünwald, 1933.

———. *The Wisdom of the Psalms*. Translated by Stella Lange. Chicago: Regnery, 1963; *Weisheit des Psalmen. Meditationen*. Würzburg: Werkbund, 1938.

———. *The Word of God: On Faith, Hope, and Charity*. Translated by Stella Lange. Chicago: Regnery, 1963; *Drei Schriftauslegunge: Im Anfang war das Wort, Die christliche Liebe, Das Harren der Schöpfung*. Würzburg: Werkbund, 1949.

———. *The World and the Person*. Translated by Stella Lange. Chicago: Regnery, 1965; *Welt und Person*. Würzburg: Werkbund, 1939.

———. *Wunder und Zeichen*. Mainz: Matthias-Grünwald, 1991.

———. *Würzeln eines großen Lebenswerk: Aufsätze und kleine Schriften*. 2 vols. Mainz: Matthias-Grünwald, 2000–2001.

———. "Zum begriffe des Befels und des Gehorsams." *Pharus* 2.7 (1916) 834–43.

Gwynne Paul. *Special Divine Action: Key Issues in the Contemporary Debate (1965–1995)*. Serie Teologia 12. Rome: Gregorian University Press, 1996.

Haas, Peter J. *Morality after Auschwitz: The Radical Challenge of the Nazi Ethic*. Philadelphia: Fortress, 1988.

Harries, Richard. *After the Evil: Christianity and Judaism in the Shadow of the Holocaust*. Oxford: Oxford University Press, 2003.

Hasker, William. *God, Time, and Knowledge*. New York: Cornell University Press, 1998.

———. *Providence, Evil and the Openness of God*. London: Routledge 2004.

Hayes, Zachary. *The Hidden Centre: Spirituality and Speculative Christology in St. Bonaventure*, New York: Paulist, 1981.

———. *Visions of a Future: A Study of Christian Eschatology*. Wilmington: Glasier, 1989.

Heidegger, Martin. *The Basic Problem of Phenomenology*. Translated by Albert Hofstadter. Indianapolis: Indiana University Press, 1982.

———. *Being and Time*. Translated by John Macquarrie and Edward Robinson. New York: Harper Row, 1962.

Helm, Paul. *The Providence of God: Contours of Christian Theology*. Downer's Grove: InterVarsity, 1994.

Henrich, Franz, ed. *Romano Guardini. Christliche Weltanschauung und Menschliche Existenz*. Regensburg: Pustet, 1999.

Hens-Piazza, Gina. *The New Historicism*. Minneapolis: Fortress, 2002.

Hitler, Adolf. *Hitler's Table Talk, 1941–1944: Hitler's Conversations Recorded by Martin Bormann*. Oxford: Oxford University Press, 1988.

———. *Mein Kamf*. Berlin: Zentralverlag Der NSAP, 1936.

———. *My New Order*. Edited by Raoul De Roussy De Sales. New York: Reynal and Hitchcock 1941.

Hoonhout, Michael. "A Grounding Providence in the Theology of the Creator: The Exemplarity of Thomas Aquinas." *Heythrop Journal* 43 (2002) 1–19.

Hudal, Bischoff Alois. *Die Grundlagen des National Socialismus*. Leipzig: Günther, 1937.

Husserl, Edmund. *Ideas: General Introduction to Pure Phenomenology*. Translated by Boyce Gibson. New York: Collier, 1962.

Hürten, Heinz. *Deutsche Katholiken 1918–1945*. Paderborn: Schöningh, 1992.

Jockmann, Werner. *Adolf Hitler: Monologue im Fürherhauptquartier 1941–1944: Die Aufzeichnungen Heinrick Heims*. Munich: Knaus, 1982.

Kasper, Walter. *The God of Jesus Christ*. New York: Continuum, 2012.

Kilby, Karen. "Perichoresis and Projection: Problems with Social Doctrines of the Trinity." *New Blackfriars* 81.957 (2000) 432–45.

Kirpatrick, Dow. *Faith Born in the Struggle for Life*. Translated by Lewistine McCoy. Grand Rapids: Eerdmans, 1988.

Kleiber, Hans Ruedi. *Glaube und Religiöse Erfrahung bei Romano Guardini*. Paderborn: Schöningh, 1993.

Knoll, Alfons. *Glaube und Kultur bei Romano Guardini*. Paderborn: Schöningh, 1994.

Kobyliński, Andrzej. *Modernità e Postmodernità: L'interpretazione Cristiana Dell'Esistenza al Tramonto Dei Tempi Moderni nel Pensiero di Romano Guardini*. Rome: Gregorian University Press, 1998.

Kreiner, Armin. "Models of Divine Action in the World." In *Naming and Thinking God in Europe Today: Theology in Global Dialogue*, edited by Norbert Hintersteiner, 331–48. Amsterdam: Rodopi, 2007.

Krieg, Robert A. *Catholic Theologians in Nazi Germany*. New York: Continuum International, 2004.

———. *Romano Guardini: A Precursor of Vatican II*. Notre Dame: University of Notre Dame Press, 1997.

———, ed. *Romano Guardini: Proclaiming the Sacred in a Modern World*. Chicago: Liturgy Training, 1995.

———, trans. *Romano Guardini: Spiritual Writings*. Maryknoll: Orbis 2005.

———. "Romano Guardini's Theology of the Human Person." *Theological Studies* 59 (1998) 457–74.

Kühn, Heinz R. *The Essential Guardini: An Anthology of the Writings of Romano Guardini*. Chicago: Liturgy Training, 1997.

———. "Fires in the Night: Germany 1920–1950." In *Romano Guardini: Proclaiming the Sacred in a Modern World*, edited by Robert A. Krieg, 1–15. Chicago: Liturgy Training, 1995.

Kühn, Regina. "Romano Guardini in Berlin." In *Romano Guardini: Proclaiming the Sacred in a Modern World*, edited by Robert A. Krieg, 87–91. Chicago: Liturgy Training, 1995.

Laubach, Jacob. "Romano Guardini." In *Theologians of Our Time*, edited by Leonhard Reinisch, 109–27. Notre Dame: University of Notre Dame Press, 1964.

Ledek, Ronald. *The Nature of Conscience and Its Religious Significance with Special Reference to John Henry Newman*. Bethesda: International Scholars, 1996.

Lee, Jane L. "Karl Rahner's Mysticism: How is It Specifically Christian?" ThM diss., Melbourne College of Divinity, 1992.

Lindsay, Mark R. *Covenanted Solidarity: The Theological Basis of Karl Barth's Opposition to Nazi Antisemitism and the Holocaust*. Issues in Systematic Theology 9. New York: Lang, 2001.

MacDermott, John. *Love and Understanding: The Relation of Will and Intellect in Pierre Rousselout's Christological Vision*. Rome: Gregorian University Press, 1983.

Macquarrie, John. *Twentieth-Century Religious Thought*. London: SCM, 1981.

———. *Principles of Christian Theology*. London: SCM, 1966.

McCool, Gerard A. "The Primacy of Intuition." *Thought* 37 (1962) 57–73.

McGrath, Alister. *The Re-enchantment of Nature: The Denial of Religion and the Ecological Crisis*. New York: Doubleday, 2002.

Meier, Hans. "Zur Totalitarianismuskritik von Romano Guardini." *Brief Aus Mooshausen* (1997) 7–10.

Mendes-Flohr, Paul. "Martin Buber and Martin Heidegger in Dialogue." *Journal of Religion* 94.1 (2014) 2–25.

Merker, Hans. *Bibliographie Romano Guardini (1885–1968): Guardinis Werke veröffentlichungen über Guardini Rezensionen*. Munich: Schöningh, 1978.

Merrigan, Terrence. *Clear Heads and Holy Hearts: The Religious and Theological Ideas of John Henry Newman*. Leuven: Peeters, 1991.

Mosse, George L. *The Crisis of German Ideology: Intellectual Origins of the Third Reich*. New York: Grosset and Dunlop, 1964.

Müller, Eberhard. *Der Heiland: Ein Buch von Jesus dem grund des Glaubens dem Fürsten des Lebens und dem Herrn der Welt*. Berlin: Fürche, 1938.

Müller, Eric. "The Philosophy of Christian Existence." *Theology* 2 (1949) 50–54.
Murphy, Francessca Aran, and Philip G. Ziegler, eds. *The Providence of God*. London: T. & T. Clark, 2009.
A New Dictionary of Christian Ethics. Edited by John Macquarrie and James Childress. London: Westminster, 1986.
The New Catholic Encyclopedia. 15 vols. 2nd ed. Washington, DC: Catholic University of America, 2003.
Newbigin, Lesslie. *Foolishness to the Greeks: The Gospel and Western Culture*. London: SPCK, 1980.
———. *The Gospel in a Pluralist Society*. Grand Rapids: Eerdmans, 1989.
Newman, John Henry. *Apologia Pro Vita Sua*. Boston: Houghton Miffin, 1956.
———. *The Benedictine Order*. London: Catholic Truth Society, 1914.
———. *An Essay in Aid of a Grammar of Assent*. London: Burns, Oats, and Co., 1870.
———. *Meditations and Devotions of the Late Cardinal Newman*. Edited by E. P. Neville. New York: Longman, Greens and Co., 1907.
Oberdorfer, Max, ed. *Romano Guardini. Zeugnisse eines Großen Lebens*. Ostfildern: Matthias-Grünewald, 2010.
O'Collins, Gerald, and Edward G. Farrugia. *A Concise Dictionary of Theology*. London: HarperCollins, 1991.
———. *Catholicism: The Story of Catholic Christianity*. Oxford: Oxford University Press, 2003.
Otto, Rudolf. *The Idea of the Holy: An Inquiry Into the Non-Rational Factor in the Idea of the Divine and its Relation to the Rational*. London: Oxford University Press, 1958; *Das Heilige: über des irrationale in der idee des Göttlichen und sein Verhältnis zum Rationalen*. Gotha: Perthes, 1923.
The Oxford Dictionary of the Christian Church. Edited by F. L. Cross. 3rd ed. revised and edited by E. A. Livingston. Oxford: Oxford University Press, 2005.
Penso, Giorgio. "L'Interpretation di Höderlin in Romano Guardini, Filosofo Dell'Esistenza." In *La Weltanschauung Cristiana di Romano Guardini*, edited by Silvano Zukal, 449–70. Trento: Instituto Trentino di Cultura, 1988.
Perry, Ralph Barton. *Philosophy of the Recent Past*. New York: Scribner's Sons, 1926.
Pinnock, Clarke, ed. *The Openness of God: A Biblical Challenge to the Traditional Understanding of God*. Downer's Grove: InterVarsity, 1980.
Pinnock, Sarah K. *Beyond Theodicy: Jewish and Christian Continental Thinkers Respond to the Holocaust*. Albany: State University of New York Press, 2002.
Pinson, Koppel S. *Modern Germany: Its History and Civilization*. New York: MacMillan, 1954.
Plantinga, Richard J., et al. *An Introduction to Christian Theology*. Cambridge: Cambridge University Press, 2010.
Porter, Stanley E., and Jason C. Robinson. *Hermeneutics: An Introduction to Interpretive Theory*. Grand Rapids: Eerdmans, 2011.
Pope Benedict XVI. "A Man of Dialogue in Search for Truth." *L'Osservatore Romano*. November 17, 2010.
Pope Francis. "Laudato Si' of the Holy Father Francis on Care for our Common Home." Encyclical Letter. May 24, 2015. http://www.vatican.va/content/francesco/en/encyclicals/documents/papa-francesco_20150524_enciclica-laudato-si.html.
Post, Stephen G. "Alzheimer's and Grace." *First Things* (2004) 12–14.

Rahner, Karl. *Theological Investigations.* Vol. 16. Translated by David Moreland. London: Dartman, Longman and Todd, 1979.

———. "Ignatian Spirituality and Devotion to the Sacred Heart." In *Jesuit Spirit in a Time of Change,* edited by Raymond A. Schoth et al., 53–58. Westminster: Newman 1967.

———. *I Remember.* Translated by Harvey D. Egan. New York: Crossroad, 1985.

Ratzinger, Joseph (Pope Benedict XVI). *Fundamental Speeches from Five Decades.* Edited by Florian Schuller. Translated by Michael J. Miller et al. San Francisco: Ignatius, 2012; *Grundsatz-Redenaus aus fünf Jahrzenten.* Regensburg: Pustet, 2005.

———. *The Spirit of the Liturgy.* San Francisco: Ignatius, 2000; *Der Geist der Liturgie.* Freiburg: Herder, 2000.

Reber, Joachim. *Die Welt des Christen: Philosophische Untersuchungen zum Welt Concept Romano Guardinis.* St. Ottilien: EOS Erzabtei, 1999.

———. *Romano Guardini Begegnen.* Augsburg: Sankt Ulrich, 2001.

Rice, Richard. *The Openness of God: The Relationship of Divine Foreknowledge and Human Free Will.* Nashville: Review and Herald, 1980.

Ricoeur, Paul. *The Symbolism of Evil.* Translated by Emerson Buchanan. Boston: Beacon, 1975.

Robson, Mark Ian Thomas. *Ontology and Providence in Creation: Taking Ex Nihilo Seriously.* London: Continuum International, 2008.

Rosenberg Alfred. *Der Mythus des 20 Jahrhunderts.* Munich: Höneichan, 1935.

Ruppert, Godehard. *Quickborn – Katholische und jugendbewegt: Ein Beitrag Zur Wirkungsgeschicte der katholische Jugendbewegung.* Opole: Wydzial Teologiczny Uniwersytetu Opolskiego, 1999.

Sagi, Avi, and Daniel Statman. *Religion and Morality.* Translated by Batya Stein. Amsterdam: Rodopi, 1995.

Sanders, John. *The God Who Risks: A Theology of Providence.* Downer's Grove: InterVarsity, 2007.

Seckler, Max. *Theologie vor Gericht: Der Fall Wilhelm Koch – Ein Bericht.* Tübingen: Mohr Siebeck, 1972.

Schall, James. "Benedetto XVI Ha un Padre, Romano Guardini." http//chiesa.espresso.repubblica.it/articolo/20716?eng=y.

———. "Guardini." http://www.ignatiusinsight.com/features2010/schall_guardini_dec2010.asp.

Scheler, Max. *On the Eternal in Man.* Translated by Bernard Noble. London: SCM, 1960; *Vom Ewigen im Menschen* Vol 5. Berne: A Frank AG, 1954.

Schilson, Arno. "La sequela di Cristo Centro dell'esistenza Cristiana." *Communio* 132 (1993) 43–57.

———. "The Major Theological Themes of Romano Guardini." In *Proclaiming the Sacred in a Modern World,* edited by Robert A. Krieg, 31–43. Chicago: Liturgy Training, 1995.

———. *Perspectiven Theologischer Erneuerung: Studien zum Werk Romano Guardinis.* Düsseldorf: Patmos, 1986.

Schmidbauer, Hans Christian. *Gottes Handeln in Welt und Geschichte: Eine Trinitarische Theologie der Vorsehung.* St. Ottilien: EOS Erzabtei, 2003.

Schreiter, Robert J. *Constructing Local Theologies.* London: SCM, 1985.

Schwöbel, Christoph. *God: Action and Revelation.* Studies in Philosophical Theology 3. Kampen: Pharos, 1992.
Sheehan, Thomas. *Karl Rahner: The Philosophical Foundations.* Athens: Ohio University Press, 1987.
Sommavilla, Guido, ed. *Romano Guardini: Scritti Filosofici.* Vol. I. Milan: Fabri, 1964.
Sweeney, David F. "Herman Schell, 1850–1906: A German Dimension to the Americanistic Controversy." *The Catholic Historical Review* 76.1 (1990) 44–70.
Swinburne, Richard. *Providence and the Problem of Evil.* Oxford: Clarendon, 1998.
Tallon, Andrew. "The Heart in Rahner's Philosophy of Mysticism." *Theological Studies* 53 (1992) 700–28.
Terlinden, Luc. "The Originality of Newman's Teaching on Conscience." *Irish Theological Quarterly* 73 (2008) 274–306.
Tiessen, Terrance. *Providence and Prayer: How Does God Work in the World?* Downers Grove: InterVarsity, 2000.
Tillich, Paul. *Systematic Theology.* Vol. I. Chicago: University of Chicago Press, 1951.
Tolliday, Phillip, and Heather Thomson, eds. *Speaking Differently: Essays in Theological Anthropology.* Canberra: Barton, 2013.
Trevor-Roper, Hugh, ed. *Final Entries 1945: The Diaries of Joseph Goebbels.* New York: Putnam's Sons, 1978.
Turabian, Kate. *A Manual for Writers of Research Papers, Theses, and Dissertations: Chicago Style for Students and Researchers.* 8th ed. Revised by Wayne Booth et al. Chicago: University of Chicago Press, 2013.
Villa, Dana R. *Politics, Philosophy, Terror: Essays on the Thought of Hannah Arendt.* Princeton: Princeton University Press, 1999.
Wiles, Maurice. *God's Action in the World: The Bampton Lectures for 1986.* London: SCM, 1986.
———, ed. *Providence.* London: SPCK, 1969.
Wright, John H. *Divine Providence in the Bible: Meeting the Living True God.* 2 vols. New York: Paulist, 2009–2010.
Zukal, Silvano. *La Weltanschauung Cristiana di Romano Guardini.* Trento: Instituto Trentino di Cultura, 1988.

Index

Abandonment to Divine Providence (Caussade), 53
accountability, 199
act of knowing, 13
Adam, Karl, 12, 41
adoration of God, 91
agreement, with God, 77, 81–82
Allen, Paul, 6n6
animals, 136
Anruf der Freiheit (Brüske), 20
Anschauung, 12–13
Aquinas, Thomas. *See* Thomas Aquinas, Saint
Arendt, Hannah, 12n37, 54
Aristotle, 130
Aryans, 58–59, 59n120, 118–19, 121n40, 156
assent to God, 83–84
attitude of mind
  changes to, 207
  contemplative, 171
  destiny and, 12, 207, 226
  importance of, 22
  overview of, 153
Augustine, Saint, 164n210
authenticity, 75n27, 138n109
Autonom, 86
autonomy, 193–94

Balthasar, Hans Urs von, 22–23, 54, 56
baptism, 122, 195
Bärsch, Claus-Ekkard, 58
Barth, Karl, 8, 41, 231
being, spheres of, 14

Beingness concept, 130
Benedictine, Saint, 31–32
Benedict XVI (Joseph Ratzinger) (pope), 54, 55, 93n96
Bericht über mein Leben (Guardini), 32
Berkouwer, G. C., 183n57
Berlin, Germany, 57. *See also* Germany
Biser, Eugene, 21n62
Bonaventure, Saint, 51–52, 85, 164n210
born again, 96–97, 228
Bougerol, J. Guy, 51–52
Brunner, Emil, 41
Brüske, Gunda, 20, 133–34
Buber, Martin, 49–51
Burg Rothenfels castle, 35, 68

call of God, 115, 127, 134–36, 223–24
care of God, 118
Catholic Theologians under Hitler (Krieg), 59
Catholic youth groups, 34–37, 34n22
Caussade, Jean-Pierre de, 53
Christians
  as child of God, 96–97, 122, 131, 160, 196
  as "co-creator" with God, 109, 205, 235
  as door for God in the world, 87, 106, 157–58
  as God-loving person, 118–19

Christians (*continued*)
   living with Providence practice of, 88–90
   responsibility of, 162–63
   See also human beings
Christocentricism, 155
Christocentric pneumatology, 107
Church, 33, 106–7
Church and the Catholic, The (Guardini), 79, 105, 163, 172
Church of the Lord, The (Guardini), 172
co-creator concept, 109, 205, 235
community, 106–7
concealment, 198–99
Confirmation, 89–90
conscience
   defined, 89
   holiness and (the Good), 76, 88–89, 188–89
   as living product, 90
   overview of, 110
   within Providence, 79–83
   spiritual dimension of a person and, 177
   writings regarding, 52–53
Conscience (Guardini), 52, 79–80, 85–86, 100n124
consciousness, 10, 140, 180, 214
Constitution on the Sacred Liturgy (*Sacrosanctum Concilium*), 34
contemplation, 115n12, 233
conversion (*metanoia*)
   destiny and, 153
   importance of, 32
   process of, 96–97, 101, 206–7, 226–27, 235
covenant, relationship with God as, 109
creation
   care for, 217, 221
   doctrine of, 19n60
   experience within, 191
   God in, 150–51
   grace in, 98
   as in movement, 121n42
   mystery within, 218
   nature as, 147–50, 226
   Providence in, 101–3
   renewal of, 97, 226
   world of, 22, 146–48
Creator, God as, 17–18, 19n60, 71–72, 110, 235

damnation, eternal, 144
Das Wesen des Christentum (Guardini), 66
Deism, 228–29
"Der Heiland" (The Savior) (Guardini), 65
destiny
   attitude of mind and, 22, 207, 226
   changes to, 231–32
   control of, 174
   conversion and, 153
   defined, 174
   harmony and, 181
   of Jesus, 178, 180, 224–25
   in life of faith, 154–55
   overview of, 18, 152–54
   Providence and, 173–75
   redemption and, 182–83
   unredeemed existence and, 193
"Die Heilige Franziskus zum Gedachtnis" (Guardini), 42
discipleship, 230
Divine Providence in the Bible (Wright), 15
Dogma und Leben (Dogma and Life) (Krebs), 45
doxology, 218–21

Ebeling, Gerhard, 41n46
empathy, 137
End of the Modern World, The (Guardini), 54, 169–70
enlightenment, 190–91
entelechy, 176, 176n26
environment/environment pole, 157, 158–61, 165–67, 226
Essence of Christianity (Das Wesen des Christentums) (Guardini), 40
eternal life, 199

Eucharist, 122
Evans, Richard J., 57–58
evil, 13–14, 15, 178–82, 193–94
exemplarity of God, 85n62
existence
    holiness of, 209–10
    of human beings, 81
    new, 97, 146–67, 205–16, 226–27
    personal, 177
    Providence in, 173–75
    redeemed, 100–101, 173, 193, 208–9
    religious, 11
    from transformation, 208
    unredeemed, 193
Existentialism, 18

fact concept, 175–76
faith
    child-like, 117
    destiny and, 154–55
    environment and, 158–61
    Jesus' indwelling through, 122
    meaning of, 193
    process of, 131, 208
Faith and Modern Man (Glaubenserkenntnis) (Guardini), 60
fleshly man concept, 155
forgiveness of God, 95–96
Francis, Saint, 43, 164
Francis I (pope), 54, 55–56, 98
freedom
    baptism and, 195
    exercising of, 195
    function of, 229
    grace of God and, 75, 98–99, 194–96, 225
    holiness of God (the Good) and, 104
    human action and, 184–86, 209
    misuse of, 203
    moral, 188–90
    overview of, 184
    personal existence within, 177
    personal relations and, 187–88
    power and, 186–87
    principles of, 186
    religious, 190–92
    in religious experience, 191
    self-realization and, 177, 195
    source of, 171
    truth and, 187
Freedom, Grace, and Destiny (Guardini)
    conversion theme within, 206–7
    destiny theme within, 173–75, 180, 181
    dominion theme within, 186
    fact concept theme within, 175–76
    freedom theme within, 186–87, 189–90
    God's restraint theme within, 199
    Good theme within, 188–89
    guidance theme within, 209–10
    human action theme within, 184–85, 210–11
    intrinsic worth theme within, 188
    judgement theme within, 196, 198, 199, 201–2
    nature theme within, 191
    new existence theme within, 208
    quote within, 129n72
    redemption theme within, 203–4
    religious experience theme within, 191
    Satan discussion within, 179
    spiritual element theme within, 176–78
free will, 16, 19, 120, 134, 235
fullness of God, 73

Gebet und Wahrheit (Prayer and Truth) (Guardini), 216–17
Germany
    Berlin, 57
    Munich, 63n141
    political and social challenges within, 116n19
    society changes within, 56–61
    World War II and, 68

4 INDEX

Germany (*continued*)
  youth movements within, 34–37, 34n22
  See also National Socialism
Gestalt, 5, 20, 112n2, 192, 223, 232
Gethsemane, 178
Glaube und Kulture bei Romano Guardini (Knoll), 20–21
God
  accountability to, 199
  adoration of, 91
  agreement with, 81–82
  allegiance to, 171
  assent to, 83–84
  call of, 115, 127, 134–36, 223–24
  care of, 118
  centrality of, 235
  communion and, 18
  in creation, 150–51
  creative power of, 132–33
  as Creator, 17–18, 19n60, 71–72, 110, 235
  emphasis on, 134
  empowerment from, 229
  exemplarity of, 85n62
  focus on, 234
  foreknowledge of, 203, 207
  forgiveness of, 95–96
  freedom from, 98–99
  as fulfillment, 163
  fullness of, 73
  glory of, 219
  as ground of all being, 18
  guidance of, 85, 109, 209–10, 228
  history's guilt and, 183
  holiness of (the Good), 76, 79–83, 88–89, 104, 199
  human being's individual importance to, 70–71, 91–93, 133–46, 196–205, 225–26
  imprint of, 203
  as incomprehensible, 109–10, 128–29
  inwardness of, 128–29
  Jesus and, 180, 181n50
  judgement of, 196–202, 226
  Lordship of, 149
  love of, 5, 70–71, 73, 225
  mark of, 92–94
  mutual understanding with, 83–84
  nature of, 71, 75–76
  obedience to, 108, 110, 182n53, 215–16
  omnipotence of, 101, 111, 199
  omnipresence of, 102, 111, 170
  omniscience of, 16, 71–72, 101, 111
  participation in, 203
  patience of, 72–73, 74–75
  power of, 72–73
  presentiment of, 77, 78–79
  Providence of, 15–16, 67
  rejection of, 203
  relationship with, 48, 75, 77–78, 83–86, 93, 109, 113–14, 120–33, 160, 182, 183–96, 204, 225
  resistance to, 199
  responsibility of, 162n204
  sharing in life of, 94–95, 129–32
  simplicity of, 73
  speaking by, 110
  suffering and, 230
  touch of, 203
  as true "Thou," 126–28
  trusting, 53, 102–3, 116, 224
  truth of, 163–64
  will of, 73, 74–75, 78, 133, 232, 234
  wisdom of, 72–73, 92, 210, 232–33
  See also grace of God; love of God
God-loving person, 118–19, 227. *See also* Christians; human beings
Gogarten, Friedrich, 50
Good (holiness of God)
  as changing and alive, 129
  conscience and human action and, 76, 88–89, 188–89
  effects of, 88–89
  freedom and, 104

function of, 199
overview of, 76
within Providence, 79–83
good and evil, contradictions of, 13–14, 15
Görres, Joseph von, 44–45
Görres *Gesselschaft* (Görres Society), 44
Gottglaübigen (believers in God), 65
grace of God
    as active, 89
    awareness from, 109
    conscience and, 80
    in creation, 98
    freedom through, 75, 98–99, 194–96, 225
    inwardness and, 167
    judgement and, 201–2
    participation with, 194
    power of, 143
    as preeminent, 207
    primacy of, 18–19
    within Providence, 119
    revelation by, 132
    transformation through, 5
Graf, Willi, 62–63
Guardini, Romano
    areas of interest of, 39–40
    as Benedictine Oblate, 31–32
    dream of, 93n96
    as educator, 37–39
    higher education of, 30–31
    illness of, 34, 39, 172
    inconsistencies of, 41–42
    as influencer, 54–56, 62–63
    influencers to, 44–53
    as Kerygmatic Theologian, 8
    as liturgical leader, 32–34
    as member of literary circle, 29–30
    mental health of, 39
    methodology of, 6–7
    overview of, 3–4, 29
    as philosopher of existence, 6n12
    preaching of, 38–39
    pseudonym of, 70
    quote of, 7
    responsibility example of, 211–13
    as theologian writer, 5n4
    use of Scripture by, 7–8
    writings of, 16–17
    as youth group leader, 34–37
    guidance of God, 85, 109, 209–10, 228

Hayes, Zachary, 166
heart, 101, 114–15, 132–33
Heidegger, Martin, 49–51, 125, 153n172
"Heilige Gestalt: Von Büchern und mehr als Büchern" (Guardini), 42
Heteronom, 86
heteronomy, 150, 179
Hitler, Adolf, 58–59, 64, 65–66, 67, 117n20, 118n26, 141–42
holiness of existence, 209–10
holiness of God (Good)
    as changing and alive, 129
    conscience and human action and, 76, 88–89, 188–89
    effects of, 88–89
    freedom and, 104
    function of, 199
    overview of, 76
    within Providence, 79–83
"the holy," religious freedom and, 190–92
Holy Spirit, 61, 64, 116–18
Hoonhout, Michael A., 17
hope, 208
human action
    freedom and, 184–86, 209
    Good (holiness of God) and, 76, 88–89, 188–89
    importance of, 61, 199–200, 220–21
    in Providence, 230
    responsibility within, 210–11
human beings
    arrangement of being for, 132
    as artisan of own fortune, 152
    authenticity of, 138n109
    changes to, 113–14

human beings (*continued*)
   as child of God, 96–97, 122, 131, 160, 196
   as "co-creator" with God, 109, 205, 235
   concrete existence of, 81
   creative tension with, 90–91
   decision capacity of, 134
   as door for God in the world, 87, 106, 157–58
   existence of, 81
   freedom of, 74, 120–21
   free will of, 120, 134
   as God-loving person, 118–19
   heart of, 101
   as individual importance to God, 70–71, 91–93, 133–46, 196–205, 225–26
   insignificance of, 72
   interiority of, 139
   living with Providence practice of, 88–90
   love and, 136–37
   nature of God and, 75–76
   poles of, 152
   relationship with God by, 77–78, 83–86, 93, 109, 113–14, 120–33, 160, 182, 183–96, 204, 225
   repentance of, 95–96
   sharing in life of God by, 94–95
   social reality of, 87–88
   spiritual elevation of, 107
   transcendence of, 93
   uniqueness of, 93, 225–26
   will of, 137–39
   See also Christians
human decision, 175–76
human experience, 6, 6n6
humility, 204, 215–16
Husserl, Edmond, 9–10

inductive theology, 7
indwelling, of Jesus Christ, 121–23, 225, 229
inner life, 88, 90
instruments, learning, 159
integrity, 86–87
intentionality, 9–10
interiority, 128–29, 139, 204
inter-subjectivity, 126
intrinsic worth, 188
intuition, 103
I-Thou concept, 49–50, 123–26, 225

Jaspers, Karl, 54
Jesus Christ
   addressing of evil by, 178–82
   atonement of, 231
   as with the believer, 155–56
   centrality of, 12, 231
   consciousness of, 180
   destiny within, 178, 180, 224–25
   as essence of Christianity, 66
   as exemplar, 85n62
   in Gethsemane, 178
   God and, 180, 181n50
   in Guardini's writing, 40–42
   humility of, 215
   indwelling of, 121–23, 225, 229
   Jewishness of, 65, 156
   kinship with, 122
   lifestyle of, 173
   liturgy and, 33
   obedience of, 182n53, 215–16
   power of, 213
   Providence and, 64, 67, 77, 116–20, 172–83, 224–25
   quote of, 104, 105
   as redemptive, 122, 231
   suffering of, 230
   transformation of, 235
   uniqueness of, 181
Jesus Christus (Guardini), 78n33
Jews
   Aryans *versus*, 59n120
   Engelbert Krebs' writings regarding, 45
   Guardini's defense of, 50, 211, 213, 227
   Jesus Christ as, 65, 156
   Nazi viewpoint regarding, 58
   rejection of Jesus by, 199
   as untermenschen (sub-human), 58
John Paul II (pope), 54

judgement of God, 196–202, 226
justice, 140–41

Kant, Immanuel, 78n35, 86, 184
Kasper, Walter, 47–48
Katholische Jugend Deutschelands (Catholic Youth of Germany), 35
kerygma, 41n46
Kingdom of God
    concern for, 110
    environment and, 165–67
    focus on, 227
    order of being and, 217–18
    overview of, 104–9, 163–65, 221, 224
    seeking, 104, 105, 119–20, 234
    as state of being, 108
    as Theocentric, 107–8
    unity and, 235
Knoll, Alfons, 20–21
knowledge, 80n46
Koch, Wilhelm, 46
Krebs, Engelbert, 44–46
Krieg, Robert, 59
Kühn, Heinz, 37, 57
Kühn, Regina, 38, 43

laity, 42–44, 163
language, significance of, 51
Last Things, The (Guardini), 145n138
Laudato Si' (Francis I), 54, 55–56
liturgy, 32–34
living conceptions, 13
living concrete concept, 30
Living Freedom (Guardini), 192
Living God, The (Guardini), 78, 79, 99, 110
Lord, The (Der Herr) (Guardini), 40, 41, 54, 65
Lord's Prayer, 116
Lord's Prayer, The (Guardini), 66, 142, 143, 144, 145, 163, 164
love
    freedom and, 187–88
    giving, 208
    human beings and, 136–37
    process of, 208
    in Providence, 207–8
love of God
    function of, 230, 235
    harmony with, 181, 182
    for individuals, 70–71
    overview of, 73, 225
    predestination and, 144–45

martyrdom, 62
Mass, 33
Mediator Dei (Pius XII), 34
meditation, 89
Meier, Hans, 64
Mein Kampf (My Struggle), 58
Melancthon, Philip, 30
middle way, 90–91
military, 92–93
mind
    attitude of, 12, 22, 153, 171, 207, 226
    person as determined by, 139–43
    unity of, 114–15
moral deeds, 99–100, 110, 226
moral freedom, 188–90. *See also* freedom
morality, 188
Moses, 95–96
Munich, Germany, 63n141. *See also* Germany
mutual understanding, 83–84
Mystical Body of Christ, 108

National Socialism
    absolutist ideas of, 190
    Aryan status within, 118–19, 121n40, 156
    Christocentrism and, 155
    destiny and, 173
    Guardini's criticism of, 65
    Guardini's writings during, 66–67, 112–14
    ideology of, 64–65
    nature elevation by, 147
    overview of, 57–61
    time period of, 113
    world view within, 117n20

nature
    as creation, 147–50, 226
    experience within, 191
    National Socialist elevation of, 147
    overview of, 216–17
nature of God, 71, 75–76
Nazis/Nazism, 45, 58. *See also* National Socialism
new creation
    human person's role within, 151–52
    new person within, 160
    overview of, 97, 146–67, 205–16, 226–27
new existence, 97, 146–67, 205–16, 226–27
New Heaven and New Earth, 61, 151–52, 160, 234–35
Newman, John Henry, 52–53
new person, 206–7
Nietzsche, Friedrich, 150, 190
Nominalism, 17

obedience to God, 108, 110, 182n53, 215–16
objects, intentionality regarding, 9–10
omnipotence of God, 101, 111, 199
omnipresence of God, 102, 111, 170
omniscience of God (all-knowing), 71–72, 101, 111
ontological difference, 58
Openness Theology, 71n6, 230
Open Theism, 16
Opposites, the *(Der Gegensatz)*, 12–15
order of being, 217–18
Otto, Rudolf, 150n159, 190–92

Parousia, 108–9
participation in God, 203
patience of God, 72–73, 74–75
Paul, Saint, 155
Paul VI (pope), 54
Pentecost, 107–8
Penzo, Giorgio, 6n12
personal integrity, 86–87

personal relations, 187–88
phenomenology, 9–12
Philosophers of Being, 11
piety, 170
Pilate, 178
Pius XII (pope), 8, 42, 54
Pneuma, 108
poles concept, 87–88, 227
power, 186–87, 213–16
Power and Responsibility (Guardini)
    attitude theme within, 171
    overview of, 170
    power theme within, 213–14
    responsibility theme within, 213, 214–15
    strength theme within, 171
power of God, 72–73
praise, 219–20
prayer, 89, 91, 220, 233
Prayers From Theology (Guardini), 236
predestination, 143–46, 156
presentiment of God, 77, 78–79
present moment, living with, 53
priesthood, 36
Providence
    anthropological aspect of, 87
    as becoming, 229
    contemporary theological literature on, 15–16
    defined, 15
    development of, 91, 113
    double agency of, 18–19, 61, 136, 227, 230
    dynamic paradigm within, 112n2
    as eschatological, 216
    fulfillment of, 223–24
    gaps in literature regarding, 23–24
    Guardini's prayer regarding, 236
    Guardini's writing changes regarding, 24
    Guardini's writing differences during National Socialist period regarding, 66–67

Guardini's writings, 1945 and
   after writings regarding, 68,
   169–72
Gunda Brüske's viewpoint
   regarding, 20
Holy Spirit's work regarding, 61,
   64, 116–18
interactive aspect of, 160–61
living with awareness of, 220,
   227, 234
mutual understanding with God
   and, 83–84
as in opposition to Hitler's
   understanding, 63–66
overview of, 4–5, 61, 66, 67,
   109–11, 203–4, 210, 233
purpose of, 167
Scripture grounding within, 8
spatial aspect of, 87–88
themes of, 69, 224
as Trinitarian, 233
viewpoints regarding, 17–19
works regarding, 69–70
purgatory, 145n138
purification, 197

Quickborn (Fountain of Youth), 35

Rahner, Hugo, 41
Rahner, Karl, 54, 56
Ratzinger, Joseph (Benedict XVI),
   54
reason, human capacity for, 11–12
Reber, Joachim, 21–22
redeemed existence, 100–101, 173,
   193, 208–9
redeemed world, 146n140. *See also*
   world
redemption
   destiny and, 182–83
   effects of, 224
   by God in Christ, 182–83
   process of, 203–4, 225
   relationship from, 207
   from sin, 194
reflection, 89, 233
religious essence, 11
religious experience, 161–62, 191

religious freedom, 190–92
renewal, 161–62
repentance, 95–96, 100–101, 153,
   228
responsibility
   as active, 221
   example of, 211–13
   within human action, 210–11
   as instrumental, 221
   overview of, 227
   power and, 213–15
revelation, 204
right thinking, 204
Romano Guardini Begegnen (Reber),
   21–22
*Romano Guardini: Reform from the
   Source* (Balthasar), 22–23
Rule (St. Benedictine), 31–32, 31n10

Saints, in Guardini's writings, 42–44.
   See also specific persons
Saints in Daily Life, The (Guardini),
   43, 53
salvation, 15, 202, 215
Satan, 178–79, 194
Scheler, Max, 10–11, 32–33, 48–49
Schell, Hermann, 30, 47–48
Scholl, Hans and Sophie, 62
science, 217, 219
Scripture, Guardini's use of, 7–8
secret writing groups, 60 n128
self-actuation, 47
self-casualty, 47
selfishness, 159
self-realization, 177, 195
service, 193
"Seventh Sunday after Pentecost:
   Divine Providence"
   (Guardini), 70–71
Sheehan, Thomas, 130
simplicity of God, 73
sin, 95–96, 194
social integrity, 86–87
Socrates, 187
solitude, 188
sovereignty, 215
spirit, interiority and, 139–40

Spirit of the Liturgy, The (Benedict XVI), 55
Spirit of the Liturgy, The (Guardini), 32–33
spiritual element, 176–78
Stations of the Cross, 40
St. Ludwig's Church (Munich, Germany), 38–39
submission theodicy, 103n135

"Tagebuch Aus Oberitalien" (Guardini), 147n143
Tallon, Andrew, 115n12
theodicy, 203–4
theological method, 6n6
Theonomy, 136, 188
Theosis, 18
things, human beings and, 147n143
Thomas Aquinas, Saint, 51, 129, 130, 202
Thoughts on the Relationship of Christianity and Culture (Guardini), 107–8
Totalitarianism, 64
transcendence, 93, 166–67, 228
transfiguration, 162
transformation, 196, 208
treaty of Versailles, 57
trials, importance of, 152
Trinitarian Theology, 47–48
Trinity, 97, 106
trust in God, 53, 102–3, 116, 224
truth, 187
truth of God, 163–64

unity, 114–15, 235
universal judgement, 198
University of Berlin, 38
University of Munich, 211
University of Tübingen, 30–31, 213
untermenschen (sub-human), 58

value, 114, 138, 187
Vatican II, 34
vision, 169–70, 171, 193

Way of the Cross of our Lord and Savior, The (Guardini), 40

What JESUS Understood about Providence (Guardini), 116
White Rose *(Die Weisse Rose)*, 62–63
Wilhelmsen, Frederick D., 170
will, human, 137–39
Wille und Wahrheit (Will and Truth) (Guardini), 121
will of God, 73, 74–75, 78, 133, 232, 234
wisdom of God, 72–73, 92, 210, 232–33
Wisdom of the Psalms, The (Weisheit des Psalmen) (Guardini), 218–21
world
  Christian, 151–52
  Christian responsibility within, 162–63
  Christians as door for God within, 87, 106, 157–58
  cosmic meaning of, 23
  as created, 150
  environment of, 158
  as experienced, 173
  as God's, 231–32
  Guardini's understanding of, 146–48
  importance of, 226
  moral deeds within, 99–100
  potential of, 158
  redeemed, 146n140
  relationship with God within, 183–96
  theological viewpoints regarding, 17
World and the Person, The (Guardini)
  attitude theme within, 153
  Christian being theme within, 155, 156
  Christian responsibility theme within, 162–63
  Christians as door for God in the world theme within, 157–58
  creation theme within, 151
  freedom theme within, 186

human beings as artisan of own
    fortune within, 152
human will theme within, 138
inwardness theme within, 129
I-Thou relationship theme
    within, 50, 124–28, 135
justice theme within, 140–41
Kingdom of God theme within,
    166
love theme within, 137
mind theme within, 139
nature theme within, 148,
    149–50
overview of, 113
Providence message within, 166,
    167
redeemed world theme within,
    146n140
religious consciousness theme
    within, 134
religious experience theme
    within, 161

as resource, 21–22
selfishness theme within, 159
self-knowledge theme within,
    131
standards theme within, 231
world of being theme within,
    131–32
worldview, 6
World War I, 92
World War II, 57–58, 68
world-word *(Welt-Wort)*, 127
Wright, John H., 15
Wunder und Zeichen (Guardini),
    217–18

youth groups, Catholic, 34–37,
    34n22

"Zur Totalitarismuskritik von
    Romano Guardini" (Meier),
    64

www.ingramcontent.com/pod-product-compliance
Lightning Source LLC
Chambersburg PA
CBHW050342230426
43663CB00010B/1960